OPEL
SERVICE · REPAIR HANDBOOK
ALL MODELS · 1966-1977

By
RAY HOY

ERIC JORGENSEN
Editor

JEFF ROBINSON
Publisher

Published by

CLYMER PUBLICATIONS

*World's largest publisher of books devoted exclusively to
automobiles, motorcycles, and boats.*

222 NORTH VIRGIL AVENUE, LOS ANGELES, CALIFORNIA 90004

FIRST EDITION
First Printing October, 1973
Second Printing April, 1974
Third Printing March, 1975

SECOND EDITION
Revised to include 1974-1975 models
First Printing October, 1975
Second Printing March, 1976
Third Printing October, 1976

THIRD EDITION
Revised to include 1976-1977 models
First Printing July, 1977

Printed in U.S.A.

ISBN: 0-89287-171-7

*Photos and illustrations courtesy of
Buick Motor Division, General Motors Corporation, Detroit, Michigan.*

CONTENTS

CHAPTER FIVE

FUEL AND EXHAUST SYSTEMS . . . .

Fuel tank
Fuel filter
Fuel lines
Fuel gauge tank sending units
Mechanical fuel pump
Electric fuel pump
Carburetors

Carburetor idle mixture adjustment
Overhaul
Fuel injection
Air cleaner
Intake manifold
Exhaust system
Gas pedal and linkages

CHAPTER SIX

COOLING AND HEATING SYSTEMS . . . .

Draining cooling system
Filling cooling system
Thermostat
Radiator
Water pump

Automatic fan clutch
Fan belt
Water hoses
Heater

CHAPTER SEVEN

EMISSION CONTROL SYSTEMS . . . .

Air injection reactor system
Opel emission control system
Controlled combustion system
Dashpot

Catalytic converter
Fuel evaporation control system
Positive crankcase ventilation system

CHAPTER EIGHT

ELECTRICAL SYSTEM . . . .

Battery
Ignition/starter switch
Starter motor
Distributor
Alternator
Generator
Generator/alternator voltage
    regulator

Ignition coil
Spark plugs
Ignition cables
Light bulbs
Fusible links
Fuses
Wiring diagrams

CHAPTER NINE

CLUTCH, TRANSMISSION, AND DRIVE SHAFT . . . .

Clutch assembly
Manual transmission

Automatic transmission
Drive shaft

QUICK REFERENCE DATA

BREAKER PLATE SCREWS

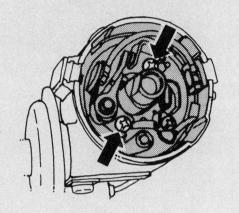

IDLE ADJUSTMENT

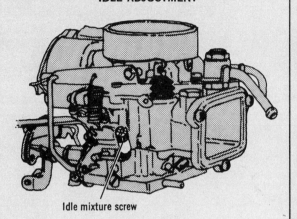

Idle mixture screw

ENGINE TUNE-UP

Cylinder firing order	1-3-4-2	
Spark plugs	AC 43FS (1.1 liter); AC 44XLO (1.5 liter);	
Type	AC 42FS (1.9 liter through 1974); AC 42.6FS (1.9 liter, 1975); AC R44 XLS (1.8 liter, 1976 on)	
Gap	0.030 in.	
Valve clearance*	**Intake:**	**Exhaust:**
1.1 liter	0.006 in.	0.010 in.
1.5 (1968) and 1.9 liter (1968-1970)	0.012 in.	0.012 in.
1.9 liter (1971-1975 models)	Zero, plus 1 turn 0.006 in. (cold)	Zero, plus 1 turn 0.010 in. (cold)
1.8 liter (1976 on)	0.008 in. (hot)	0.012 in. (hot)
Breaker point gap		
1966-1973 models	0.018 in.	
1974-1975 models	0.016 in.	
1976 models on	0.018 in.	
Dwell		
1966-1973 models	50 ± 2°	
1974-1975 models	50 ± 3°	
1976 models on	52 ± 2°	
Idle speed		
1.1 liter	950-1,000 rpm	
1.5 liter (1968)	750-850 rpm	
1.9 liter (1968-1970)	750-780 rpm	
1.9 liter (1971)	850-900 rpm (manual transmission) 800-850 rpm (automatic transmission)	
All models, 1972 on	Refer to specifications on tune-up label under hood	

*All engines through 1970 require valve adjustment with engine running; all engines from 1971 on require valve adjustment with engine off.

CHASSIS ADJUSTMENT

Model	Clutch Pedal Free Play
1.1 liter (1966-1968)	¾-1 in.
1.1 liter (1969)	½-1 in.
1.1 liter (1970-1971)	¾-1¼ in.
1.5 liter (1968)	¾-1 in.
1.9 liter (1968)	¾-1 in.
1.9 liter (1969-1970)	½-1 in.
1.9 liter (1971-1975)	Operates without clutch pedal free play
1.8 liter (1976 on)	⅝ in.

RECOMMENDED LUBRICANTS

	Temperature	Type	Capacity
Engine	Below 20°F	SE, 5W-20, 5W-30*	1966-1975: 3.0 U.S. qt. (2.84 liter)
	0°F to 60°F	SE, 10W, 5W-30, 10W-30, 10W-40*	
	20°F and above	SE, 20W,10W-30, 10W-40, 20W-40, or 20W-50*	1976 and later: 5.0 U.S. qt. (4.73 liter)
Rear axle	Below 50°F	GL-5, SAE 80	2½ U.S. pt. (1.25 liter)
	0° to 90°F	GL-5, SAE 90	
Manual transmission 1966-1975	Below 50°F	Multipurpose gear lubricant MIL-L-2105B, SAE 80	2.64 U.S. pt. (1.25 liter)
	Above 50°F	Multipurpose gear lubricant MIL-L-2105B, SAE 90	
1976 and later	Below 50°F	SE engine oil, SAE 10W-30	2.64 U.S. pt. (1.25 liter)
	Above 50°F	SE engine oil, SAE 40	
	Between 0° and 90°F	SE engine oil, SAE 30	
Automatic transmission	All temperatures	DEXRON II ATF	6.5 U.S. qt. (6.15 liter)

* SAE 5W-20 oils are not recommended for sustained high-speed driving.
  SAE 30 oils may be used at temperatures above 40°F.

DRIVE BELT ADJUSTMENT

Center-to-center distance between pulleys:	When pressure is applied midway between pulleys, belt should depress:
7-10 in.	¼ in.
13-16 in.	½ in.

TIRE PRESSURE RECOMMENDATIONS

Load	Front*	Rear*
Up to vehicle load capacity (4 occupants, 600 lb. total; and trunk load of 125 lb., for total of 725 lb.)	24 psi	28 psi
Four occupants (600 lb. total)	24 psi	24 psi

* Check when cold.

CHAPTER ONE

GENERAL INFORMATION

This service and repair handbook provides complete information and procedures for all Opel cars imported into the United States from 1966 on. To use it, you need only know your car's engine size and model year.

Four different engines have been used: 1.1, 1.5, 1.8, and 1.9. In 1966 and 1967, the only engine available was the 1.1 liter. In 1968, 1.5 and 1.9 engines were added. All 1969-1971 models use either the 1.1 or 1.9 engine. Models from 1972 through 1975 use the 1.9 engine, only. Models from 1976 on use the 1.8 engine, manufactured in Japan (models from 1966 through 1975 were manufactured in Germany).

All engines are of 4-cylinder, inline, overhead valve design. The valves in the 1.1 engine are operated by pushrod-driven rocker arms: the camshaft is the engine block. On 1.5, 1.8, and 1.9 engines, the valves are operated by camshaft-driven valve lifters. The camshaft is in the cylinder head.

Transmissions include fully synchronized 4-speed (and, introduced in 1976, a 5-speed) manual transmission, and a 3-speed automatic. The 5-speed transmission is not available in California and certain high altitude areas.

Several different types of carburetion have been used, depending on model year, horsepower output, and emission control require-

ments. The 1976 Opel models use Bosch L-Jetronic Fuel Injection, a Pulse Time Manifold Injection System that injects metered fuel into the intake manifold near the intake valves by electronically controlled injection valves. All 1976 and later cars use a 2-barrel downdraft carburetor.

NOTE: *The 1976 and later models are covered in the* Supplement *section at the back of this manual.*

MANUAL ORGANIZATION

This chapter provides general information on the Opel line, plus valuable service hints and a brief description of recommended hand tools and test equipment useful for preventive maintenance, tune-up, and troubleshooting.

Chapter Two explains all periodic lubrication and routine maintenance, and recommended tune-up procedures required to keep your car in top running condition.

Chapter Three provides methods and suggestions for finding and fixing troubles fast. Troubleshooting procedures discuss typical symptoms and logical methods to pinpoint the trouble.

Subsequent chapters describe specific systems such as the engine; fuel and exhaust systems; cooling and heating systems; emission control systems; electrical system; clutch; transmission and drive shaft; front suspension, wheels, and steering; differential, rear axle, and rear suspension; and brakes.

Each chapter provides disassembly, repair, and assembly procedures in easily followed, step-by-step form. All procedures are given in the most practical sequence. Complex and lengthy operations are described in detail and are thoroughly illustrated. The exploded views show the correct sequence of all parts as well as a listing of the parts needed for replacement. These can be of considerable help as a reference during disassembly and reassembly.

Installation and assembly procedures are given where they differ from removal and disassembly procedures.

Italic notes of caution or operation emphasis appear throughout the text to ensure safety and working efficiency.

U.S. standards are used throughout and are accompanied by metric equivalents in parentheses where such reference might have practical value. See **Table 1**.

MODEL IDENTIFICATION

See **Figure 1**. The manufacturer's identification plate does not identify the car by model year, but rather by model and number. The identification plate is attached to the front of the cowl between the battery and heater plenum on standard models, inside the right front inner fender panel on 1900 models, and on the top right side of the cowl in GT models. Information included on the plate includes type and model, allowable front axle load, allowable maximum vehicle weight, chassis serial number, allowable rear axle load, and paint color code.

The first 2 digits of the identification number indicate the vehicle model. The rest of the number is the vehicle serial number.

The engine number is stamped on a boss on the left side of the engine. The first 2 digits designate engine size; the following letters designate destination and model. For example: *1.1R US* is an 1100cc ECONO Opel engine imported into the United States. The rest of the number is the engine serial number.

RECOMMENDED TOOLS

Some of the procedures in this manual specify special tools, which are generally expensive. It is usually more practical to have an Opel dealer or repair shop perform only the step which requires the special tool. However, if you prefer to do your own work, no matter how involved it gets, special tools can be ordered through the Kent-Moore Organization, Inc., 28635 Mound Road, Warren, Michigan, 48092.

. Most of the procedures in this manual can be carried out with simple hand tools and test equipment familiar to the average home mechanic.

For proper servicing, you will need an assortment of ordinary hand tools. Recommended are:

a. Combination wrenches
b. Sockets, socket extension(s), and a socket wrench
c. Plastic mallet
d. Small hammer
e. Snap ring pliers
f. Pliers
g. Phillips and straight-blade screwdrivers
h. Feeler gauges
i. Tire pressure gauge

Table 1   CONVERSION CHART — MILLIMETERS TO INCHES

mm	in.	mm	in.	mm	in.
0.01	0.0004	0.51	0.0201	1	0.0394
0.02	0.0008	0.52	0.0205	2	0.0787
0.03	0.0012	0.53	0.0209	3	0.1181
0.04	0.0016	0.54	0.0213	4	0.1575
0.05	0.0020	0.55	0.0217	5	0.1969
0.06	0.0024	0.56	0.0221	6	0.2362
0.07	0.0028	0.57	0.0224	7	0.2756
0.08	0.0032	0.58	0.0228	8	0.3150
0.09	0.0035	0.59	0.0232	9	0.3543
0.10	0.0039	0.60	0.0236	10	0.3937
0.11	0.0043	0.61	0.0240	11	0.4331
0.12	0.0047	0.62	0.0244	12	0.4724
0.13	0.0051	0.63	0.0246	13	0.5118
0.14	0.0055	0.64	0.0252	14	0.5512
0.15	0.0059	0.65	0.0256	15	0.5906
0.16	0.0063	0.66	0.0260	16	0.6299
0.17	0.0067	0.67	0.0264	17	0.6693
0.18	0.0071	0.68	0.0268	18	0.7087
0.19	0.0075	0.69	0.0272	19	0.7480
0.20	0.0079	0.70	0.0276	20	0.7874
0.21	0.0083	0.71	0.0280	21	0.8268
0.22	0.0087	0.72	0.0284	22	0.8661
0.23	0.0091	0.73	0.0287	23	0.9055
0.24	0.0095	0.74	0.0291	24	0.9449
0.25	0.0098	0.75	0.0295	25	0.9843
0.26	0.0102	0.76	0.0299	26	1.0236
0.27	0.0106	0.77	0.0303	27	1.0630
0.28	0.0110	0.78	0.0307	28	1.1024
0.29	0.0114	0.79	0.0311	29	1.1417
0.30	0.0118	0.80	0.0315	30	1.1811
0.31	0.0122	0.81	0.0320	31	1.2205
0.32	0.0126	0.82	0.0323	32	1.2598
0.33	0.0130	0.83	0.0327	33	1.2992
0.34	0.0134	0.84	0.0331	34	1.3386
0.35	0.0138	0.85	0.0335	35	1.3779
0.36	0.0142	0.86	0.0339	36	1.4173
0.37	0.0146	0.87	0.0343	37	1.4567
0.38	0.0150	0.88	0.0347	38	1.4961
0.39	0.0154	0.89	0.0350	39	1.5354
0.40	0.0158	0.90	0.0354	40	1.5748
0.41	0.0161	0.91	0.0358	41	1.6142
0.42	0.0165	0.92	0.0362	42	1.6535
0.43	0.0169	0.93	0.0366	43	1.6929
0.44	0.0173	0.94	0.0370	44	1.7323
0.45	0.0177	0.95	0.0374	45	1.7716
0.46	0.0181	0.96	0.0378	46	1.8110
0.47	0.0185	0.97	0.0382	47	1.8504
0.48	0.0186	0.98	0.0386	48	1.8898
0.49	0.0193	0.99	0.0390	49	1.9291
0.50	0.0197			50	1.9685

Any owner-mechanic intent on saving money and aggravation by doing his own repair and maintenance work should invest in the following test instruments:

1. *Hydrometer* (**Figure 2**). The hydrometer gives a useful indication of battery condition and charge by measuring the specific gravity of the electrolyte in each cell. Such an instrument is available at any auto parts store and through most large mail order outlets. Refer to Chapter Eight for details on the correct use and interpretation of hydrometer readings.

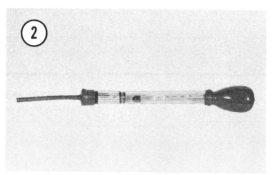

2. *Compression Gauge* (**Figure 3**). The compression gauge measures the compression pressure built up in each cylinder. Interpretation of compression test results can indicate general cylinder and valve condition. The gauge shown has a flexible stem, which enables it to reach cylinders where there is little clearance. Inexpensive ones are available at most auto accessory stores or by mail from large catalog order outlets. See Chapter Two for complete details on the correct use and interpretation of compression readings under the *Compression Test* heading in the *Tune-Up* section.

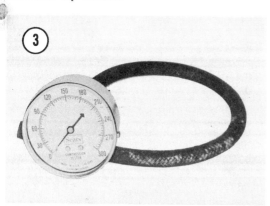

3. *Vacuum Gauge* (**Figure 4**). The vacuum gauge is one of the easiest instruments to use, but one of the most difficult for the inexperienced mechanic to interpret. Used in conjunction with the compression gauge, the results can provide valuable information as to an engine's condition.

4. *Dwell Meter* (**Figure 5**). A dwell meter measures the distance in degrees of cam rotation that the breaker points remain closed while the engine is running. Since this angle is determined by the breaker point gap, the dwell angle is an accurate indication of point gap.

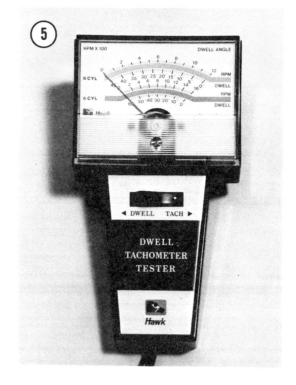

5. *Tachometer* (Figure 5). A tachometer measures engine speed and is necessary for setting ignition timing and adjusting the carburetors.

The best instrument for this purpose is one with a range of 0-2,000 rpm. Tachometers with an extended range (0-6,000 or 0-8,000 rpm) lack accuracy at lower speeds. The tachometer should be capable of detecting changes of 25 rpm.

Many tachometers intended for testing and tuning incorporate a dwell meter.

6. *Strobe Timing Light* (**Figure 6**). This instrument permits extremely accurate engine timing. The light flashes precisely at the same instant that the No. 1 cylinder fires, so the position of the crankshaft pulley relative to a fixed timing mark at that instant can be seen. The timing mark on the pulley must be in alignment with the stationary timing mark. This is accomplished by adjusting the distributor.

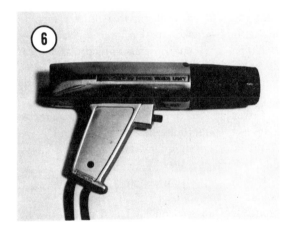

Suitable lights are neon bulb and xenon strobe types. Neon bulb timing lights are difficult to see and must be used in dimly lit areas. Xenon strobe timing lights can be used in bright sunlight. Use the light according to the manufacturer's instructions.

7. *Fuel Pressure Gauge.* This instrument is vital for evaluating fuel pump performance. It measures the force that the pump is exerting to push gasoline through the fuel lines. Often a fuel pressure gauge is combined with a vacuum gauge.

8. *Voltmeter, Ammeter, and Ohmmeter* (**Figure 7**). A good voltmeter is required for testing the ignition and electrical systems. The meter should range from 0 to 20 volts, and have an accuracy of ½ volt.

The ohmmeter measures electrical resistance and is required to check continuity (open and short circuits), and to test fuses and lights.

The ammeter measures electrical current. One for automotive use should cover 0 to 10 amperes and 0 to 100 amperes. An ammeter is useful for checking battery charging and starting current. The starter and generator (alternator) inspection and repair procedures use an ammeter to check for shorted windings.

Some inexpensive VOM's (volt-ohmmeters) combine all 3 instruments into one. The ammeter ranges are usually too small for automotive work, however.

9. *Exhaust Analyzer* (**Figure 8**). This instrument is necessary to check emission control adjustments accurately. It samples the exhaust gases from the tailpipe and measures the thermal conductivity of the exhaust. Since different gases conduct heat at varying rates, thermal conductivity of the exhaust is a good indicator of the gases present.

Exhaust analyzers are relatively expensive to buy, but some large rent-all dealers have them available at a modest price.

SERVICE HINTS

Observing the following practices will save time, effort, and frustration, as well as prevent possible injury.

Throughout this manual keep in mind 2 conventions: "Front" refers to the front of the car.

The front of any component such as the engine is that end which faces towards the front of the car. The left and right side of the car refer to a person sitting in the car facing forward. For example, the steering wheel is on the left side.

When working under a car, do not trust a hydraulic or mechanical jack alone to hold the car up. Always use jackstands.

Disconnect the battery ground cables before working near electrical connections and before disconnecting wires. But, *never* run the engine with the battery disconnected; the alternator could be seriously damaged.

Tag all similar internal parts for location and mark all mating parts for position. Record number and thickness of any shims as they are removed. Small parts such as bolts can be identified by placing them in plastic sandwich bags and sealing and labeling the bags with some kind of masking tape.

Protect finished surfaces from damage or corrosion. Keep gasoline and brake fluid off painted surfaces.

Frozen or very tight bolts and screws can often be loosened by soaking with penetrating oil, then sharply striking the bolt head a few times with a hammer and punch (or screwdriver for screws). Avoid heat, unless absolutely necessary, since it may melt, warp, or remove the temper from many parts.

Avoid flames or sparks when working near a charging battery or flammable liquids such as brake fluid or gasoline.

No parts, except those assembled with a press fit, require unusual force during assembly. If a part is hard to remove or install, find out why before proceeding.

Cover all openings after removing parts to keep dirt, small tools, etc., from falling in.

When assembling 2 parts, start all fasteners, then tighten evenly.

Read each procedure in its entirety while looking at the actual part before beginning. Many procedures are complicated and errors can be disastrous. When you thoroughly understand what is to be done, follow the procedure step-by-step.

In procedural steps, the term "replace" means to discard a defective part and replace it with a new or exchange unit. "Overhaul" means to remove, disassemble, inspect, measure, repair or replace defective parts, reassemble, and install major systems and parts.

CHAPTER TWO

LUBRICATION, MAINTENANCE, AND TUNE-UP

This chapter provides lubrication, maintenance, and tune-up procedures for all 1966-1975 Opel models. Refer to the *Supplement* section, Chapter Two, at the back of this book for additional procedures for 1976 and later models.

ROUTINE CHECKS

The following simple checks should be performed at each fuel stop.

1. Check engine oil. The engine should be warm and the car parked on level ground. Turn the engine off. Remove the oil gauge rod (dipstick), wipe it clean, and reinsert it for an accurate reading. The oil level should be maintained in the safety margin, neither going above the FULL mark, nor below the ADD OIL mark. See **Figure 1**. Replenish as necessary with oil of the proper viscosity (see **Table 1**).

2. Check the battery electrolyte level. It should be ½ in. above the top of the battery plates. Replenish with distilled water if it is low. See **Figure 2**.

3. Check tire air pressure, preferably when the tires are cold.

PREVENTIVE MAINTENANCE

Performed less frequently than the routine checks described preceding, scheduled checks

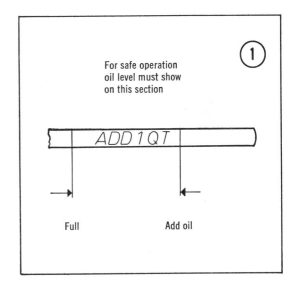

For safe operation oil level must show on this section

ADD 1 QT

Full   Add oil

Table 1   OIL VISCOSITY CHART

Temperature	Recommended SAE Viscosity
Below 20°F	5W-20, 5W-30
0°F to 60°F	10W, 5W-30, 10W-30, 10W-40
20°F and over	20W, 10W-30, 10W-40, 20W-40
Note: SAE 5W-20 oils are not recommended for sustained high-speed driving. SAE 30 oils may be used at temperatures above 40°F.	

and maintenance keep a car running smoothly. Adherence to the following recommendations will ensure top performance.

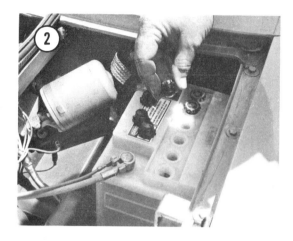

Engine Compartment

Check the entire engine compartment for leaking or deteriorated oil and fuel lines. Check electrical wiring for breaks in insulation caused by deterioration or chafing. See **Figure 3**. Check for loose or missing nuts, bolts, and screws.

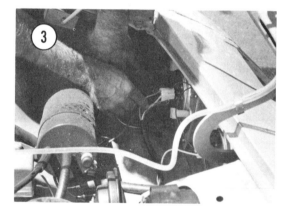

Radiator Coolant

Check the radiator level only at oil change intervals, unless there is evidence of leakage or overheating. The coolant level should be 2 in. below the top of the filler neck when the engine is cold. Add a 50/50 mixture of high quality ethylene glycol anti-freeze and water if coolant additions are necessary. Do not overfill.

WARNING
Use care when removing radiator cap on a warm or hot engine. Hot water under pressure can boil out when pressure is released and cause severe scalding or burns. Loosen radiator cap to

first notch and wait for pressure to escape before removing cap.

The cooling system should be drained, flushed with clean water, and refilled with anti-freeze at least every 2 years.

Replace any hoses that are cracked, deteriorated, or extremely soft. Make sure all hoses are correctly installed, and all clamps secure. See **Figure 4**.

See Chapter Six for radiator removal and installation procedures.

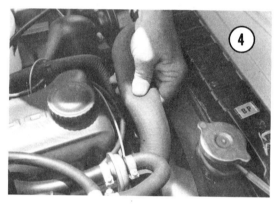

Drive Belts

Inspect all drive belts at the first 4 months, or 6,000 miles, and every 4 months or 6,000 miles thereafter, for wear, fraying, cracking and improper tension. A belt should be retightened only when it deflects more than ½ in. with moderate thumb pressure applied midway between pulleys. See **Figure 5**.

A wise move is to automatically replace belts every 24 months or 24,000 miles.

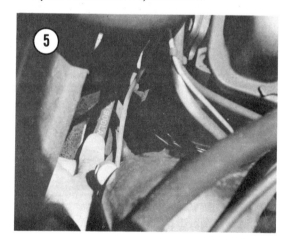

Battery

Water is the only component of the battery which is lost as the result of charging and discharging. It must be replaced before the electrolyte level falls to the tops of the battery plates. (If the plates become exposed they may become permanently sulphated, which would impair the performance of the battery. Also, the plates cannot take part in the battery action unless they are completely covered by the electrolyte.) Add distilled water as often as necessary to keep the electrolyte level at ½ in. above the top of the battery plates. Do not overfill.

When working with batteries, use extreme care to avoid spilling or splashing the electrolyte. This electrolyte is sulfuric acid, which can destroy clothing and cause serious chemical burns. If any electrolyte is spilled or splashed on clothing or body, it should immediately be neutralized with a solution of baking soda and water, then flushed with plenty of clean water.

WARNING
Electrolyte splashed into the eyes is extremely dangerous. Safety glasses should always be worn when working with batteries. If electrolyte is splashed into the eyes, call a physician immediately, force the eyes open, and flood with cool, clean water for about 5 minutes.

If electrolyte is spilled or splashed onto painted or unpainted surfaces, it should be neutralized immediately with baking soda and water solution and then rinsed with clean water.

Keep the battery clean by brushing it with an ammonia or baking soda solution; flush off with clean water. Apply petroleum jelly to the battery terminals to retard corrosion. See **Figure 6**.

Refer to Chapter Eight for battery removal, installation, and battery charging information.

Emission Control Maintenance

a. *Catalytic Converter*—All 1975 Opels to be sold in California only are equipped with a catalytic converter—an emission control device added to the exhaust system to reduce hydrocarbon and carbon monoxide pollutants from the exhaust gas stream. The converter contains

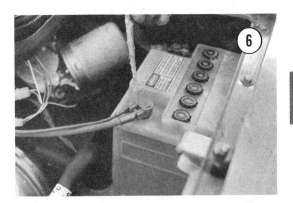

beads which are coated with a catalytic material containing platinum and paladium. The catalytic converter (**Figures 7 and 8**) requires the use of unleaded fuel.

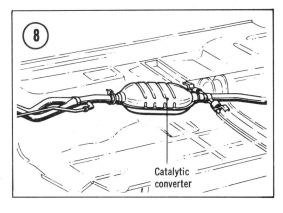

Catalytic converter

b. *Positive Crankcase Ventilation System*—The PCV metered orifice should be cleaned at 12,000 mile intervals under normal use, and at 6,000 mile intervals when the car is used under adverse conditions (trailer pulling, short trip operation at below freezing temperatures, dusty driving conditions, etc.).

c. *Evaporation Control System* — Check all vapor and fuel lines for proper connections and condition. Remove canister and check for damage. Replace the filter in the open end of the canister at 24 month/24,000 mile intervals. See **Figure 9**.

d. *Exhaust Gas Recirculation System*—Every 12 months or 12,000 miles, check and clean the EGR passages. See **Figure 10**.

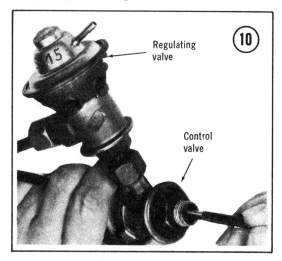

Regulating valve

Control valve

e. *Carburetor Fuel Inlet Filter*—Replace every 12 months or 12,000 miles. See **Figure 11**.

f. *Fuel Cap, Fuel Lines, and Fuel Tank*—Inspect for damage. The fuel cap should seal properly. See **Figure 12**.

g. *Air Cleaner (Thermostatically Controlled)*— Be sure that all hoses and ducts are securely connected. Check valve for proper operation. See **Figure 13**.

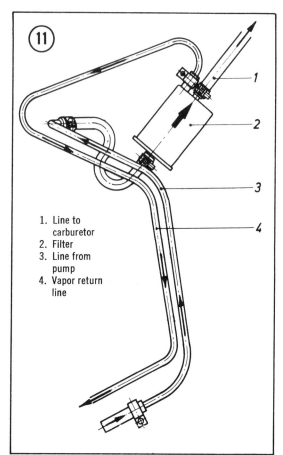

1. Line to carburetor
2. Filter
3. Line from pump
4. Vapor return line

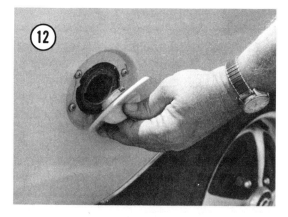

h. *Air Cleaner (Conventional)*—Inspect the filter element every 6,000 miles and replace if necessary. Replace every 24,000 miles (more often under extremely dusty conditions). See **Figure 14**. The engine air cleaner should be installed at all times during engine operation to avoid the possibility of engine backfiring causing a fire in the engine compartment.

Refer to Chapter Seven for detailed procedures on the emission control system.

Engine Oil Change

The oil change interval varies depending on the type of driving you do. For normal driving, including some city traffic, change oil every 4 months or 3,500 miles, whichever occurs first. If driving is primarily short distance with considerable stop-and-go city traffic, or if conditions are particularly dusty, change oil more often (possibly even twice as often). Change oil at least twice a year if the car is driven only a few hundred miles a month. To drain oil:

1. Warm the engine to operating temperature.

2. Remove the drain plug from the oil pan. See **Figure 15**.

3. Let the oil drain for at least 10 minutes.

4. Install the oil drain plug.

5. Change the oil filter (see procedure below).

6. Remove the oil filler cap. Refill with SE engine oil (SE oils meet quality standard GM 6041-M). See Table 1 for recommended viscosity.

Engine Oil Filter

Replace the oil filter at the first oil change, and at every other oil change thereafter. Install the new filter after the oil has been drained and before the new oil is poured in.

To remove the filter, unscrew it by hand or use a filter wrench. See **Figure 16**. Wipe the gasket area of the base with a clean, lint-free cloth. Coat the gasket on the new filter with clean oil. Install the filter by hand until the gasket just touches the base, then tighten ½ turn by hand. Snug down with a filter wrench, but do not overtighten.

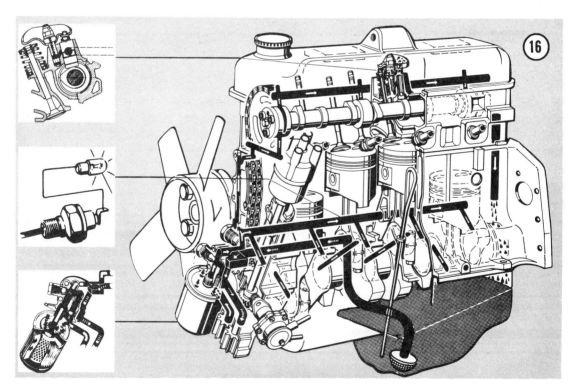

Engine Oil Pump

The oil pump and filter screen should be cleaned whenever the oil pan and/or timing gear cover are removed.

See Chapter Four for removal and installation procedures.

Clutch

Check the clutch pedal free-play by depressing the pedal by hand. Free-play on cars equipped with the 1.1 engine should be ¾ to 1 in. for 1966-1968 models; and ¾ to 1¼ in. for 1970-1971 models. Early cars (and all GT's) fitted with the 1.5 and 1.9 engines use the same adjustments as those fitted with the 1.1 engine. See **Figure 17**.

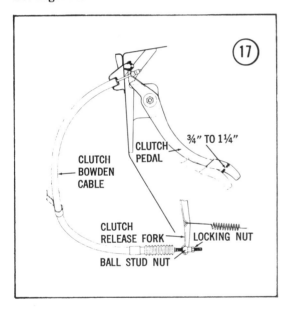

On late models, clutch actuation works without clutch pedal free-play. Readjustment of the clutch is required only if the indicator lamp on the instrument panel lights up.

CAUTION
If the indicator lights up, it is possible that the emergency brake is partially on. Make sure the emergency brake is completely disengaged. If the indicator is still on, the clutch must be adjusted.

Late model clutch adjustment is accomplished by loosening the ball stud locknut (see **Figure 18**), then adjusting the ball stud until the distance between the clutch housing contacting surface and clutch release lever is 4¼ in. After the adjustment has been completed, tighten the ball stud locknut and check to make certain the indicator light is not on.

See Chapter Nine for removal and installation procedures.

Manual Transmission

Check the oil level in the transmission. With the transmission at normal operating temperature, remove the filler plug. See **Figure 19**. The oil level should just reach the bottom of the filler plug hole. If the lubricant level is checked with the unit cold, the level should be ½ in. below the filler plug hole. If the quantity is low, top the transmission up with SAE 80 or 80-90 Multi-Purpose Gear Lubricant MIL-L-2105B.

See Chapter Nine for removal and installation procedures.

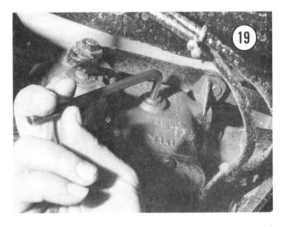

Automatic Transmission

Check the fluid level on the dipstick with the car parked on a level surface, engine idling, selector lever in PARK, parking brake set, and the transmission at operating temperature (approximately 180-190 degrees F). Pull out the dipstick, wipe it with a clean cloth, and reinsert it until the cap seats firmly. Pull the dipstick out again and check that the level is between the 2 marks (see **Figure 20**). If necessary, add fluid (GM DEXRON or equivalent), but do not overfill. If level is above the top-mark, fluid must be drained to restore proper level, or seals may be damaged.

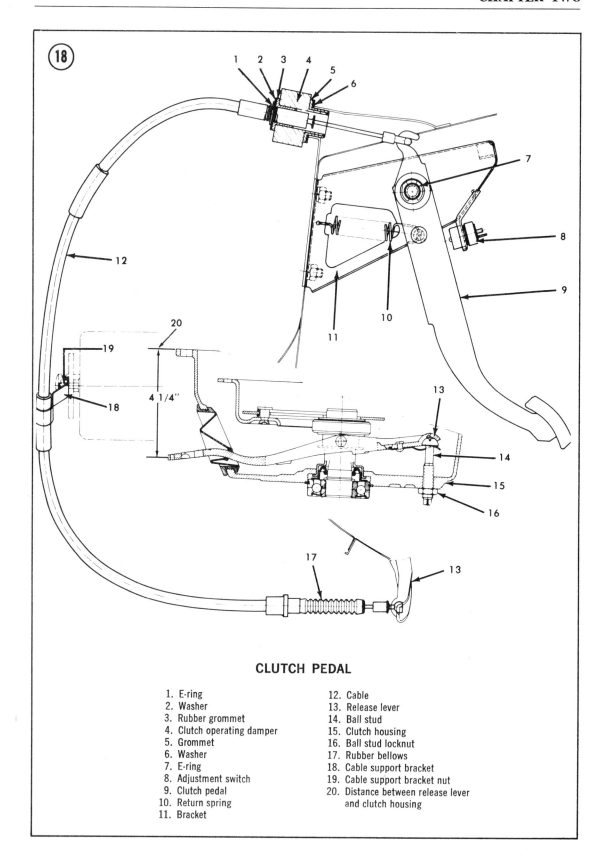

CLUTCH PEDAL

1. E-ring
2. Washer
3. Rubber grommet
4. Clutch operating damper
5. Grommet
6. Washer
7. E-ring
8. Adjustment switch
9. Clutch pedal
10. Return spring
11. Bracket
12. Cable
13. Release lever
14. Ball stud
15. Clutch housing
16. Ball stud locknut
17. Rubber bellows
18. Cable support bracket
19. Cable support bracket nut
20. Distance between release lever
    and clutch housing

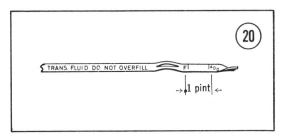

Automatic transmission fluid in the transmission sump must be changed every 24,000 miles in normal driving, 12,000 miles in heavy duty driving. See Chapter Nine for removal and installation procedures.

Rear Axle

Check the lubricant level every 4 months or 6,000 miles. Remove the filler plug. See **Figure 21**. The oil level should just reach the bottom of the filler plug hole. If necessary, top up with SAE 80 or SAE 90 GL-5 Gear Lubricant.

See Chapter Eleven for removal and installation procedures.

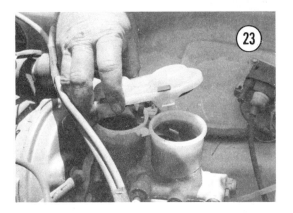

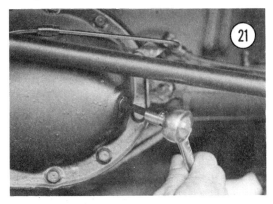

Exhaust System

Examine the exhaust pipes, mufflers, and hangers for rust, holes, and other damage. See **Figure 22**. Replace any worn parts.

See Chapter Five for removal and installation procedures.

Brakes

Check the fluid level in the master cylinder. See **Figure 23**. Maintain level between minimum and maximum reservoir level marks. Use Delco

Supreme II Hydraulic Brake Fluid or equivalent. Never use reclaimed fluid, mineral oil, or fluid inferior to SAE J 1703.

On disc brake models, check the condition of the pads and discs while the wheels are being removed during tire rotation. See **Figure 24**. Have scored or corroded discs turned down. Replace pads that are worn or contaminated with oil, grease, or brake fluid.

Check the wheel cylinders and calipers for brake fluid leaks. Rebuild or replace defective calipers or cylinders.

Check the brake lines and hoses for leaks and wear. If worn spots are visible, replace the line or hose after determining what is causing the wear and correcting the problem.

On drum brakes, remove the drums and inspect the linings. See **Figure 25**. Replace the brake shoes if the linings are worn or contaminated with oil, grease, or brake fluid. Check the drums for scoring or uneven wear. Have the drums turned if necessary. Check the drums and shoes for blue-tinted areas indicating overheating. Replace any overheated parts. In addition,

2

replace brake springs if overheated parts are found.

The parking brake should be adjusted and inspected for signs of wear, cracks, leakage, etc., and defective parts replaced if necessary.

See Chapter Twelve for removal and installation procedures.

Tire and Wheel Inspection

Check the condition of all tires, including the spare. Check local traffic regulations concerning minimum tread depth. Most recommend replacing tires when tread depth is less than 1/32 in. The original equipment tires on the Opel incorporate built-in tread wear indicators. These indicators will appear as ½ in. wide bands when the tire tread depth is 1/16 in. or less. When the indicators appear in 2 or more adjacent grooves, tire replacement is recommended. See **Figure 26**.

To equalize wear it is recommended that the tires be rotated every 6,000 miles. Tire pressure should be adjusted after tires are rotated. Check wheel lug nuts for tightness.

NOTE: *1975 Opels have larger brakes than previous models, therefore a larger wheel (5½J x 13) with an 8 vent hole design is used. The old style wheel (4 vent holes) cannot be used on 1975 vehicles but 1975 wheels can be used on older models. All 1975 Opels use 165SR x 13 steel belted radial tires.*

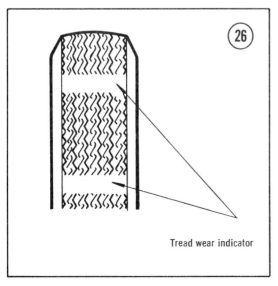

Tread wear indicator

Wheel Bearings

Clean, pack, and adjust the front wheel bearings every time the brakes are inspected or serviced. See **Figure 27**. Use high melting point grease conforming to GM Specification 6031-M. See Chapter Ten for removal and installation procedures.

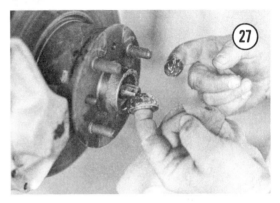

Steering and Suspension

No lubrication of the steering or suspension is required. However, the bushings and rubber parts should be inspected for damage or looseness. See **Figure 28**. Step-by-step procedures pertaining to the front suspension, wheels, and steering can be found in Chapter Ten.

Shock Absorbers

Inspect shock absorbers for damage and seal leaks. See **Figure 29**. Push down on each corner of the car with all of your weight, then release it. The car should rebound upward to its normal height and remain there without further "bobbing." If the car continues to oscillate the shock absorber(s) need replacement. Always replace

the upper and lower rubber grommets when replacing a shock absorber.

See Chapter Ten for removal and installation procedures.

Body

Check all glass for scratches or breakage which could obscure vision. Check all latches (seat backs, doors, hood, trunk) for positive closing, latching, and locking. Lubricate sparingly (see **Figure 30**). Replace defective windshield wiper blades.

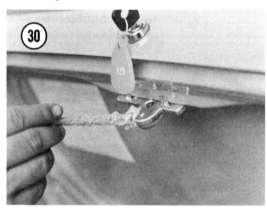

ENGINE TUNE-UP

The purpose of a tune-up is to restore power and performance lost over a gradual period of time due to normal wear.

Because of Federal laws limiting exhaust emissions, it is important that the engine tune-up is done accurately, using the specifications listed and the tune-up sticker found in each engine compartment.

Economical, trouble-free operation can better be assured if a complete tune-up is performed at the first 4 months or 6,000 miles of operation, and at 12 month or 12,000 mile intervals thereafter.

Tune-ups generally consist of 3 distinct categories: compression, ignition, and carburetion. Carburetion adjustments should not be attempted until the compression and ignition phases have been completed. Carry out the tune-up in the same sequence as in this chapter for best results. See **Table 2** at end of chapter.

Tune-up Equipment Hook-up

A description of the various tools and specialized test instruments can be found in Chapter One. Always follow the manufacturer's recommendations for use of test instruments. If such instructions are not available, the following can be used as a general guide:

a. *Voltmeter*—Connect the positive lead to the resistor side of the coil, and the negative lead to the ground.

b. *Timing Light*—Connect the positive lead to the positive battery terminal; connect the trigger lead to the No. 1 spark plug; and connect the negative lead to ground.

c. *Tachometer*—Connect the positive lead to the distributor side of the coil, and the negative lead to ground.

d. *Dwell Meter*—Connect the positive lead to the distributor side of the coil, and the negative lead to ground.

Valve Clearance Adjustment

Noisy valves and valve lifters generally affect the driver's nerves more than they do engine performance. It is quite a simple problem to correct, however, so there is no point in enduring the din produced by clattering valve train components.

Before attempting to judge the valve noise level, warm the engine to operating temperature. Listen for valve noise while sitting in the driver's seat with the hood closed. Run the engine at idle and various higher speeds.

If the valve mechanism is abnormally noisy, remove the bolts fixing the rocker arm cover to the cylinder head. Remove the rocker arm cover and the gasket. Do not damage the gasket.

A piece of heater hose may be used as a "stethoscope" quite effectively to locate the particular valve that is causing the noise. With the engine running at a speed where the noise is pronounced, hold one end of the hose to an ear and the other end about ½ in. from the point of contact between the rocker arm and valve stem.

Noisy valves can be caused by one or more of the following conditions:

a. *Sticking, warped, or eccentric valves, and/or worn guides*—Sticking valves can cause irregular engine operation or missing on a low speed pull. Pour penetrating oil over the valve spring cap and let it drain down the valve stem. Apply pressure to first one side of the valve spring, then the other. Rotate the valve spring about ½ turn. If any of these operations affect the valve noise, the valves should be reconditioned or replaced.

b. *Worn or scored parts in the valve train*—Inspect the rocker arm and pushrod ends for scoring. Check the pushrods for bends, and the valve lifters and camshaft surfaces for scoring. Replace faulty parts.

All 1.1, 1.5, and early model (through 1970) 1.9 engines require valve adjustment with the engine running at slow idle, as follows.

1. Start the engine and run it until it reaches normal operating temperatures.

2. Remove the bolts holding the rocker arm cover to the cylinder head. Remove the rocker arm cover and gasket, being careful not to damage the gasket. See **Figure 31**.

3. With the engine running at slow idle, insert a proper size feeler gauge between the valve stem and the rocker arm mating face (see Table 2 for the required specifications). Use a wrench to loosen or tighten the adjusting nut on the top of the rocker arm until the clearance is correct. The feeler gauge should slide with a slight drag when the adjustment is correct. The adjusting nut is self-locking. For identification of the intake and exhaust valves, refer to Chapter Four.

Late model (1971 and after) 1.9 engines require valve adjustment with the engine off, as follows.

1. Valves can be adjusted satisfactorily with the engine hot or cold. Remove the spark plugs and bring the No. 1 piston up to TDC on the firing stroke. This can be accomplished by removing the distributor cap and observing the rotor. Check the position of the rotor (see **Figure 32**). Follow the spark path for the rotor tip through the distributor cap, high tension wire to the spark plug. This determines which cylinder is at the upper top center on the firing stroke.

2. Intake and exhaust valves should be closed for the No. 1 cylinder. Loosen the adjusting nuts on the top of the intake and exhaust rocker arms until clearance exists between the rocker arm and valve stem, and the rocker arm and hydraulic lifter. See **Figure 33**.

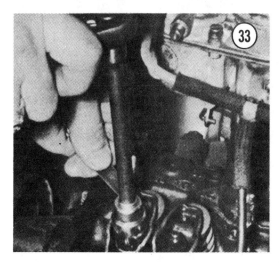

3. Slowly tighten the adjusting nut until clearance is eliminated. When clearance is eliminated,

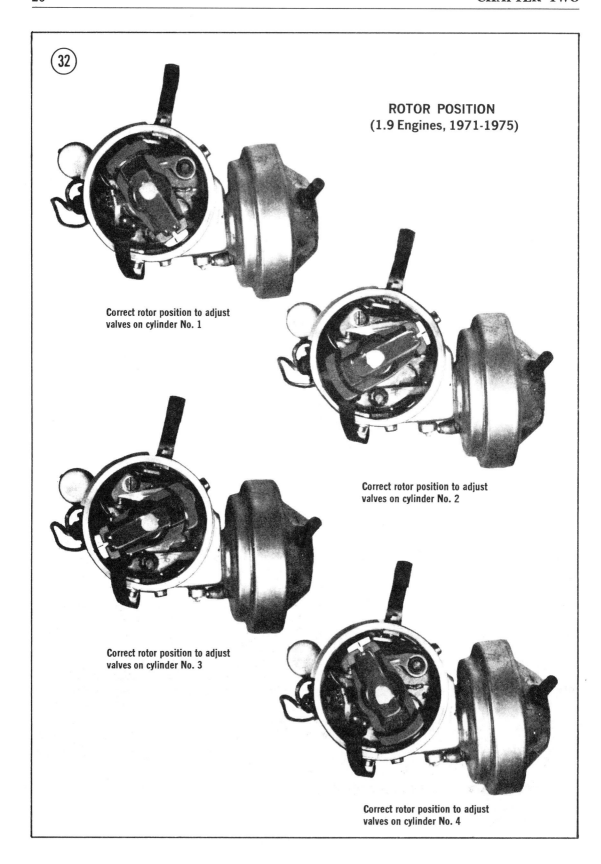

32

ROTOR POSITION
(1.9 Engines, 1971-1975)

Correct rotor position to adjust
valves on cylinder No. 1

Correct rotor position to adjust
valves on cylinder No. 2

Correct rotor position to adjust
valves on cylinder No. 3

Correct rotor position to adjust
valves on cylinder No. 4

turn the adjusting nut one full turn (clockwise). This positions the hydraulic piston of the hydraulic lifter midpoint in its total available travel. No further adjustment is necessary. The nuts are self-locking.

4. Repeat the above steps for the other cylinders in firing order: 1-3-4-2. This is accomplished by turning the engine so that another cylinder is at TDC on the firing stroke. Adjust the 2 valve lifters for that cylinder. Repeat the process until all the valves are adjusted.

Compression Test

A compression test is performed to check for worn piston rings and/or valves. After adjusting valves (see *Valve Clearance Adjustment*, above), check compression as follows.

1. Start the engine and run it until normal operating temperature is reached. Shut the engine off, remove the air cleaner, and block the throttle and choke in the wide open position. See **Figure 34**.

2. Remove the spark plugs and washers from the cylinder head. (See *Spark Plug Inspection*

and *Service*, following, for proper removal procedure). See **Figure 35**.

3. Connect a jumper wire between the distributor terminal of the coil and the ground on the engine to avoid high tension sparking while cranking the engine.

4. Firmly insert the compression gauge into the spark plug hole (see **Figure 36**). Have an assistant crank the engine over several revolutions to obtain the highest possible reading on the compression gauge. Write it down on a piece of paper.

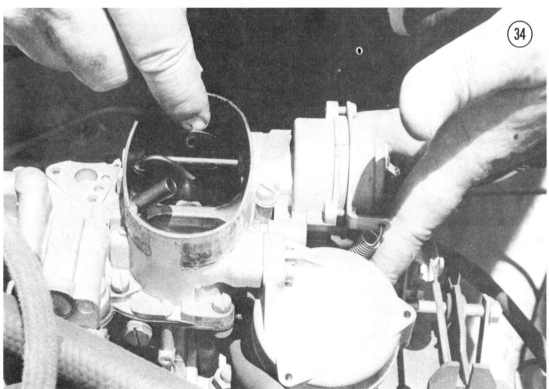

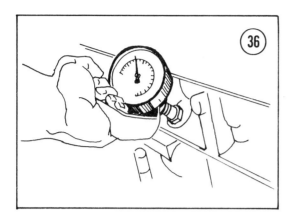

(36)

Table 3 COMPRESSION PRESSURE LIMITS

Pressure (psi)		Pressure (psi)	
Maximum	Minimum	Maximum	Minimum
134	101	188	141
136	102	190	142
138	104	192	144
140	105	194	145
142	107	196	147
146	110	198	148
148	111	200	150
150	113	202	151
152	114	204	153
154	115	206	154
156	117	208	156
158	118	210	157
160	120	212	158
162	121	214	160
164	123	216	162
166	124	218	163
168	126	220	165
170	127	222	166
172	129	224	168
174	131	226	169
176	132	228	171
178	133	230	172
180	135	232	174
182	136	234	175
184	138	236	177
186	140	238	178

5. Check the compression of each cylinder. Then repeat the compression check once more on each cylinder. Select the highest compression reading for each cylinder. The compression is considered normal if the lowest reading cylinder is more than 75 percent of the highest reading cylinder. See **Table 3**. This table may be used as a quick reference when checking cylinder compression pressures. It has been calculated so that the lowest reading number is 75 percent of the highest reading number.

Example: After checking the compression pressures in all cylinders it was found that the highest pressure obtained was 182 psi. The lowest pressure reading was 145 psi. By locating 182 in the maximum column, it is seen that the minimum allowable pressure is 136 psi. Since the lowest reading obtained was 145 psi, the compression is within satisfactory limits.

6. If one or more cylinders read low, pour a tablespoon of engine oil through the spark plug hole in the low reading cylinders. Repeat the compression check on these cylinders. If the compression improves considerably, the rings are worn. If the compression does not improve, the valves are sticking or seating poorly. If 2 adjacent cylinders indicate low compression and injecting oil does not increase compression, the cause may be the head gasket leaking between the cylinders. Engine coolant and/or oil in the cylinders could result from this defect.

Spark Plug Inspection and Service

Spark plugs are available in various heat ranges hotter or colder than the plug originally installed at the factory.

Select plugs of a heat range designed for the loads and temperature conditions under which the engine will run. Use of incorrect heat ranges can cause seized pistons, scored cylinder walls, or damaged piston crowns.

In general, use a lower-numbered plug for low speeds, low loads, and low temperatures. Use a higher-numbered plug for high speeds, high engine loads, and high temperatures.

> NOTE: *Use the highest numbered plug that will not foul. In areas where seasonal temperature variations are great, the factory recommends a high-numbered plug for slower winter operation.*

The reach (length) of a plug is also important. A longer than normal plug could interfere with the piston, causing permanent and severe damage. Refer to **Figures 37 and 38**.

A quick test can be made to determine if the plug is correct for your usage. Accelerate hard

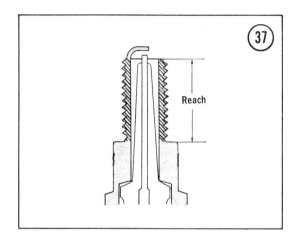

Reach

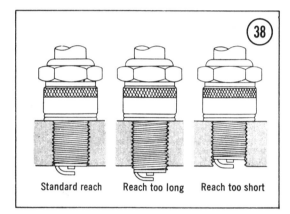

Standard reach   Reach too long   Reach too short

and maintain a high, steady speed. Shut the throttle off, and kill the engine at the same time, allowing the car to slow, out of gear. Don't allow the engine to slow the car. Remove the plug and check the condition of the electrode area. A spark plug of the correct heat range, with the engine in a proper state of tune, will appear light tan. See **Figure 39**.

If the insulator is white or burned, the plug is too hot and should be replaced with a colder one. Also check the setting of the carburetor for it may be too lean.

A too-cold plug will have sooty deposits ranging in color from dark brown to black. Replace with a hotter plug and check for too-rich carburetion.

If any one plug is found unsatisfactory, discard the set.

Changing spark plugs is generally a simple operation. Occasionally heat and corrosion can cause the plug to bind in the head, however, making removal difficult. Don't use force; the

head is easily damaged. Here is the proper way to replace a plug.

1. Blow out any debris which has collected in the spark plug wells. It could fall into the hole and cause severe damage.

2. Gently remove the spark plug leads by pulling up and out on the cap. Don't jerk the wires or pull on the wire itself.

3. Apply penetrating oil to the base of the plug and allow it to work into the threads.

4. Back out the plugs with a socket that has a rubber insert designed to grip the insulator. Be careful not to drop the plugs where they could become lodged. See **Figure 40**.

5. Remove the spark plug gaskets from the spark plug holes. Clean the seating area after removal.

6. Remove all grease and dirt from the insulator with a clean rag. Inspect the insulator and body of each spark plug for signs of cracks and chips. Replace if defective.

7. Clean the tips of the plugs with a sandblasting machine (some gas stations have them) or with a wire brush and solvent.

8. File the center electrode flat. Clean and file all surfaces of the outer electrode. All surfaces should be clean, flat, and smooth.

9. Using a round feeler gauge, adjust the clearance between the electrodes as specified in Table 2. See **Figure 41**. Do not try to bend the inner electrode or damage to the insulator may result.

10. Always use a new gasket if the old plugs are to be reused after cleaning. Apply a dab of

(39)

Normal plug appearance noted by the brown to grayish-tan deposits and slight electrode wear. This plug indicates the correct plug heat range and proper air fuel ratio.

Red, brown, yellow and white coatings caused by fuel and oil additives. These deposits are not harmful if they remain in a powdery form.

Carbon fouling distinguished by dry, fluffy black carbon deposits which may be caused by an over-rich air/fuel mixture, excessive hand choking, clogged air filter or excessive idling.

Shiny yellow glaze on insulator cone is caused when the powdery deposits from fuel and oil additives melt. Melting occurs during hard acceleration after prolonged idling. This glaze conducts electricity and shorts out the plug.

Oil fouling indicated by wet, oily deposits caused by oil pumping past worn rings or down the intake valve guides. A hotter plug temporarily reduces oil deposits, but a plug that is too hot leads to pre-ignition and possible engine damage.

Overheated plug indicated by burned or blistered insulator tip and badly worn electrodes. This condition may be caused by pre-ignition, cooling system defects, lean air/fuel ratios, low octane fuel or over advanced ignition timing.

Spark plug condition photos courtesy of AC Spark Plug Division, General Motors Corporation.

2

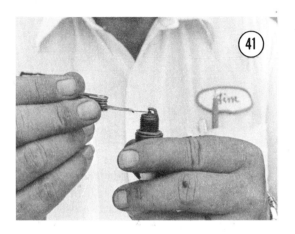

graphite to the spark plug threads to simplify future removal.

11. Thread the plug into the spark plug holes finger-tight then tighten ¼ turn more with a wrench. Further tightening will flatten the gasket and cause binding. If a torque wrench is available, torque the plugs to the recommended tightness (see Table 2).

12. Connect the spark plug wires to the spark plugs, making sure you do not get the wires crossed. Push the plug wire connectors firmly onto the spark plug tips.

Distributor Inspection and Service

The distributor is the heart of the ignition system, which consists of the distributor, contact breaker points, condenser, coil, high and low tension circuit parts. The low tension (primary) circuit consists of the power source (battery), contact breaker points, condenser, and ignition coil primary winding. The high tension (secondary) circuit consists of the ignition coil secondary winding, rotor arm, distributor cap electrical contacts, high tension cables, and spark plugs.

Most of the difficulties encountered in the distributor will be in the cap, rotor, contact points, condenser, or wiring. The distributor should operate noiselessly. If noise is apparent, the bearings or gears are worn and should be replaced.

Unless it is essential to remove the distributor from the engine for disassembly and parts replacement, all services can be performed with the distributor in place.

To adjust or replace the points, unsnap the clips or loosen the screws fixing the distributor cap to the distributor body. On late model 1.9 engines, push back the rubber boot covering the distributor cap. Remove the cap and examine the inside for signs of carbon tracks (arcing) from contact to contact. Carbon tracks indicate defects, such as cracks. If any are found, replace the cap.

Figure 42 shows the inside of the distributor used on the 1.1 engine with the distributor cap removed. Note how the rotor and body alignment marks are positioned when the No. 1 cylinder is at TDC on the compression stroke.

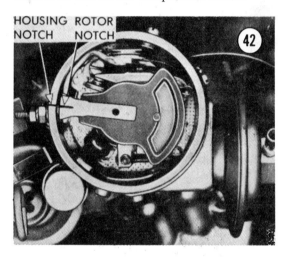

HOUSING ROTOR
NOTCH NOTCH

Remove the rotor by pulling it off the distributor shaft. Inspect it carefully for excessive wear or burning around the top metal contact surface. If defective, replace. As a matter of good practice, replace the rotor whenever the contact points are replaced.

Figure 43 shows the distributor used on the 1.5 and 1.9 engines with the rotor removed. Note how the rotor, drive shaft, and body alignment marks are positioned when the No. 1 cylinder is at TDC on the compression stroke.

Once the rotor is removed, the contact point assembly can be adjusted or replaced.

NOTE: *Late model distributors are equipped with an insulator between the rotor and distributor contact point assembly to prevent contamination of the point assembly. After removing the rotor, lift up and remove the insulator.*

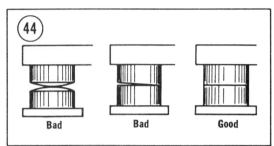

Adjust contact points by following these steps.
1. Rotate the distributor drive shaft cam by turning the crankshaft pulley until the moving contact (rubbing arm) is positioned at the highest point on the cam lobe. The contact points should be separated (open).

> NOTE: *Removal of the spark plugs will make it easier to turn the crankshaft pulley.*

2. Check that the insulation between the breaker contacts and the contact breaker base is not defective. A short-circuit will prevent the engine from running. To test for this condition, disconnect the wire or wires on the points, and with the points still blocked open, measure insulation resistance between the movable point and a good ground, using the highest range on the ohmmeter. If there is any indication at all on the ohmmeter, the points are shorted.

3. Contact surfaces may become pitted or worn from normal use. See **Figure 44**. If they are not too damaged, they can be dressed with a few strokes of a clean point file. Do not use sandpaper, as particles may remain on the points and cause arcing and burning. If a few strokes of a file don't smooth the points completely, they will have to be replaced.

4. Use a feeler gauge to measure the gap between the moveable and stationary contact points. For the correct gap, refer to Table 2.

5. Loosen the screw fixing the contact breaker assembly to the breaker plate. Move the stationary point until the correct gap is achieved. Tighten the screw. The feeler gauge should have a slight drag as the gauge is moved back and forth, but you should not be able to see the moveable point move. Recheck the gap after tightening the screw. If incorrect, readjust.

Replace the contact points by following these steps:

1. Unsnap the distributor cap clamps, remove the distributor cap, the rotor, and the insulating plate (if so equipped).

2. Disconnect the breaker point wire by pulling it off the connector (1.5, 1.9 engine) or by loosening the screw fixing it to the contact post (1.1 engine).

3. Remove the screw fixing the contact point assembly to the breaker plate. Pull up and remove the breaker point assembly.

4. Discard the old points and install new ones by reversing the above steps. Make sure the pivot shaft at the spring end of the assembly fits into the guide hole in the breaker plate.

5. See **Figure 45**. Lightly lubricate the sliding parts of the breaker plate (B) and the felt in the drive shaft (C) with oil. Apply a thin coating of high-melting-point grease to the cam (A).

6. Adjust the points as described above. Make sure the points mate exactly (see Figure 44). If not, bend the moveable arm until they do.

7. The condenser is a sealed unit and requires no maintenance. During a tune-up most mechanics prefer to discard the condenser and replace it with a new one. Remove the screw fixing the condenser to the distributor body. Then disconnect the condenser wire and remove the condenser. To replace it, reverse the procedure. Be sure the connections are clean and tight.

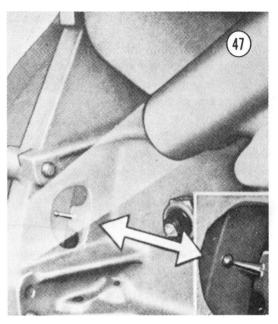

Ignition Timing

Ignition timing can be adjusted with the engine running or turned off. The following procedures should be followed when the engine is running. For details on setting the timing with the engine turned off, refer to Chapter Eight.

The timing mark on the pulley and the stationary pointer for the 1.1 engine are shown in **Figure 46**. The flywheel timing ball and flywheel housing pointer and access hole for the 1.5 and 1.9 engines are shown in **Figure 47**.

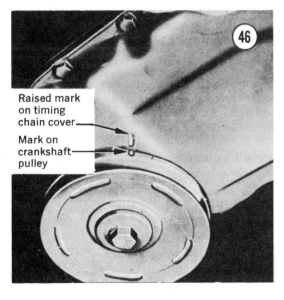

Raised mark on timing chain cover

Mark on crankshaft pulley

The timing marks for the 1975 models are located at the lower left front of the engine. The pointer is part of a bracket attached to the engine block. A timing mark is located on the crankshaft pulley. See **Figure 48**.

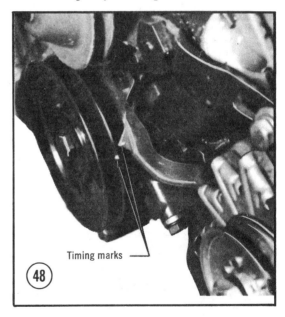

Timing marks

1. Be sure that the spark plug and distributor breaker point gaps are set accurately, as previously described.

2. Disconnect the distributor end of the vacuum line from the carburetor to the distributor. Plug the end of the vacuum line with a suitable stopper.

3. Hook up the stroboscopic timing light and tachometer per the manufacturer's instructions, or the simple hook-up directions given in the beginning of the *Tune-up* section, preceding.

4. Start the engine and warm it up to normal operating temperature.

5. Refer to Table 2 for correct timing figures. Check the engine idle speed with the tachometer. Adjust if necessary as described in Chapter Five.

6. Once the idle speed is adjusted accurately, aim the timing light at the crankshaft pulley or the flywheel timing hole. When the light flashes, the timing mark or ball should line up with the stationary pointer. Timing is accurate when the center of the mark or ball lines up directly opposite the stationary pointer.

7. If the timing is not accurate, loosen the nut at the base of the distributor and rotate the distributor body until the timing is correct. Tighten the nut.

8. Once the timing is correct, shut off the engine, remove the timing light and tachometer, and connect the vacuum advance line to the distributor.

Dwell Angle Setting

"Dwell" is the number of degrees of distributor rotation during which the breaker points are closed. The "dwell angle" is the angle formed by the distributor drive shaft as it passes in between the closing and opening of the points. See **Figure 49** (S = dwell angle). Refer to Table 2 for dwell angle and point gap specifications.

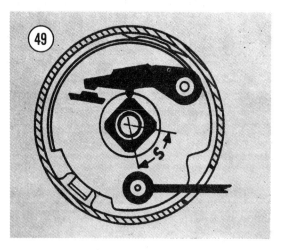

1. Check and adjust the contact breaker points, as previously described.

2. Connect and calibrate the dwell angle tester, according to the manufacturer's instructions. Connect the tachometer.

3. Remove the distributor cap and rotor. Turn the engine over and check the dwell angle. Adjust the contact point gap until the dwell angle is correct. If the dwell angle is too large, the point gap must be increased; if too small, reduce the point gap.

> NOTE: *If it is necessary to reduce the point gap to less than 0.013 in., the distributor is defective and must be overhauled or replaced.*

4. Install the rotor and cap. Start the engine.

5. Adjust the idle speed to 2,000-2,500 rpm. The dwell meter must not show a deviation of more than 2.5° from the reading previously taken. If the deviation is larger, the distributor is defective and must be overhauled or replaced. Turn off the engine.

6. Check the ignition timing, as previously discussed. Adjust as required.

Carburetor and Idle Speed

Torque the carburetor attaching bolts and/or nuts to 12 ft.-lb. to compensate for compression of the gasket. Adjust the idle speed. See Chapter Five for procedures. Proper carburetor functioning is essential to control of emissions. The correct mixtures for emission compliance and idle quality have been preset by Opel. Plastic idle mixture limiters have been installed on the idle mixture screw, idle air screw, and throttle stop screw to preclude unauthorized adjustment. The plastic caps on the idle mixture screw and the idle adjustment screw must be removed to perform an idle speed adjustment. See **Figure 50**. The plastic cap on the throttle stop screw is not to be removed unless major carburetor repair or replacement is necessary.

Carburetor Choke

Petroleum gum formation on the choke shaft occasionally results in a binding condition. Another cause is overtightening of the air cleaner

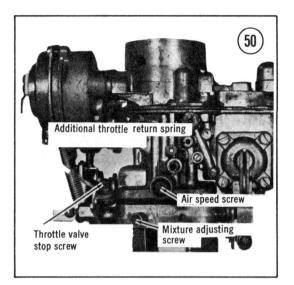

Additional throttle return spring

Air speed screw

Throttle valve stop screw

Mixture adjusting screw

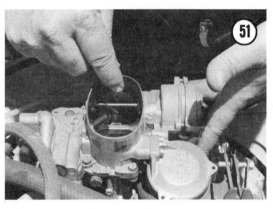

2

clamp. Check the choke mechanism for free operation. See **Figure 51**. Also check the electric choke terminal connections and fuse.

Accelerator Linkage

Lubricate ball sockets every 15,000 miles by removing retaining clips, snapping the ball socket off ball stud with a screwdriver, and cleaning and lubricating parts with silicone grease. Reassemble, making sure that clips are reinstalled properly.

See next page for tune-up specifications.

Table 2   TUNE-UP SPECIFICATIONS

Description	1.1	1.5	1.9	1.9 (1974)	1.9 (1975)
Distributor type	VJU4(R)	JFU4	JFU4	JFU4	
Breaker point gap (in.)	0.018	0.018	0.018	0.016	0.016
Breaker point spring pressure (oz.)	14-19	14-19	14-19	14-19	18-23
Dwell angle (degrees)	50 ± 2	50 ± 2	50 ± 2	50 ± 3	50 ± 3
Firing order	1 - 3 - 4 - 2	1 - 3 - 4 - 2	1 - 3 - 4 - 2	1 - 3 - 4 - 2	1 - 3 - 4 - 2
Condenser capacity (μfd)	0.23-0.32	0.23-0.32	0.23-0.32	0.15-0.20	0.23-0.32
Distributor/coil cable resistance (ohms)	100-500	100-500	100-500	10,000	10,000
Spark plug cable resistance (ohms)	500-1,000	500-1,000	500-1,000	10,000	10,000
Total advance (degrees @ rpm)	40-53 @ 2,500	43-55 @ 2,500	43-55 @ 2,500	29-37 @ 3,600	21-25 @ 3,400
Centrifugal advance (degrees @ rpm)					
Start	900-1,200	800-1,100	800-1,100	1,000-1,200	1,100-1,400
Medium	24-31 @ 1,700	17-23 @ 1,500	17-23 @ 1,500	7.5-15 @ 1,400	7.5-15 @ 1,400
Maximum	39-46 @ 4,200	31-37 @ 3,200	31-37 @ 3,200	28-32 @ 3,600	21-25 @ 3,400
Vacuum advance (degrees @ inches vacuum)					
Start	900-1,200	800-1,100	800-1,100	−5 @ 2.9-4.1 in.	0 @ 1,100-1,400
Maximum	39-46 @ 4,200	31-37 @ 3,200	31-37 @ 3,200	28-32 @ 3,600	21-25 @ 3,400
Vacuum retard (engine degrees at closed throttle — 1974-1975 models only)	*N/A	*N/A	*N/A	−5	—4
Spark plug make and type	AC 43FS	AC 44XLO	AC 42FS	AC 42FS	AC 42.6FS
Spark plug gap (in.)	0.030	0.030	0.030	0.030	0.030
Spark plug torque (ft.-lb.)	30	30	30	30	29

*N/A = Not Applicable

CHAPTER THREE

3

TROUBLESHOOTING

Troubleshooting mechanical problems can be relatively simple if you use orderly procedures and keep a few basic principles in mind.

The troubleshooting procedures in this chapter analyze typical symptoms, and show logical methods of isolating causes. These are not the only methods. There may be several ways to solve a problem, but only a systematic, methodical approach can guarantee success.

Gather as many symptoms together as possible to aid in diagnosis. Note whether the engine lost power gradually or all at once, what color smoke (if any) came from the exhaust, and so on. After the symptoms are defined, areas which could cause the problems are tested and analyzed. Guessing at the cause of a problem may eventually provide the solution, but it can easily lead to frustration, wasted time, and a series of expensive, unnecessary parts replacements.

You don't need exotic, complicated test gear to determine whether repairs can be made at home. A few simple checks could save a large repair bill and time lost while the engine sits in a dealer's service department. On the other hand, be realistic and don't attempt repairs beyond your abilities. Service departments tend to charge heavily to correct other people's mistakes. Some won't even take on such a job, so use your head.

The following are commonly encountered problems.

STARTER TROUBLESHOOTING

Starter system troubles are relatively easy to isolate. The following are common symptoms.

Engine Cranks Very Slowly or Not at All

Turn on the headlights. If the lights are very dim, the battery or connecting wires most likely are at fault. Check battery condition with hydrometer. Check wiring for breaks, shorts, and dirty connections. If the battery and wires are all right, turn the headlights on and crank the engine. If the lights dim drastically, the starter is probably shorted to ground.

If the lights remain bright or dim slightly when cranking, the trouble may be in the starter, solenoid, or wiring. To isolate the trouble, short the 2 large solenoid terminals together (not to ground); if the starter cranks normally, check the solenoid and wiring to the ignition switch. If the starter still fails to crank properly, remove and test it and overhaul as required.

Starter Turns, but Does Not Engage With Flywheel

Usually caused by defective starter pinion gear in starter or solenoid shifting fork. The pinion gear teeth, flywheel ring gear teeth, or both may be worn or stripped, preventing proper meshing.

Starter Engages, but Will Not Disengage When Ignition Switch Is Released

Usually caused by defective solenoid, but occasionally the pinion may jam on the flywheel. The pinion can be temporarily freed by rocking the car in fourth gear.

Loud Grinding Noises When Starter Runs

The teeth on the pinion and flywheel ring gears are not meshing properly or the over-running clutch mechanism is defective. Remove the starter and examine the gears for damage.

CHARGING SYSTEM TROUBLESHOOTING

Charging system troubles may be in the alternator (generator), voltage regulator, or fan belt. The following symptoms are typical.

Dashboard Indicator Shows Continuous Discharge

This usually means battery charging is not taking place. Check fan belt tension. Check battery condition with hydrometer and electrical connections in the charging system. Finally, check the alternator (generator) and/or voltage regulator.

Dashboard Indicator Shows Intermittent Discharge

Check fan belt tension and electrical connections. Trouble may be traced to defective alternator or generator parts, as described in Chapter Eight.

Battery Requires Frequent Addition of Water or Lamps Require Frequent Replacement

Alternator or generator is overcharging the battery or the voltage regulator output is faulty.

Excessive Noise From Alternator (Generator)

Check for loose mountings and/or worn bearing. Check condition of belt.

ENGINE TROUBLESHOOTING

These procedures assume the starter cranks the engine. If not, refer to the *Starter Troubleshooting* section of this chapter.

Engine Won't Start

Could be caused by the ignition or fuel system. First, check to make sure the car has fuel in the fuel tank. Secondly, determine if high voltage to the spark plug occurs. To do this, disconnect one of the spark plug wires. Hold the exposed wire terminal about ¼ to ½ inch from ground (any metal in the engine compartment) with an insulated screwdriver. Crank the engine. If sparks don't jump to ground or the sparks are very weak, the trouble is probably in the ignition system. If sparks occur properly, the trouble is probably in the fuel system.

Engine Misses Steadily

Using a heavily insulated tool, remove one spark plug wire at a time and ground the wire. If engine miss increases, that cylinder is working properly. Reconnect the wire and check the other spark plugs. When a wire is disconnected and engine miss remains the same, that cylinder is not firing. Check spark as described above. If no spark occurs for one cylinder only, check distributor cap, wire, and spark plug. If spark occurs properly, check compression and intake manifold vacuum.

Engine Misses Erratically at All Speeds

Intermittent trouble can be difficult to find. It could be in the ignition system, exhaust system, or fuel system. Follow troubleshooting procedures for these systems to isolate trouble.

Engine Misses at Idle Only

Trouble could be ignition or carburetor idle adjustment. Check idle mixture adjustment and check for restrictions in the carburetor idle circuit.

Engine Misses at High Speed Only

Trouble is in the fuel or ignition system. Check accelerator pump operation, fuel pump delivery, fuel lines, etc. Check the spark plugs and wires.

Low Performance at All Speeds, Poor Acceleration

Trouble is usually in ignition or fuel system. Tune up engine as described in Chapter Two.

Excessive Fuel Consumption

Could be caused by a number of seemingly unrelated factors. Check for clutch slippage, brake drag, defective wheel bearings, poor front end alignment, faulty ignition, leaks in gas tank or lines, and carburetor condition.

Low Oil Pressure Indicated by Oil Pressure Indicator

If the oil pressure indicator lights with the engine running, stop the engine immediately. Coast to a stop with the clutch disengaged. The trouble may be caused by low oil level, blockage in an oil line, defective oil pump, overheated engine, or defective pressure sending unit. Check the oil level and fan belt tension. Check for a shorted oil pressure sending unit with an ohmmeter or replace with a new unit. Remove and clean the oil pressure relief valve. Do not start the engine until you know why the low indication was given and are sure the problem has been corrected.

Engine Overheats

Usually caused by trouble in the cooling system. Check level of coolant in radiator, condition and tension of the fan belt, and water hoses for leaks and loose connections. Can also be caused by late ignition or valve timing.

Engine Stalls as It Warms Up

The choke may be stuck closed, the manifold heat control valve may be stuck, the engine idle speed may be set too low, or the emission control system valves may be defective. Low speed carburetor idle circuit may be faulty.

Engine Stalls After High-Speed Driving

Vapor lock within the fuel lines caused by an overheated engine is the usual cause. Inspect and service the cooling system. If the trouble persists, changing to a different fuel or shielding the fuel line from engine heat may be helpful.

Engine Backfires

Several causes are possible; ignition timing, overheating, excessive carbon buildup in combustion chambers, worn ignition points, wrong heat range spark plugs, hot or sticking valves, and/or defective distributor cap.

Smoky Exhaust

Blue smoke indicates excessive oil consumption usually caused by worn rings. Black smoke indicates an excessively rich fuel mixture.

Excessive Oil Consumption

Can be caused by external leaks through broken seals or gaskets, or by burning oil in the combustion chambers. Check the oil pan and the front and rear of the engine for oil leaks. If oil is not leaking externally, valve stem clearance may be excessive, piston rings may be worn, cylinder walls may be scored, rod bearings may be worn, or carburetor vacuum pump diaphragm may be ruptured.

Noisy Engine

1. *Regular clicking sound*—valves out of adjustment or defective valve lifters.

2. *Ping or chatter on load or acceleration*—spark knock due to low octane fuel, carbon buildup, overly advanced ignition timing, and causes mentioned under engine backfire.

3. *Light knock or pound with engine not under load*—worn connecting rod bearings, misaligned piston pin, and/or lack of engine oil.

4. *Light metallic double knock, usually heard during idle*—worn or loose piston pin or bushing and/or lack of oil.

5. *Chattering or rattling during acceleration*—worn rings or cylinder walls, low ring tension, and/or broken rings.

6. *Hollow, bell-like muffled sound when engine is cold*—piston slap due to worn pistons or cylinder walls, collapsed piston skirts, excessive clearances, misaligned connecting rods, and/or lack of oil.

7. *Dull, heavy, metallic knock under load or acceleration, especially when cold*—regular noise indicates worn main bearings; irregular noise, worn thrust bearings.

IGNITION SYSTEM
TROUBLESHOOTING

The following procedures assume the battery is in good enough condition to crank the engine normally.

No Spark to One Plug

The only causes are defective distributor cap, rotor, or spark plug wire. Examine the distributor cap for moisture, dirt, carbon tracking caused by flashover, and cracks. Check condition of rotor and spark plug wire for breaks and loose connectors.

No Spark to Any Plug

This could indicate trouble in the primary or secondary ignition circuits. First, remove the coil wire from the center post of the distributor. Hold the wire end about ¼ inch from ground with an insulated screwdriver. Crank the engine. If sparks are produced, the trouble is in the rotor or distributor cap. Remove the cap and check for burns, moisture, dirt, carbon tracking, cracks, etc. Check rotor for excessive burning, pitting, and cracks.

If the coil does not produce any spark, check the secondary wire for a break. If the wire is good, turn the engine over so the breaker points are open. Check the points for excessive gap, burning, pitting, and loose connections. With the points open, check voltage from the coil to ground with a voltmeter or test lamp. If voltage is present, the coil is probably defective. Have it checked or substitute a coil known to be good.

If voltage is not present, check wire connections to the coil and distributor. Disconnect wire leading from the coil to the distributor and measure from the coil terminal to ground. If voltage is present, the distributor is shorted. Examine breaker points and connecting wires carefully. If voltage is still not present, measure the other coil terminal. Voltage on the other terminal indicates a defective coil. No voltage indicates a broken wire between the coil and the battery.

Weak Spark

If the spark is so small it cannot jump from the wire to ground, check the battery. Other causes are defective breaker points, condenser, incorrect point gap, dirty or loose connection in the primary circuit, or dirty or burned rotor or distributor. Check for worn cam lobes on distributor shaft.

Missing

This is usually caused by fouled or damaged plugs, plugs of the wrong heat range, or incorrect plug gap.

FUEL SYSTEM
TROUBLESHOOTING

Fuel system troubles must be isolated to carburetor, fuel pump, or fuel lines. The following procedures assume the ignition system has been checked and is in proper working order.

Engine Will Not Start

First, determine that fuel is being delivered to the carburetor. If it is, check the carburetor and choke system for dirt and/or defects. If fuel is not delivered, the trouble is either a defective fuel pump or blockage in fuel line.

Engine Runs at Fast Idle

Misadjustment of fast idle screw or defective carburetor.

EXHAUST EMISSION CONTROL TROUBLESHOOTING

Failure of the exhaust emission control system to maintain exhaust emissions within acceptable limits is usually due to defective carburetor, general engine condition, or defective exhaust control valves. Generally, if defects are suspected in the emission control system, refer testing and service to your Opel dealer.

CLUTCH TROUBLESHOOTING

Several clutch troubles may be experienced. Usually the trouble is quite obvious and will fall into one of the following categories:
1. Slipping, chattering, or grabbing when engaging.
2. Spinning or dragging when disengaged.
3. Clutch noises, clutch pedal pulsations, and rapid clutch disc facing wear.

Clutch Slips While Engaged

Improper adjustment of clutch linkage, weak or broken pressure springs, worn friction disc facings, defective flywheel, and grease, dirt, or oil on clutch disc.

Clutch Chatters or Grabs When Engaging

Usually caused by misadjustment of clutch linkage, defective release bearing, dirt or grease on clutch/flywheel/pressure plate mating surfaces, or broken and/or worn clutch parts.

Clutch Spins or Drags When Disengaged

The clutch disc normally spins briefly after disengagement from the flywheel and pressure plate and takes a moment to come to rest. This sound should not be confused with drag. Drag is caused by the friction disc not being fully released from the flywheel or pressure plate as the clutch pedal is depressed. The trouble can be caused by clutch linkage misadjustments or defective or worn clutch parts.

Clutch Noises

Clutch noises are usually most noticeable when the engine is idling. First, note whether the noise is heard when the clutch is engaged or disengaged. Clutch noises when engaged could be due to a loose clutch disc hub, loose friction disc springs, and misalignment or looseness of engine or transmission mountings. When disengaged, noise can be due to a worn release bearing, defective pilot bearing, or misaligned release lever and clutch linkage.

Clutch Pedal Pulsates

Usually noticed when slight pressure is applied to the clutch pedal with the engine running. As pedal pressure is increased, the pulsation stops. Possible causes include misalignment of engine and transmission, bent crankshaft flange, distortion or shifting of clutch housing, release lever misalignment, warped friction disc facing, and/or damaged pressure plate and flywheel.

Rapid Friction Disc Facing Wear

This trouble is caused by any condition that permits slippage between facing and the flywheel or pressure plate. Probable causes are "riding" the clutch, slow releasing of the clutch after disengagement, weak or broken pressure springs, pedal linkage misadjustment, and warped clutch disc or pressure plate.

TRANSMISSION TROUBLESHOOTING

Hard Starting into Gear

Common causes are failure of clutch to release, misadjustment of linkage, linkage in need of lubrication, bent shifter forks, sliding gear tightness on shaft splines, damaged sliding gear teeth, and damaged synchronizer.

Transmission Sticks in Gear

May be caused by clutch not releasing, gearshift linkage out of adjustment, linkage needing lubrication, detent ball stuck, or gears tight on shaft splines.

3

Transmission Slips Out of Gear

Gearshift linkage out of adjustment, misalignment between engine and transmission, excessive main shaft end-play, worn gear teeth, insufficient shift-lever spring tension, worn bearings, or defective synchronizer. Gear may be loose on the main shaft.

No Power Through Transmission

May be caused by clutch slippage, stripped gear teeth, damaged shifter fork linkage, broken gear or shaft, and stripped drive key.

Transmission Noisy in Neutral

Transmission misaligned, bearings worn or dry, gears worn, countershaft worn or bent, and excessive countershaft end-play.

Transmission Noisy in Gear

Defective clutch disc, worn bearings, loose gears, worn gear teeth, and faults listed above.

Gears Clash During Shifting

Caused by the clutch not releasing, defective synchronizer, or gears sticking on main shaft.

Oil Leaks

Most common causes are foaming due to wrong lubricant, lubricant level too high, broken gaskets, damaged oil seals, loose drain plug, and cracked transmission case.

DIFFERENTIAL/REAR AXLE TROUBLESHOOTING

Usually, it is noise that draws attention to trouble in the differential, rear axles, drive shaft, or rear wheels. It is not always easy to diagnose the trouble by determining the source of noise and the operating conditions that produce the noise. Defective conditions in the universal joints, rear wheel bearings, muffler, or tires may be wrongly diagnosed as trouble in the differential or rear axles.

Some clue as to cause of trouble may be gained by noting whether the noise is a hum, growl, or knock; whether it is produced when the car is accelerating under load or coasting; and whether it is heard when the car is going straight or making a turn.

Noise During Acceleration: May be caused by shortage of lubricant, incorrect tooth contact between drive gears and drive pinion, damaged or misadjusted bearings in axles or side bearings, or damaged gears.

Noise During Coasting: May be caused by incorrect backlash between drive gear and drive pinion gear or incorrect adjustment of drive pinion bearing.

Noise During Turn: This noise is usually caused by loose or worn axle shaft bearing, pinion gears too tight on shaft, side gear jammed in differential case, or worn side gear thrust washer and pinion thrust washer.

Broken Differential Parts: Breaking of differential parts can be caused by insufficient lubricant, improper use of clutch, excessive loading, misadjusted bearings and gears, excessive backlash, damage to axle case, or loose bolts.

Rear Wheel Wobble: Usually indicates a bent axle or worn wheel bearings. If wheel bearings, a rumbling noise would probably be heard.

Humming Noise: A humming noise in the differential is often caused by improper drive pinion or ring gear adjustment that prevents normal tooth contact between gears. If ignored, rapid tooth wear will take place and the noise will become more like a growl. Repair as soon as the humming is heard so that new gears will not be required. Tire noise will vary considerably, depending on the type of road surface. Differential noises will be the same regardless of road surface. If noises are heard, listen carefully to the noise over different road surfaces to help isolate the problem.

BRAKE TROUBLESHOOTING

Brake Pedal Goes to Floor

Worn linings or pads, air in the hydraulic system, leaky brake lines, leaky wheel cylinders, or leaky or worn master cylinder may be the cause. Check for leaks and worn brake linings or pads. Bleed and adjust brakes. Rebuild wheel cylinders, calipers, and/or master cylinder.

Spongy Pedal

Usually caused by air in the brake hydraulic system. Bleed and adjust brakes.

Brakes Pull

Check brakes adjustment and wear on linings and disc pads. Check for contaminated linings, leaky wheel cylinders, loose calipers, lines, or hoses. Check front end alignment and look for suspension damage such as broken front or rear springs and shock absorbers. Tires also affect braking; check tire pressures and condition.

Brakes Squeal or Chatter

Check brake shoe and pad lining thickness and brake drum and rotor condition. Ensure that shoes are not loose. Clean away all dirt on shoes, drums, rotors, and pads.

Brakes Drag

Check brake adjustment, including handbrake. Check for broken or weak shoe return springs, swollen rubber parts due to improper brake fluid or contamination. Check for defective master cylinder or brake servo unit.

Hard Pedal

Check brake linings and pads for contamination. Check for brake line restrictions.

High Speed Fade

Check for distorted or out-of-round drums and rotors and contaminated linings or pads.

Pulsating Pedal

Check for distorted or out-of-round brake drums or rotors. Check for excessive rotor runout.

COOLING SYSTEM TROUBLESHOOTING

Engine Overheats

May be caused by insufficient coolant, loose fan belt, defective fan belt, defective thermostat, defective water pump, clogged water lines and passages, incorrect ignition timing, and/or defective or loose hoses. Inspect radiator and all parts for leaks.

Engine Does Not Warm Up

Usually caused by defective thermostat or extremely cold weather.

Loss of Coolant

Radiator leaks, loose or defective hoses, defective water pump, leaks in cylinder head gasket, cracked cylinder head or engine block, or defective radiator cap may be the cause.

Noisy Cooling System

Usually caused by defective water pump bearings, loose or bent fan blades, or a defective fan belt.

STEERING AND SUSPENSION TROUBLESHOOTING

Trouble in the suspension or steering is evident when any of the following occur:

1. Hard steering
2. Car pulls to one side
3. Car wanders
4. Front wheels wobble
5. Excessive play in steering
6. Abnormal tire wear

Unusual steering, pulling, or wandering is usually caused by bent or misaligned suspension parts. If the trouble seems to be excessive play, check the wheel bearing adjustment first. Next, check steering free-play and king pins or balljoints. Finally, check tie rod ends for looseness by shaking each wheel.

Abnormal tire wear should always be analyzed to determine the cause. The most common are incorrect tire pressure, improper driving, overloading, and incorrect wheel alignment. **Figure 1** (next page) identifies wear patterns and their most probable causes.

Wheel Balancing

All 4 wheels and tires must be in balance along 2 axes. To be in static balance (**Figure 2**), weight must be evenly distributed around the

Underinflation—Worn more on sides than in center.

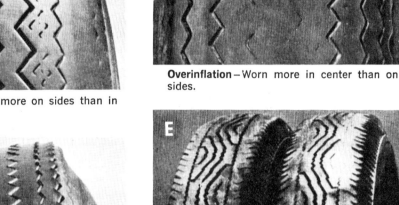

Overinflation—Worn more in center than on sides.

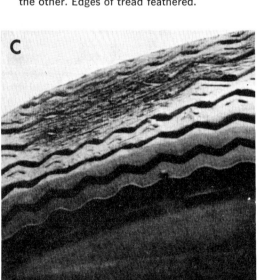

Wheel Alignment—Worn more on one side than the other. Edges of tread feathered.

Wheel Balance — Scalloped edges indicate wheel wobble or tramp due to wheel unbalance.

Road Abrasion—Rough wear on entire tire or in patches.

Combination—Most tires exhibit a combination of the above. This tire was overinflated (center worn) and the toe-in was incorrect (feathering). The driver cornered hard at high speed (feathering, rounded shoulders) and braked rapidly (worn spots). The scaly roughness indicates a rough road surface.

axis of rotation. (A) shows a statically un-balanced wheel. (B) shows the result — wheel tramp or hopping. (C) shows proper static balance.

To be in dynamic balance (**Figure 3**), the centerline of weight must coincide with the centerline of the wheel. (A) shows a dynamically unbalanced wheel. (B) shows the result — wheel wobble or shimmy. (C) shows proper dynamic balance.

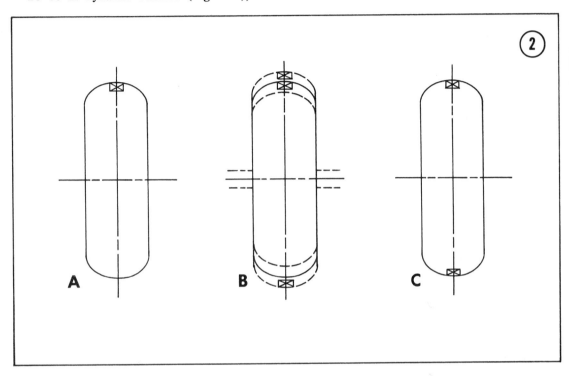

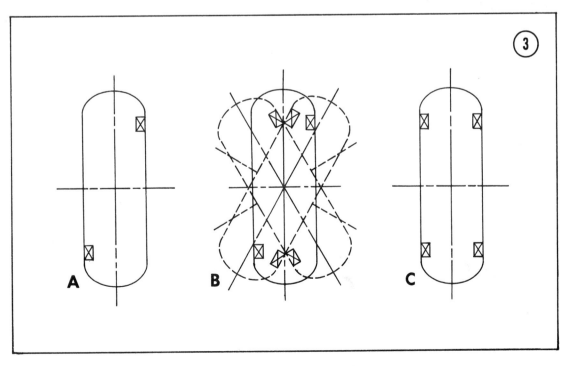

CHAPTER FOUR

ENGINE

This chapter covers the 1.1, 1.5, and 1.9 engines for models from 1966-1975. Refer to the *Supplement* section, Chapter Four, at the back of this manual, for 1976 and later models.

If major work is to be done on the engine, it is easier if the engine is on a bench or engine stand, rather than in the car.

It is easier to work on a clean engine than a dirty one, and you'll do a better job. Before starting, have the engine and under-chassis steam cleaned or clean them with a good commercial degreaser, following manufacturer's instructions. Make certain you have the necessary tools available and a clean place in which to work.

It's a good idea to identify and mark parts as they are removed so that errors will be avoided during assembly and installation. Make certain all parts related to a particular cylinder, piston connecting rod, and/or valve assembly are identified for installation in the proper place. Do not rely too heavily on your memory; it may be days or weeks before you complete the job.

Detailed specifications, clearances, and torque tightening information are given at the end of this chapter or in the procedure to which they pertain. Use and comply with this information. If a part is marginal according to specification, repair or replace it so that your work will not be wasted.

ENGINE DESCRIPTION

The various Opel models are equipped with one of three engines: 1.1, 1.5, and 1.9 liter. The 1.5 and 1.9 engines are almost identical except for cylinder bore size. All three engines are 4-cylinder, overhead valve designs. The major differences are camshaft location and the number of crankshaft main bearings. The 1.1 engine has three main bearings; the 1.5 and 1.9 engines have five. The main bearings and connecting rod bearings are replaceable shell types. The camshaft is located in the cylinder block on the 1.1 engine and in the cylinder head on the 1.5 and 1.9 engines. **Figures 1 and 2** are side and front cross section views of the 1.1 engine; **Figures 3 and 4** the 1.5 and 1.9 engines.

The crankshaft, through pulleys, sprockets, and chain, drives the water pump, generator (alternator), and emission control air pump (if equipped). On the 1.1 engine, the camshaft lobes and gearing drive the fuel pump, oil pump, and distributor. On the 1.5 and 1.9 engines, the crankshaft drives the distributor and oil pump. The fuel pump is driven by a lobe on the distributor drive shaft.

Until 1971, the 1.5 and 1.9 engines had a 9.0 to 1 compression ratio. Since then, the compression ratio has been 7.6 to 1. Compression

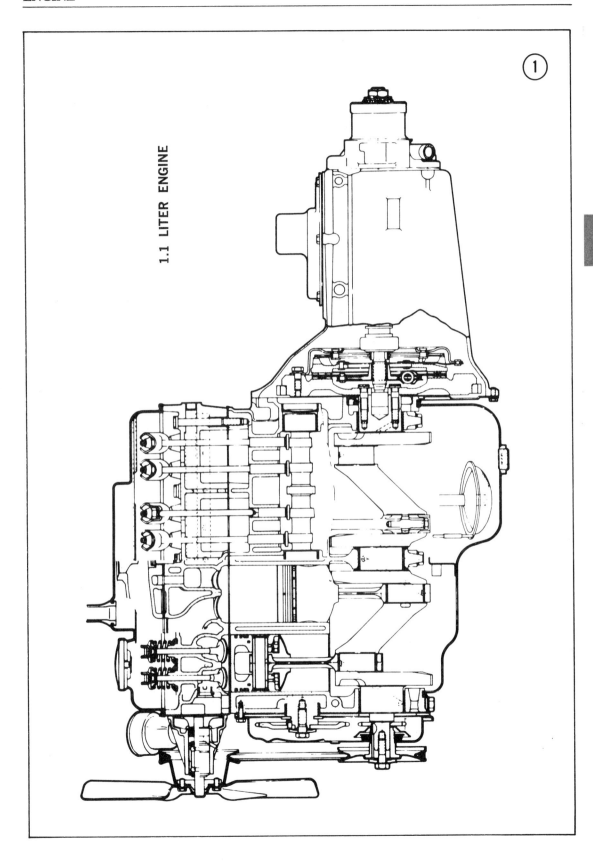

1.1 LITER ENGINE

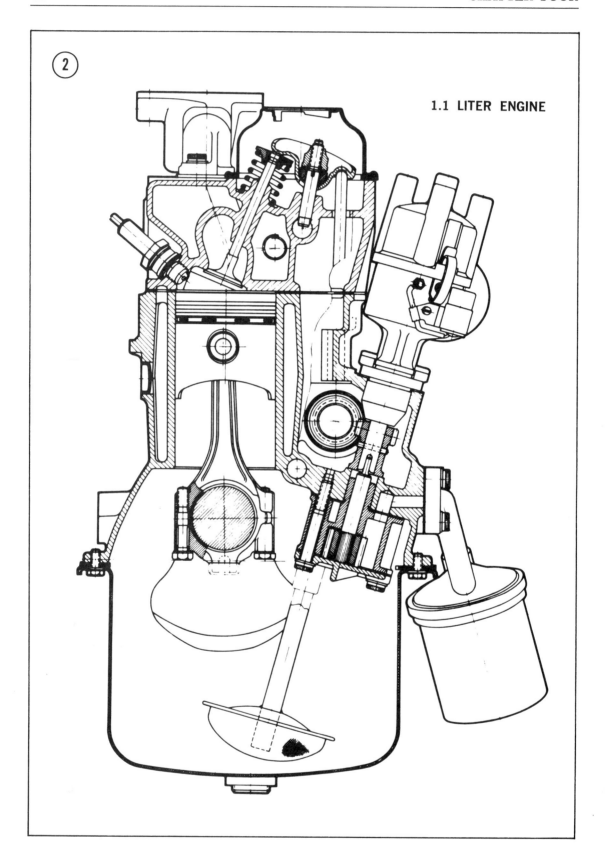

② 1.1 LITER ENGINE

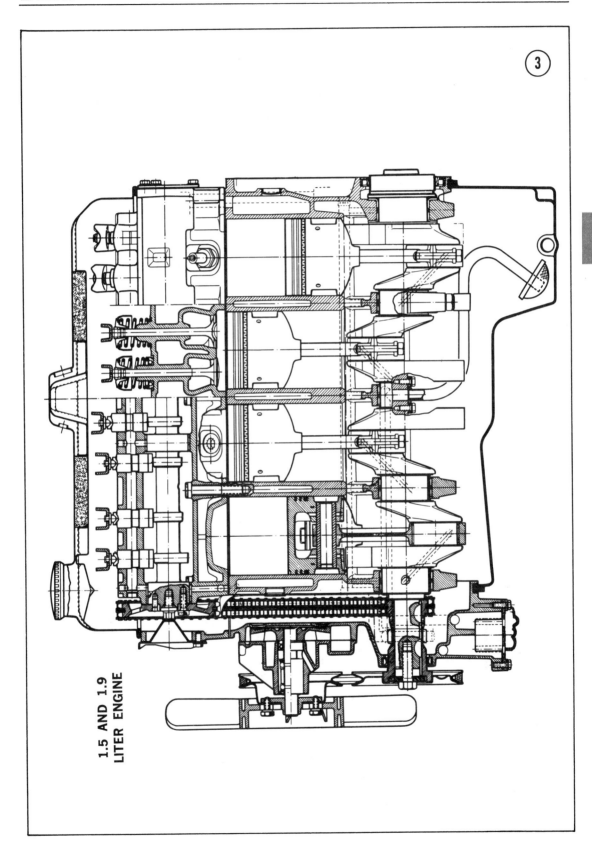

1.5 AND 1.9
LITER ENGINE

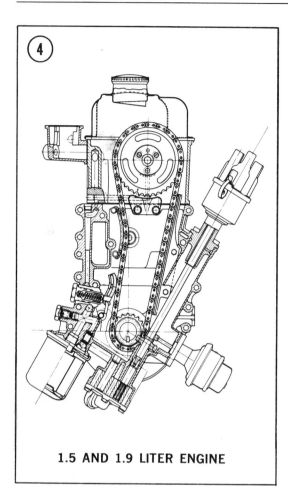

1.5 AND 1.9 LITER ENGINE

ratio in the 1.1 engine has been 7.8, 8.2, 8.8 or 9.2 to 1, depending on model and year.

ENGINE REMOVAL/INSTALLATION

Before proceeding, read all instructions carefully and study the illustration so that you have in mind the steps to be taken. Removal of the engine should only be necessary to perform major overhaul of the cylinder block and camshaft (1.1 engine). Other repairs can be done with the engine in place.

1.1 Engine

1. Jack up the front of the car and support it securely with jackstands or sturdy wooden blocks.

2. Open the hood. Cover fender surfaces with protective aprons.

3. Mark hood hinge-to-hood mounting location. Remove hood.

4. Disconnect cables from battery.

5. Drain the cooling and heating systems as described in Chapter Six.

6. Remove radiator as described in Chapter Six.

7. Remove gear shift lever as described in Chapter Nine.

8. Remove the air cleaner.

9. Disconnect throttle rod from carburetor and rear support.

10. Disconnect fuel line from intake side of fuel pump.

11. Disconnect bowden control wires from carburetor and heater.

12. Disconnect heater hoses as described in Chapter Six.

13. Disconnect electrical wires at the starter, generator, distributor, and back-up lamp switch at transmission.

14. Drain engine oil as specified in Chapter Two. Remove oil filter housing and oil filter.

15. Detach exhaust pipe from exhaust manifold.

16. Remove the drive shaft as described in Chapter Nine.

17. Use a floor jack to support transmission. Do not damage transmission case.

18. Attach a suitable hoist or block-and-tackle equipment to the engine. Lift up on the engine slightly to ease tension on mounting brackets.

19. Remove the transmission case-to-crankcase bolts.

20. Remove transmission mounting bolts.

21. Carefully inspect the engine compartment to make certain that all lines, hoses, linkages, and wires have been disconnected from the engine and transmission.

22. Remove engine mounting bolts. There are two on each side of engine.

23. Pull backward on the transmission until the transmission splines are completely extracted from the clutch plate and pressure plate.

24. Lift up on the engine and remove it from the engine compartment. During lifting, go slowly and check constantly that the engine is not obstructed by other parts in the engine compartment.

25. Place the engine on a workbench or install it on an engine stand.

26. After engine removal and if the engine is to be completely disassembled, remove generator, emission control air pump (if equipped), fan and water pump, carburetor, starter motor, oil pan and pump, and distributor, as described in other chapters.

27. To install the engine, reverse the preceding steps. During installation, make certain the transmission drive shaft splines mate with the slots in the clutch plate. Install mounting bolts of engine and transmission loosely. Then tighten finger-tight and rock engine back and forth to seat it and the transmission in a tension-free position. Torque all bolts as specified at the end of this chapter.

> NOTE: *The transmission may have to be lowered with a floor jack to align the engine properly.*

1.5/1.9 Engines

Engine removal is only possible by lowering the engine from the engine compartment. The most practical method is with the engine and transmission mounted to the front suspension. Proceed as follows:

1. Disconnect battery negative cable.

2. Remove air cleaner.

3. Drain radiator and heater. Remove upper and lower radiator hoses. It is not necessary to remove radiator.

4. Disconnect electrical connections at the starter, generator (alternator), distributor, and oil pressure sending unit.

5. Disconnect vacuum hoses at intake manifold T-connection. Remove T-connection from manifold to avoid interference during engine removal.

6. Disconnect choke cable, heater control cable, and throttle linkage.

7. Remove heater hoses from heater.

8. Disconnect the water valve bracket from the manifold.

9. Remove gearshift lever as specified in Chapter Nine.

10. Use a hoist to raise the front and rear ends of the car.

11. Disconnect fuel line at fuel pump. Plug the end of the line to prevent loss of fuel.

12. Disconnect speedometer cable, clutch cable, and drive shaft from transmission. Remove drive shaft as specified in Chapter Nine.

13. Disconnect exhaust pipe at exhaust manifold. It is not necessary to remove exhaust flange bolts on inboard side; just loosen them.

14. Remove tailpipe and muffler hangers.

15. Detach ground strap from engine and side rail.

16. Support the front of the car by placing jackstands under the jacking brackets.

17. Disconnect brake lines at brake hoses. Plug ends of hoses.

18. See **Figure 5**. Remove the clamp bolt, and mark the position of the flange with respect to the shaft.

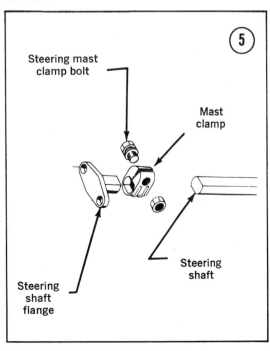

19. See **Figure 6**. Remove stop bolt and pull the column out of the steering mast flange.

> **CAUTION**
> *Use care when working with the steering mast. Energy absorbing columns are easily damaged.*

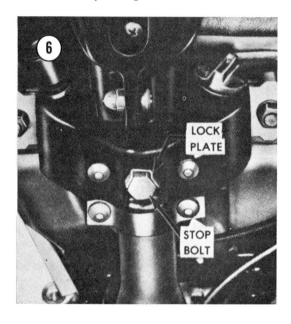

20. Chain front suspension to hoist to prevent engine and transmission from tilting when lowered.

21. Disconnect shock absorber mountings at upper shock mounting bolts. See Chapter Ten.

22. Remove front suspension mounting bolts (Chapter Ten).

23. Remove nuts securing engine mounts and front suspension crossmember. See **Figure 7**.

24. Remove transmission support bracket bolts.

25. Lower engine and front suspension assembly from car.

26. Remove transmission from engine by removing mounting bolts and pulling the transmission backwards until the transmission drive shaft clears the clutch and pressure plate.

27. Place the engine on a workbench or install it on an engine stand.

28. After engine removal, and if the engine is to be completely disassembled, remove generator (alternator), fan and water pump, emission control air pump (if equipped), carburetor, starter motor, oil pan and pump, and distributor, as described in other chapters.

29. To install reverse the preceding steps. Torque engine-to-front suspension mounting bolts to 30 ft-lbs. and the crossmember bolts to 36 ft.-lbs. Install steering column so there is ⅛ in. clearance between the hub and switch cover. Torque steering column clamp bolt to 15 ft.-lbs. Bleed brakes.

Model 1900 and Manta

The engine can be removed together with the transmission through the top of the engine compartment. Proceed as follows:

1. Mark the hood hinge-to-hood mounting position. Remove the hood.

2. Disconnect battery cables.

3. Drain coolant and remove upper and lower radiator hoses. Remove radiator and fan shroud

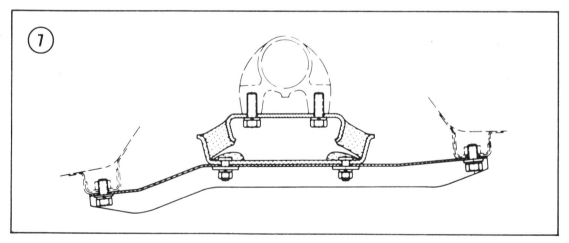

as described in Chapter Six.

4. Disconnect heater hoses and brake booster vacuum hose.

5. Remove air cleaner.

6. Disconnect electrical connections and accelerator linkage.

7. Inside the car, remove console, shift lever boot, plate, and shift lever, as described in Chapter Nine.

8. Jack up the car and place it on jackstands.

9. Disconnect fuel line from intake side of fuel pump. Block the end of the fuel line to prevent loss of fuel.

10. From under the car, remove front stone shield.

11. Disconnect the speedometer cable, back-up light switch wire, and clutch cable from the transmission.

12. Remove the drive shaft as described in Chapter Nine.

13. Disconnect the exhaust pipe from exhaust manifold. Unbolt bell housing support.

14. See **Figure 8**. Disconnect transmission support by removing fixing bolts.

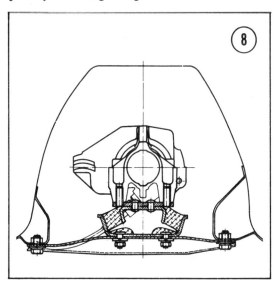

15. See **Figure 9**. Remove bolts at engine mounts.

16. Attach suitable hoist to the engine.

17. Lift the engine and transmission upward and out of the engine compartment. Go slowly

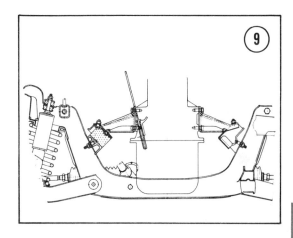

and check that the engine and transmission do not damage parts during removal.

18. To install, reverse the preceding steps. Torque bolts as specified at the end of this chapter.

GT Engine

Engine removal is only possible by lowering the engine. The engine rests on its own crossmember, so the front suspension crossmember need not be removed. **Figures 10 and 11** show details of the left and right crossmember attachments, respectively.

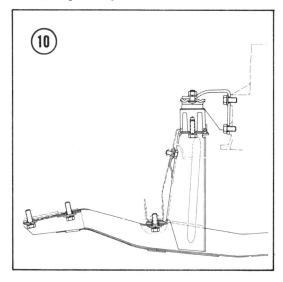

1. Disconnect battery cables.

2. Remove air cleaner.

3. Drain radiator and remove upper and lower radiator hoses.

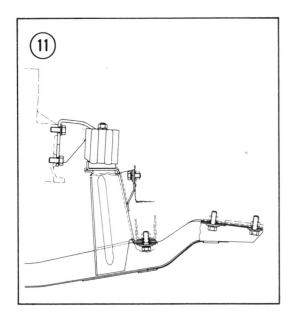

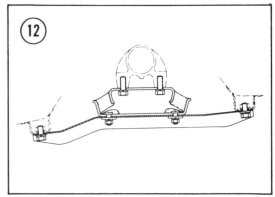

18. Detach engine crossmember from engine and frame.

19. Slowly lower engine and transmission and remove from under car, as shown in **Figure 13**.

4. Disconnect electrical connections at the starter, alternator, distributor, and oil pressure switch.

5. Disconnect vacuum hoses from intake manifold T-connection. Remove T-connection from manifold.

6. Disconnect throttle and choke connections at carburetor.

7. Disconnect heater hoses.

8. Disconnect water valve bracket from manifold.

9. Remove gearshift lever.

10. Use a hoist to lift the car. Attach a chain lift to engine and lift up slightly to ease tension on mounts.

11. Disconnect fuel line at intake of fuel pump. Plug end of fuel line. Disconnect fuel line from engine and transmission clips.

12. Disconnect speedometer cable and clutch cable from transmission.

13. Disconnect drive shaft at rear universal joint and transmission. Remove drive shaft.

14. Remove tailpipe and muffler hangers.

15. Disconnect exhaust pipe at exhaust manifold.

16. Detach ground strap from engine and side rail.

17. Detach transmission crossmember from transmission and frame. See **Figure 12**.

20. Place the engine and transmission on a workbench or on the floor. Separate the transmission from the engine by removing the bell housing mounting bolts. Pull the transmission backwards until the transmission drive shaft splines are clear of the clutch plate and pressure plate.

21. Mount the engine to a suitable work stand or place it on a workbench.

22. To install, reverse the preceding steps.

ENGINE SERVICING/OVERHAUL

The following sections deal with repair and overhaul of the main engine assemblies including the cylinder block, cylinder head, timing gearing, crankshaft, flywheel, connecting rods, pistons, camshaft, valves, and manifolds.

Since repair and overhaul techniques are similar for the 1.1, 1.5, and 1.9 engines, the discussion below applies specifically to the 1.9 engine. Important differences in the other engines are noted or discussed separately. Use the specifications, tolerances, and torque tightening information at the end of this chapter for your particular engine.

Remove all traces of old gasket material from joint faces with a scraper or electric drill fitted with a wire brush. Make certain all engine parts are clean and free from damage or defects. Clean and degrease parts in a suitable solvent.

If possible, have the cylinder block and cylinder head "hot tanked" to clean out oil and water passages. At any rate, pay special attenion to the passages to make certain they are not clogged. Check all parts and wear surfaces carefully for conformity with specifications and wear tolerances.

When overhauling or repairing an engine, always use new gaskets and lockplates. Replace damaged studs, nuts, bolts, spring washers, and leaking core plugs. Clean threads on nuts, bolts, and studs thoroughly and lightly lubricate them before installation. Tighten nuts, bolts, and studs to the correct torque with an accurate torque wrench. When using the torque wrench, do not torque to the required reading in one step; use two or three steps to gradually reach the proper tightness and move from one bolt, stud, or nut to another to prevent uneven tension and distortion of parts.

Use a good quality gasket and joining compound on gaskets, joints, and sealing faces. Use the compound according to manufacturer's instructions.

CYLINDER HEAD/INTAKE MANIFOLD

Some of the following procedures must be performed by a dealer or machine shop, since they require special knowledge and expensive machine tools. Others, while possible for the home mechanic, are difficult or time-consuming. A general practice among those who do their own service is to remove the cylinder head, perform all disassembly except valve removal, and take the head to a machine shop for inspection and service. Since the cost is relatively low in proportion to the required effort and equipment, this may be the best approach, even for more experienced owners.

Servicing of the cylinder head and valve assemblies includes:

1. Removal of cylinder head from engine and removal of intake manifold from cylinder head.

2. Cleaning and decarbonizing.

3. Inspecting all parts for damage and specification compliance.

4. Repairing or overhauling as required.

The following procedures can be performed with the engine installed or removed from the car. Unless otherwise noted, installation is the reverse of the steps used during removal and disassembly.

Cylinder Head Removal (1.1 Engine)

1. Disconnect battery cables.

2. Remove air cleaner.

3. Disconnect throttle rod from carburetor and rear support.

4. Disconnect fuel line and control cables from carburetors.

5. Detach vacuum lines from carburetors, and heater hose and control wire from heater temperature control valve.

6. Disconnect compound linkage at center. Remove hose leading from rocker arm cover to intake manifold.

7. Remove carburetors and carburetor support bracket, as described in Chapter Five. Remove O-ring seals between carburetors and intake manifold.

8. See **Figure 14**. Use serrated bit J-21736 (or equivalent) to remove three star-type bolts fixing intake manifold to cylinder head. The center bolt is accessible only after carburetors have been removed.

9. Remove intake manifold.

10. Drain coolant, as described in Chapter Six. Loosen drain plug on right side of engine to avoid coolant entering into cylinder bores.

11. Disconnect wires from spark plugs and remove distributor cap.

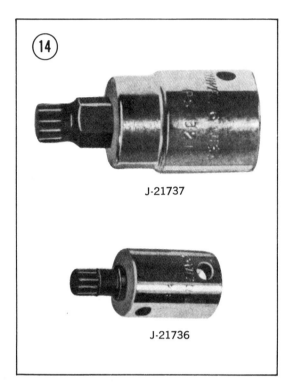

J-21737

J-21736

12. Loosen and remove generator (alternator) bracket bolt and remove fan belt.

13. Disconnect exhaust pipe from exhaust manifold.

14. Remove exhaust manifold-to-cylinder head bolts. Remove exhaust manifold.

15. Remove temperature switch from cylinder head.

16. Remove heater intake hose from cylinder head.

17. Remove rocker arm cover and gasket. Take care not to damage gasket if it is to be reused.

18. Remove self-locking nuts from rocker arms. Remove rocker arms and rocker arm ball seats. Withdraw pushrods from head. Mark all parts for later replacement in same location. Make certain to note which end of the push rod mates with the rocker arm.

19. See Figure 14. Use serrated bit J-12737 (or equivalent) to loosen and remove ten star bolts fixing cylinder head to cylinder block.

20. Separate the cylinder head from cylinder block. Remove and discard head gasket. Remove spark plugs from cylinder head. Remove plug gaskets.

Cylinder Head Installation (1.1 Engine)

To install the cylinder head and intake manifold, reverse the preceding steps and observe the following:

1. Coat cylinder head gasket on both sides with graphite grease. Place head gasket on cylinder block with word "OBEN" upward.

2. Carefully lower cylinder head onto gasket. Make certain the cylinder head is properly aligned for installation of head bolts.

3. Install head bolts and tighten finger-tight.

4. See **Figure 15**. Tighten head bolts in gradual steps following the tightening pattern shown. Torque to 35 ft.-lbs.

5. Install pushrods, rocker arms, ball seats, and adjusting nuts. **Figure 16** shows details of the valve and rocker arm assembly.

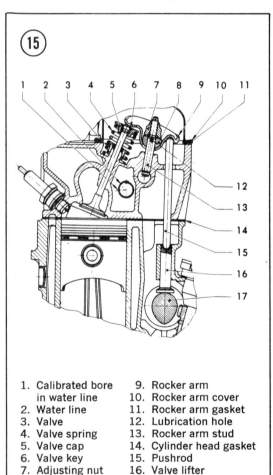

1. Calibrated bore in water line	9. Rocker arm
2. Water line	10. Rocker arm cover
3. Valve	11. Rocker arm gasket
4. Valve spring	12. Lubrication hole
5. Valve cap	13. Rocker arm stud
6. Valve key	14. Cylinder head gasket
7. Adjusting nut	15. Pushrod
8. Ball seat	16. Valve lifter
	17. Camshaft

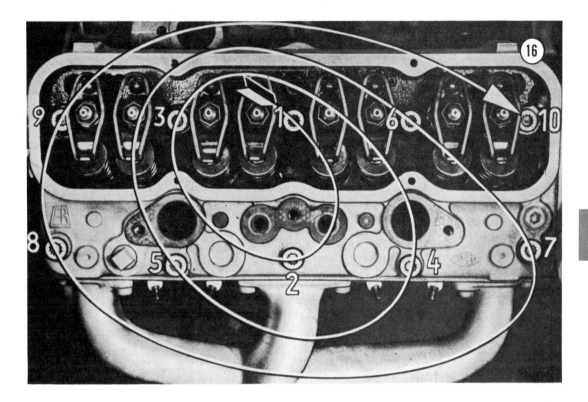

6. See **Figure 17**. Rotate crankshaft pulley until No. 1 position is at TDC on the compression stroke. Use feeler gauge and wrench to adjust valve clearances to 0.008 in. (0.203mm) for intake valve and 0.012 in. (0.304mm) for exhaust valve.

7. Sequentially position each of the other pistons at TDC on the compression stroke and adjust valves as specified above.

8. Install intake manifold and gasket. Torque bolts to 15 ft.-lbs. Start with center bolts and work towards the ends.

9. Install all parts previously removed.

10. Warm engine to normal operating temperature. Adjust intake valves to 0.006 in. (0.1524mm) and exhaust valves to 0.010 in. (0.254mm) as described in Steps 6 and 7.

Cylinder Head Removal (1.5, 1.9 Engines)

1. Disconnect battery.

2. Remove air cleaner.

3. Disconnect throttle linkage at carburetor. Disconnect vacuum advance line from carburetor.

4. Disconnect fuel line at carburetor.

5. Disconnect the positive crankcase ventilation hose at rocker arm cover.

6. Disconnect exhaust gas recirculation system lines (if equipped) from carburetor and intake manifolds. Details of the exhaust gas recirculation system are given in Chapter Seven.

7. Disconnect exhaust pipe from exhaust manifold.

8. Remove bolts fixing intake/exhaust manifold assembly to cylinder head. Remove manifolds and carburetor as an assembly. Discard manifold gasket.

9. If necessary to separate intake and exhaust manifolds, remove carburetor and use serrated bit J-23016 (or equivalent) to remove bolts fixing the manifolds together. Serrated bits are shown in Figure 14. Always install a new gasket if the manifolds are separated.

10. See **Figure 18**. During installation of manifold assembly to cylinder head, install and torque tighten bolts according to the pattern shown. Torque to 33 ft.-lbs.

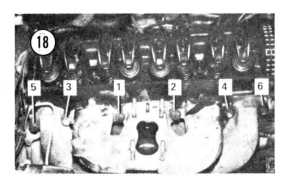

11. Drain radiator and coolant from cylinder block, as described in Chapter Six. Loosen drain plug on right side of engine to prevent coolant from entering cylinder bores.

12. Remove hoses from thermostat housing.

13. Remove spark plug wires from plugs. Mark each wire with its cylinder number for correct installation.

14. Remove bracket holding spark plug wires away from cylinder head.

15. Remove rocker arm cover.

16. Use serrated bit J-22915 (or equivalent), such as shown in Figure 14, to loosen and remove bolts fixing cylinder head to cylinder block and timing cover.

17. Remove plastic screw from end of camshaft.

18. Remove three bolts fixing camshaft sprocket to camshaft. Slide sprocket off of camshaft. Lift up and remove cylinder head. Discard gasket.

19. Place head on bench. Support both ends with wooden blocks to prevent damage to valves.

Cylinder Head Installation (1.5, 1.9 Engines)

To install cylinder head, reverse the preceding steps and observe the following:

1. See **Figure 19**. Install new coolant passage rubber gasket ring in timing case.

1. Timing chain	5. Support timing mark
2. Camshaft sprocket	6. Support
3. Sprocket timing mark	7. Cylinder block
4. Timing case	8. Rubber gasket ring

2. Apply silastic sealer (or equivalent) to both sides of cylinder head gasket where the gasket mates with the timing chain cover. Place new cylinder head gasket onto cylinder block.

3. Carefully install cylinder head. Be careful to place head squarely over guide pins.

4. See **Figure 20**. Rotate camshaft so that recesses are in vertical position to allow installation of left row of head bolts.

5. Install and finger tighten head bolts. Torque head bolts gradually following pattern shown in **Figure 21**. Tighten to 72 ft.-lbs.

6. Install bolts fixing cylinder head to timing chain cover. Torque tighten to 17 ft.-lbs.

7. Slide camshaft sprocket with assembled chain onto the camshaft and guide pin. Install bolts

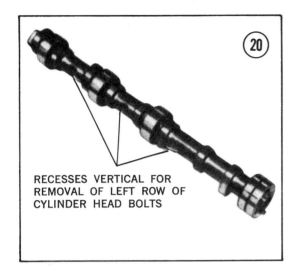

RECESSES VERTICAL FOR
REMOVAL OF LEFT ROW OF
CYLINDER HEAD BOLTS

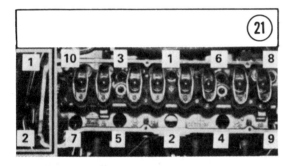

and tighten. Install nylon adjusting screw. Check alignment to see that chain has not slipped. Close front access hole.

8. Use a feeler gauge to check clearance between end of nylon screw and timing gear cover. Clearance should be 0.004 to 0.008 in. (0.016 to 0.203mm). Eliminate excess clearance by adjusting cover with suitable drift.

Cylinder Head Decarbonizing

Removal of carbon from combustion chambers and valves should be done with the valves installed in the cylinder head. By doing so, damage to valve guides and seats will be avoided.

1. Remove all traces of carbon buildup with a scraper and a wire brush fitted to an electric drill.

2. Remove valves from head, as discussed later.

3. Polish combustion chambers and ports with fine emery cloth. Clean head thoroughly to prevent abrasive material from entering engine.

Cylinder Head Inspection

1. After cleaning and decarbonizing, check head carefully for signs of damage, such as cracks and defective core plugs. Replace core plugs if they show any signs of rust, leaks, or weakness.

2. Use a long straightedge and thin feeler gauge to check head and block mating surfaces. The surfaces must be flat to prevent leaks and blowing of head gasket. If high spots are found, they can sometimes be eliminated with a scraper. If the cylinder head is distorted, have it resurfaced with a surface grinder. Refer this service to an automotive machine shop.

Valve Removal/Installation

1. Remove cylinder head, as previously described.

2. On the 1.5 and 1.9 engines, do not lay the head flat on a workbench or the valves may be damaged. Support both ends with wooden blocks.

3. See **Figure 22**. Use spring compressor J-8062 (or equivalent) to compress valve spring. Remove valve cap retainers. Release tool and remove valve cap and spring. Mark all parts to simplify later installation in the correct sequence and position.

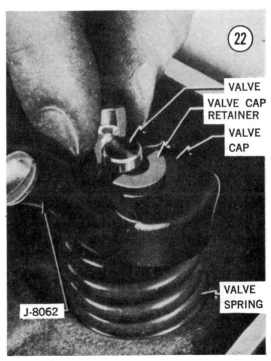

VALVE

VALVE CAP
RETAINER

VALVE
CAP

VALVE
SPRING

J-8062

4. Push valve out through bottom of cylinder head. Take care not to damage valve seats or valve guides as excessive oil consumption may result.

5. Inspect and service valves, as discussed later.

6. To install valves, reverse above steps.

Valve Servicing

1. Clean valves with a wire brush and solvent. Discard burned, warped, or cracked valves. Check critical valve dimensions against specifications. If a valve head must be ground until the outer edge is sharp, discard the valve as it will run too hot.

2. Clean carbon and gum deposits from valve guide bores. Be careful not to damage valve seats and valve guides.

3. Measure valve length and stem diameter. Check dimensions against specifications at end of chapter. If tolerances are exceeded, replace defective valves.

4. If valves are in good enough condition to be refaced, have a machine shop reface them to an angle of 44 degrees.

5. Check condition of valve seats. Inspect for scores, burns, and ridges. If the valve seats will not clean up easily by valve-to-seat lapping, have a machine shop regrind the valve seats to 45 degrees.

6. If the valves and seats are in good enough condition to be hand lapped, proceed as follows. Put a light spring under the head and use medium-grade grinding paste. If the seats are in good condition, fine-grade paste may be used. Use a suction cup tool to hold the valve head. Grind with a semi-rotary motion and let the valve rise off the seat occasionally. Use grinding paste sparingly and when pitting has been removed, clean away paste. Use fine-grade paste until valve seat has an even grey finish. Clean away all traces of grinding paste from the valves, seats, and valve guides.

7. After refacing and reseating valves, cover valve head lightly with red lead and insert valve into valve guide. Rotate the valve back and forth several times under light pressure. Remove valve

and measure contact pattern width. Valve seat width should be as follows:

1.1 Engine		
	Intake Valve	0.050 to 0.060 in. (1.270 to 1.524mm)
	Exhaust Valve	0.065 to 0.075 in. (1.651 to 1.905mm)
1.5, 1.9 Engine		
	Intake Valve	0.049 to 0.059 in. (1.334 to 1.498mm)
	Exhaust Valve	0.063 to 0.073 in. (1.600 to 2.854mm)

8. Inspect valve guides. Worn or pitted guides can be reamed, as shown in **Figure 23**, to accept valves with oversize stems.

NOTE: *Oversize valves were sometimes installed as original equipment. Such valves are stamped on the valve stem end with "1," "2," or "A" to show the size installed. Always check for the mark and replace any defective valves with ones with the same mark.*

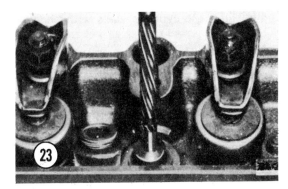

9. To install valves, reverse removal procedure. Lubricate valve stems with clean engine oil before installation into guides. Install valve springs as shown in **Figure 24**.

NOTE: *Use new valve seats whenever valves are replaced or ground.*

10. Install head, as previously described, and adjust valve clearances.

Valve Lifter Service

The valve lifters can be removed, cleaned, replaced, and installed whenever the rocker arm

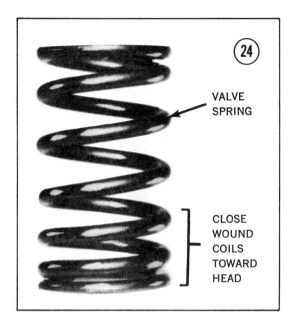

VALVE SPRING

CLOSE WOUND COILS TOWARD HEAD

assembly is disassembled. To remove the valve lifters on the 1.1 engine, the engine must be removed from the car and the camshaft removed from the engine. On the 1.5 and 1.9 engine, the valve lifters are easily removed by pulling them out of the cylinder head.

Check the valve lifters for sticking and damage. Clean sticky valve lifters with suitable solvent and replace defective valve lifters.

To adjust the valve lifters on the 1.5 and 1.9 engine proceed as specified below. Valve lifters on the 1.1 engine do not require adjustment.

1. Rotate crankshaft until piston No. 1 is at TDC on compression stroke.

2. Back off adjusting nut on intake rocker arm until clearance barely exists between valve stem, rocker arm, and lifter. Do the same on exhaust rocker arm.

3. Slowly tighten adjusting nut on each rocker arm until clearance is eliminated.

4. When clearance is eliminated, turn adjusting nut one full turn in clockwise direction.

5. Repeat above steps for each cylinder.

CAMSHAFT/TIMING SPROCKET TIMING CHAIN (1.1 ENGINE)

The camshaft, valve lifters, and camshaft bearings cannot be removed with engine in the car. The timing sprocket, drive chain, and tensioner can be serviced with the engine installed.

Chain Removal/Installation

1. Remove fan belt (see Chapter Six).

2. Remove bolt fixing crankshaft pulley to crankshaft. Pull off crankshaft pulley.

3. Remove bolts fixing timing chain cover to cylinder block. Remove cover and gasket.

4. Remove oil slinger.

5. See **Figure 25**. Remove nut bolt, and washers fixing chain tensioner to cylinder block. Remove chain tensioner.

NOTE: *The tensioner is spring loaded. Hold body and slipper pad together during removal to prevent loss of parts.*

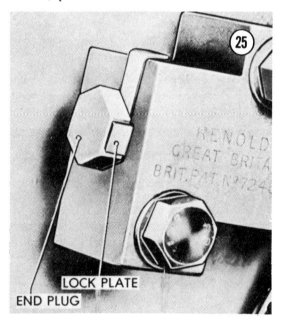

LOCK PLATE

END PLUG

6. See **Figure 26**. Rotate crankshaft until punch marks on camshaft and crankshaft sprockets are aligned.

7. Remove bolt fixing camshaft sprocket to camshaft. Mark position of timing chain relative to camshaft sprocket for later installation.

8. Pull off camshaft sprocket, crankshaft sprocket, and timing chain. Take care not to lose Woodruff key on crankshaft.

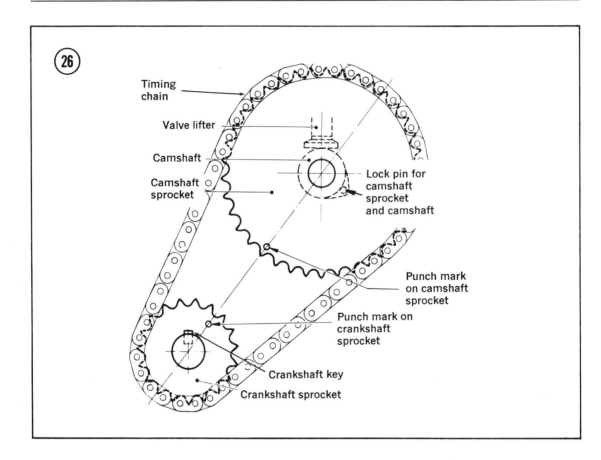

Timing chain

Valve lifter

Camshaft

Camshaft sprocket

Lock pin for camshaft sprocket and camshaft

Punch mark on camshaft sprocket

Punch mark on crankshaft sprocket

Crankshaft key

Crankshaft sprocket

9. Clean all parts and inspect for damaged teeth and general wear. Replace defective parts.

10. See **Figure 27**. Open up lock plate and remove plug from tensioner body. Extract compression spring and adjusting piston from slipper pad and tensioner body. Clean and inspect parts. Pay special attention to spring and adjusting piston. If any part is defective, replace the entire assembly.

11. To install, reverse the above steps and perform the following.

12. Fit woodruff key and crankshaft sprocket to crankshaft.

13. Install camshaft sprocket with lock plate and bolt. Make certain punch marks are located as shown in Figure 26. Install chain over camshaft and crankshaft sprockets. Torque camshaft bolt to 30 ft.-lbs.

NOTE: *Align timing chain match mark made during Step 7.*

14. Insert compression spring into chain tensioner adjusting piston. Install compression spring and adjusting piston into slipper pad sleeve so that adjusting piston helical slot and guide pin fit into each other in sleeve.

15. See **Figure 28**. Use an Allen wrench to turn adjusting piston clockwise into slipper pad sleeve until guide pin emerges on top of helical slot. This blocks the piston for installation.

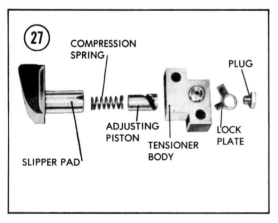

COMPRESSION SPRING

PLUG

ADJUSTING PISTON

TENSIONER BODY

LOCK PLATE

SLIPPER PAD

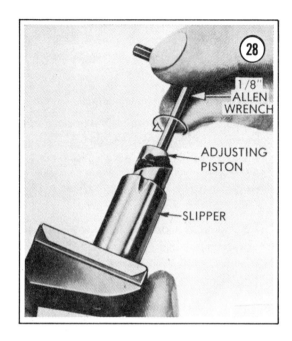

16. Lubricate sliding parts with engine oil. Slide slipper pad sleeve into tensioner body. Install tensioner assembly onto cylinder block with washers, nut, and bolt.

17. See **Figure 29**. Use Allen wrench to release adjusting piston, as shown. This releases piston and slipper pad so that tension to the chain is supplied. No further adjustment is required. Install lock plate and end plug. Turn over tab on lock plate.

18. Slide oil slinger on to crankshaft. Make certain slot engages with woodruff key.

19. Fit new gasket to timing chain cover. Mount timing chain cover to cylinder block and install bolts. Tighten finger-tight, then torque to 60 in.-lbs.

20. Install crankshaft pulley, washer, and bolt. Torque to 30 ft.-lbs.

Timing Chain Cover Seal Replacement

1. Whenever timing chain is removed, inspect seal for signs of leaks or damage. If defective, replace as follows.

2. See **Figure 30**. Use a punch to drive outer seal retainer and cork seal from cover. Do not remove inner seal retainer.

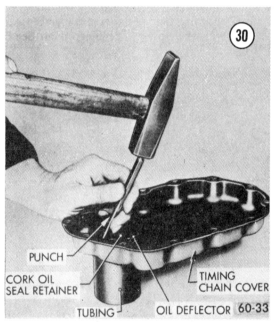

3. Install new seal through front of cover. Drive it in until it is flush with cover.

Camshaft/Valve Lifters/Camshaft Bearing Removal/Installation

1. Remove engine from car, as previously described.

2. Remove rocker arm cover and disassemble rocker arms, as previously described.

3. Remove crankshaft pulley, timing chain cover, and timing chain.

4. Remove distributor and turn engine upside down.

5. See **Figure 31**. Remove bolts fixing camshaft thrust plate to cylinder block. Remove camshaft thrust plate.

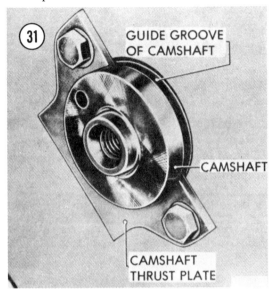

6. Carefully pull camshaft out of cylinder block. Take care not to scratch or damage camshaft journals or lobes. Remove engine front plate.

7. Inspect camshaft journals and lobes for signs of seizing, wear, and scoring. If defective, the camshaft must be replaced. If the camshaft must be replaced, the camshaft bearings in the cylinder block must be replaced. Refer such service to your dealer or a machine shop as the bearings must be line bored after installation.

8. If the valve lifters are to be removed, remove the oil pan, as described in Chapter Five, and extract the lifters from the cylinder block.

9. Clean the valve lifters with a suitable solvent and inspect for damage and sticking. Replace if defective.

10. To install, reverse above steps. Lubricate all parts liberally with clean engine oil. Take extreme care not to damage camshaft or camshaft bearings.

CAMSHAFT, SPROCKETS, AND TIMING (1.5, 1.9 ENGINE)

The camshaft and valve lifters can be removed only if the cylinder head is removed. The engine may be in or out of the car. Service to the timing chain, camshaft sprocket, and crankshaft sprocket can be done with the engine installed.

Timing Chain Removal/Installation

1. Support the engine with a lifting device or a tool such as the one shown in **Figure 32**.

2. Remove the radiator and shroud assembly (Chapter Six).

3. Remove the cylinder head, as previously described.

4. Remove alternator belt and alternator support bracket.

5. Remove fuel pump (Chapter Five).

6. Remove distributor. Unbolt and remove chain tensioner assembly from timing chain cover.

7. Remove bolt fixing crankshaft pulley to crankshaft. Remove pulley.

8. Remove bolts fixing water pump to timing chain cover. Remove water pump.

9. See **Figure 33**. Remove bolt behind water pump, as shown.

10. Remove oil pan.

11. Remove bolts fixing timing chain cover to cylinder block. Make certain to remove bolt shown in Figure 33.

12. Rotate the crankshaft until the timing marks

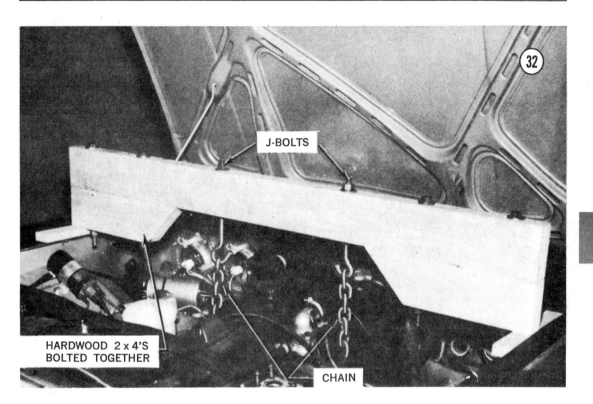

on the camshaft sprocket and crankshaft sprocket are aligned (see **Figure 34**). Number 4 piston should be at TDC on compression stroke.

13. Mark timing chain for installation. Pull off sprockets and remove chain.

14. Inspect all parts for wear and damage. Replace as required. If one sprocket must be replaced, the other must be also.

15. Inspect timing chain cover oil seal for signs of leaks. Replace as discussed in the next procedure.

16. To install, reverse preceding steps. Make certain timing marks on sprockets are aligned exactly as shown in Figure 33 so that valve timing will be correct.

17. During installation, position timing cover onto guide pin in upper left corner of cylinder block and insert centering bolt through timing chain cover into lower right corner of cylinder block. Sealing is not required.

18. Tighten crankshaft pulley bolt to 72 ft.-lbs.

Timing Chain Cover Oil Seal Replacement

1. Remove timing chain cover, as previously described.

2. Use a suitable drift to drive out oil seal from rear of timing chain cover.

> NOTE: *Replacement of the oil seal with the timing gear cover in place can be done by removing the crankshaft pulley and prying the seal out of the cover.*

3. Coat outer circumference of new oil seal lightly with suitable sealer. Press seal into cover, using suitable installer, as shown in **Figure 35**. If the timing chain cover has not been removed, put the seal into place, position the installer over the crankshaft, thread crankshaft bolt (with washer) into crankshaft, and tighten bolt until seal seats properly in timing chain cover. Remove bolt, washer, and installer.

4. Install pulley, washer, and bolt. Tighten them to 72 ft.-lbs.

Camshaft/Valve Lifter Removal/Installation

1. Remove cylinder head, as previously described.

2. Loosen self-locking rocker arm nuts and swing rocker arms off valve lifters.

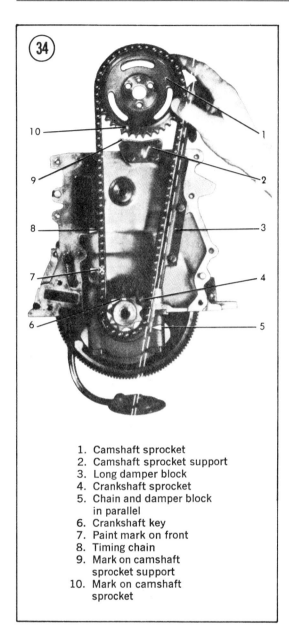

1. Camshaft sprocket
2. Camshaft sprocket support
3. Long damper block
4. Crankshaft sprocket
5. Chain and damper block
   in parallel
6. Crankshaft key
7. Paint mark on front
8. Timing chain
9. Mark on camshaft
   sprocket support
10. Mark on camshaft
    sprocket

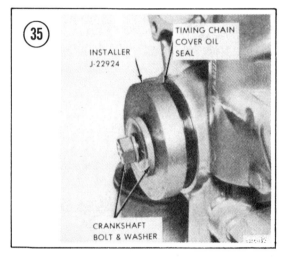

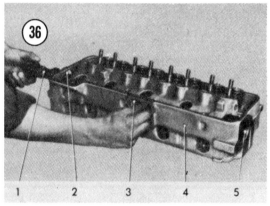

1. Camshaft
2. Front access hole
3. Lateral access hole
4. Cylinder head
5. Rear access hole

3. Remove valve lifters from cylinder head. Mark for installation.

4. See **Figure 36**. Remove cover from access hole on left side and rear of cylinder head.

5. Use your hand through the access hole to support camshaft. Remove camshaft toward front of cylinder head. Take care not to damage bearing surfaces or camshaft journals.

6. Inspect camshaft journals for wear and damage. Check condition of cam lobes. Replace camshaft if defective. Measure outside diameter of camshaft journals and inside diameter of camshaft bearings. Clearance should meet specifications at the end of this chapter. If clearance is excessive, replace camshaft and cylinder head.

7. Support camshaft on V-grooved wooden blocks or other suitable support.

8. Mount dial gauge so that feeler arm rests on center camshaft journal. Preload and zero dial gauge. Rotate camshaft and measure runout of center journal. If runout is excessive (see specifications), replace camshaft.

9. To install, reverse above steps. Liberally lubricate camshaft and bearings with clean engine oil. Take care when inserting camshaft not to damage camshaft or bearings.

10. After installation, use feeler gauge to check end play of camshaft by pushing camshaft back and forth. See specifications for maximum permissible end play.

CYLINDER BLOCK SERVICING

Cylinder block servicing requires removing the block from car, dismantling and cleaning it, inspecting and replacing worn parts, checking and reboring block as necessary, and reassembly. Remove and disassemble engine as described in this chapter. Procedures that do not require engine removal are so noted.

Measuring Cylinder Bore

Cylinder bore can be measured with the engine in the car. Proceed as follows:

1. Remove cylinder head from cylinder block.

2. Stuff clean rags into cylinder bore so that foreign material cannot enter engine. Clean top of cylinder block thoroughly. Remove all traces of gasket, rust, and other foreign material.

3. Remove rags and foreign material from cylinder bore. Check general wear of cylinder bore by feeling for ridge at top of bore. Use end of fingernail to check for ridge. If there is a definite ridge, the cylinder may be excessively worn, which requires reboring of all cylinders and installation of new oversize pistons and rings.

4. If the ridge buildup is relatively small, use a ridge reamer according to manufacturer's instructions to remove ridge.

5. See **Figure 37**. Use a cylinder gauge to measure cylinder bore. Take several readings at different locations. Determine the maximum bore wear, which normally occurs toward the top of the bore across the connecting rod thrust axis. Check readings not only for maximum bore, but also for taper and out-of-round.

6. Check readings against wear limit specification. If wear limit has been exceeded, rebore the cylinders and install oversize pistons and rings. If wear limit has not been exceeded, hone the cylinders to remove glaze and to give a good surface for the rings to seat against.

NOTE: *Cylinder block reboring requires equipment not normally available to the home mechanic. Refer such service to dealer or automotive machine shop.*

7. If the pistons have been removed, measure them, as shown in **Figure 38**. Measure the piston 2½ inches below bottom of oil ring groove, from side to side. Clearance between cylinder wall and piston should be:

1.1 Engine	0.0004 to 0.0008 in. (0.010 to 0.020mm)
1.5, 1.9 Engine	0.0008 to 0.0012 in. (0.020 to 0.030mm)

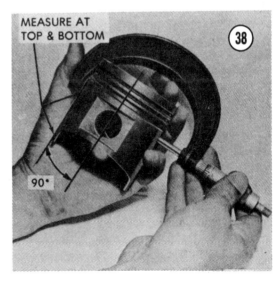

MEASURE AT TOP & BOTTOM
38
90°

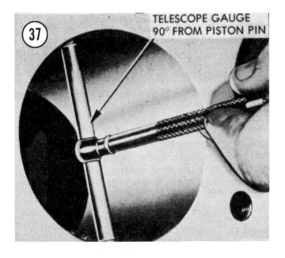

37
TELESCOPE GAUGE 90° FROM PISTON PIN

CONNECTING RODS

Removal of the connecting rods can be done with the engine in place if the oil pan is removed.

Normally, remove the engine. Whenever removal of the connecting rods is required, service the cylinder head, pistons, rings, cylinder bore, bearings, and crankshaft.

1. Remove engine from car.

2. Remove cylinder head.

3. Remove oil pan.

4. Remove rod bearing caps and bearings from crankshaft. Mark each with cylinder number and position for later installation. Inspect for ridge at top of cylinder bore. Use ridge reamer to remove ridge.

5. With ridge removed, push connecting rod and piston assembly out of top of cylinder.

6. Use ring expander to remove rings from piston. Mark each with cylinder number for later installation.

Piston Pin Removal/Installation

The piston pin is press fitted to the connecting rod. Removal and installation requires the use of a press and special tools, as shown in **Figures 39** (removal) **and 40** (installation).

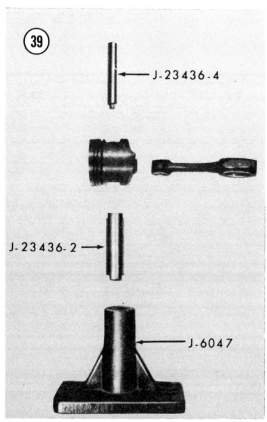

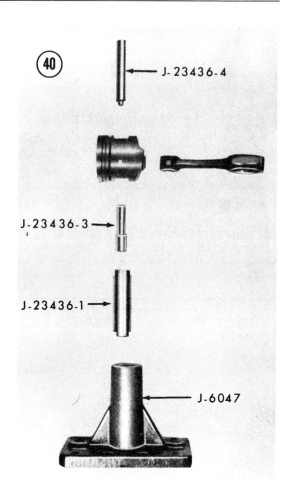

1. To remove piston pin, position base support J-6047 on press.

2. Place tool J-23436-2 in base support with large diameter bore facing upward.

3. Position piston and rod assembly on tool J-23436-2. Make certain pin is aligned on tool.

4. Position tool J-23436-4 in opposite end of piston pin and press pin out.

5. Inspect piston pin bores and piston pins for wear. Piston pin bores and piston pins must be free of varnish or scuffing.

6. Measure piston pin bore and piston pin diameter. If clearance is in excess of 0.001 in. (0.025mm), replace the piston and piston pin assembly.

7. To install, lubricate piston pin holes in piston and connecting rod.

8. Position base support J-6047 on hydraulic press.

9. Place tool J-23436-1 with large diameter bore facing upward in support J-6047.

10. Place large end of tool J-23436-3 in bore of tool J-23436-1.

11. Position piston, rod, and pin on guide J-23436-3.

12. Line up pin on piston. Use tool J-23436-4 to press pin into piston.

13. Remove piston assembly from tools and press. Check piston for freedom of movement on piston pin.

PISTONS, PISTON PINS, AND PISTON RINGS

The piston assembly consists of the connecting rod, piston pin, piston rings, and piston. Removal of this assembly is as described for connecting rods. **Figure 41** shows the piston assembly used on the 1.1 engine, **Figure 42** the piston assembly used on the 1.5 and early 1.9 engines, and **Figure 43** the piston assembly used on late 1.9 engines. Note that instructions are given for each piston assembly for installation in the engine. Make certain to follow these instructions so that the valves do not hit the top of the pistons.

Inspection and Repair

1. Remove piston and connecting rod assembly, as previously described.

2. Use ring expander to remove rings from pistons.

3. Inspect all parts for wear and damage. Replace as required.

4. Remove all carbon from piston with a scraper or broken hacksaw blade. Clean out the ring grooves with a broken ring or suitable groove cleaning tool. The tool should be the same width as the groove being cleaned.

5. Clean out oilways inside piston and connecting rod.

6. Measure clearance between the piston and cylinder wall, as previously described. If clearance is excessive, rebore cylinder and install oversize piston and rings. Always install pistons and rings in complete sets of four.

7. Check piston ring end gap by placing rings in cylinder bore about one inch from top of bore.

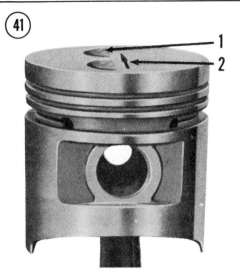

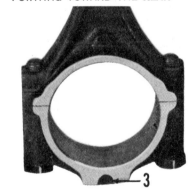

1. NOTCH IN PISTON HEAD FOR VALVES
2. RUBBER STAMPED ARROW POINTING TOWARD THE **FRONT**
3. NOTCH IN CONNECTING ROD CAP POINTING TOWARD THE **REAR**

Square it in the bore by tapping gently with the top of the piston. Use a feeler gauge to measure end gap. Check against specification at end of chapter. If gap is excessive, replace rings, or rebore cylinder and replace pistons and rings with proper oversize.

8. Use ring expander to install rings in proper grooves in piston. Use feeler gauge to measure clearance between ring and top of ring groove. Check reading against specification. If excessive, replace piston and rings.

Installation

Figure 44 shows the proper installation of the rings to the piston for the 1.5 and 1.9 engines.

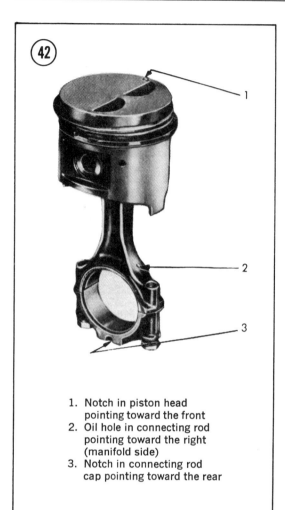

1. Notch in piston head
   pointing toward the front
2. Oil hole in connecting rod
   pointing toward the right
   (manifold side)
3. Notch in connecting rod
   cap pointing toward the rear

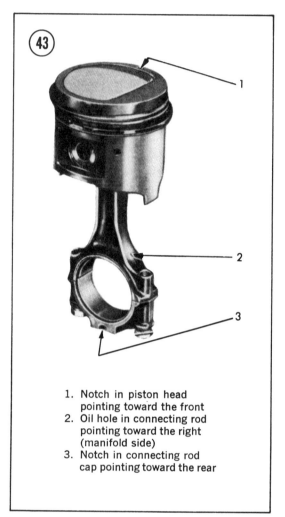

1. Notch in piston head
   pointing toward the front
2. Oil hole in connecting rod
   pointing toward the right
   (manifold side)
3. Notch in connecting rod
   cap pointing toward the rear

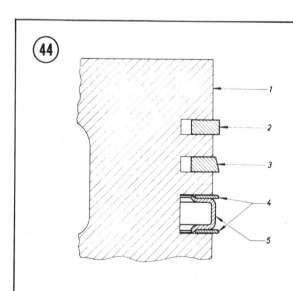

1. Piston
2. No. 1 compression ring—installed
   with either side up.
3. No. 2 compression ring—installed
   with "top" marking towards the
   top.
4. Upper and lower steel band ring—
   installed with either side up.
5. Intermediated ring—installed with
   either side up.

On the 1.1 engine, the chrome plated upper ring can be installed either way, the middle ring must be installed with the "top" mark facing the top of the piston, and the bottom ring can be installed either way.

For 1.5 and 1.9 engines, position the ring gaps around the piston as shown in **Figure 45**. For the 1.1 engine, position the ring gaps 90 degrees away from each other; no gap should be directly above another gap.

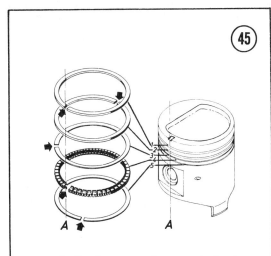

1. No. 1 compression—gap in front
2. No. 2 compression—gap in rear
3. Upper steel band—1-2 in. towards the left of intermediate ring gap
4. Intermediate ring—gap in front
5. Lower steel band—1-2 in. towards the right of intermediate ring gap.

"A" vertical line for piston and rings, front

1. Install rings to pistons.
2. Install pistons to connecting rods and piston pins, as previously described.
3. Lubricate piston and ring assembly liberally with engine oil.
4. Make certain ring gaps are properly located.
5. Use a piston ring compress to compress the rings into the piston grooves.
6. Carefully lower the piston assembly into the cylinder bore. Make certain that each piston is inserted into its proper bore and that the piston is properly positioned, as shown in Figures 41, 42, and 43.

CAUTION
When installing the piston assembly into the cylinder bore, be careful not to damage or scratch crankshaft bearing journal.

7. When the bottom of the ring compressor is flat against the top of the block, push on the top of the piston until it is free of the compressor and the rings are in contact with the cylinder walls.
8. Lubricate connecting rod bearings and crankshaft connecting rod journals with clean engine oil.
9. Insert connecting rod bearing into connecting rod. Make certain that locating tabs mate with recess in connecting rod.
10. Insert connecting rod bearing into connecting rod cap. Lubricate with clean engine oil.
11. Install cap to crankshaft, insert rod cap bolts, and tighten to specified torque.
12. Repeat above steps for each piston. Rotate the crankshaft as necessary to gain access to rod cap bolts for tightening.

CONNECTING ROD BEARINGS

Inspection/Replacement

1. Remove connecting rod bearings from cylinder block and connecting rod caps. Mark each with cylinder number and position for later installation.
2. Inspect the upper and lower halves for signs of scratches, seizing, and general wear. Do not scrape or attempt to polish defects from bearings. If they are defective, replace them.
3. If the bearings appear to be serviceable, measure the clearance between them and the crankshaft journals with Plastigage or equivalent.
4. See **Figure 46**. Fit the connecting rod/piston assembly to the crankshaft journal. Make certain to install upper bearing half.
5. Place piece of Plastigage across end cap lower bearing, as shown.
6. Install cap, bearing, and Plastigage to crankshaft. Insert end cap bolts and torque tighten to specification. Do not turn crankshaft with Plastigage on bearing.

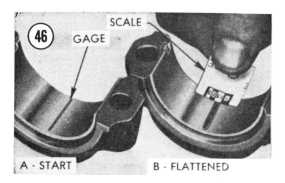

A - START   B - FLATTENED

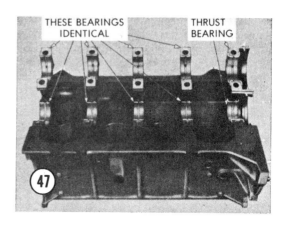

7. Remove cap, bearing, and Plastigage. The flattened piece of Plastigage will stick to either the bearing or crankshaft journal. Do not remove it.

8. Use a piece of the Plastigage envelope to measure the width of the Plastigage at its widest point. This gives bearing clearance measurement.

9. Check clearance against specification. If clearance is excessive, regrind crankshaft to nearest undersize and replace bearings with proper size according to crankshaft grind. If the crankshaft cannot be satisfactorily reground, replace it.

CRANKSHAFT/FLYWHEEL SERVICING

Servicing of the crankshaft requires removal of the engine from the car. Servicing of the flywheel requires removal of the transmission, pressure plate, and clutch assemblies from the engine.

Whenever the crankshaft is removed from engine, service or overhaul all other engine assemblies including oil pump, timing gear, cylinder head and valves, camshaft and valve lifters, connecting rod and main bearings, connecting rods and piston pins, pistons and rings, rear seals, cylinder block, and flywheel.

The crankshaft on the 1.5 and 1.9 engines has five main bearings; the main bearing closest to the flywheel is the thrust bearing, as shown in **Figure 47**.

The crankshaft on the 1.1 engine has three main bearings; the middle bearing is the thrust bearing.

Removal/Installation

1. Remove the engine, as previously described.

2. Remove the transmission, pressure plate, and clutch disc from the flywheel, as described in Chapter Nine.

3. Remove timing chain, crankshaft sprocket, and camshaft sprocket, as previously described.

4. Remove oil pan, oil pump, and distributor from engine.

5. Invert the engine so that the crankshaft is accessible.

6. Use a dial gauge on the end of the crankshaft to measure end play by moving the crankshaft toward the front and back of the engine. Check end play against specification. If end play is excessive, install proper size thrust bearings or washers at thrust bearing.

7. Check condition of flywheel. The flywheel-to-clutch disc mating surface should not be marred, burned, or grooved; it should have a mirror-like finish. If it is defective, remove flywheel and have it resurfaced or replace it with new flywheel.

8. Check condition of teeth on flywheel ring gear. If the teeth are cracked or broken, replace the flywheel and/or the ring gear.

9. With flywheel removed, check condition of rear main seal. Inspect for damage and signs of leaks. If defective, replace as described below. Before removing flywheel, mark its position relative to crankshaft for later installation.

10. Check the center main bearing for runout by removing center main bearing cap, installing dial gauge so that gauge arm rests on center main

bearing journal, and rotating crankshaft. Check readings against specification. Another method of checking runout is to remove crankshaft from cylinder block, installing it in V-blocks so the front and rear journals are supported, and using a dial gauge to check runout at the center main bearing.

11. Rotate crankshaft until No. 1 piston is at BDC. Remove bolts fixing No. 1 connecting rod cap to connecting rod. Remove end cap and end cap bearing. Gently push connecting rod up into cylinder until the crankshaft can be rotated without hitting the connecting rod. Do not push the connecting rod so far up into the cylinder bore that the rings hit the ridge at the top of the cylinder bore. If the piston and rod assemblies are to be removed, remove the ridge and push the connecting rod and piston clear out of the cylinder bore. Repeat this procedure for each connecting rod and piston assembly.

12. Remove bolts fixing the main bearing caps to the cylinder block and crankshaft. Remove main bearing caps and bearings from crankshaft. Mark all parts for later installation.

13. Lift out crankshaft and remove upper half of main bearings from cylinder block. Mark parts for later installation.

> NOTE: *If the main bearings (five-bearing models) are to be removed without removal of crankshaft, special tool J-8080 (**Figure 48**) is required. Insert the end of the tool in the crankshaft oil hole and slowly rotate crankshaft until the tool pushes the bearing out of place. Remove bearing and tool. Do not scratch the crankshaft journal.*

14. Lift out crankshaft and rear main seal. Separate rear main seal from crankshaft. Remove upper half of main bearings from cylinder block. Mark for installation.

15. Check main bearings and connecting rod bearings for signs of scoring, wear, and seizing. If the bearings appear satisfactory, check the clearance between them and the crankshaf journals with Plastigage, as described under *Connecting Rod Bearings*. Check clearance against specification. If excessive, replace with new

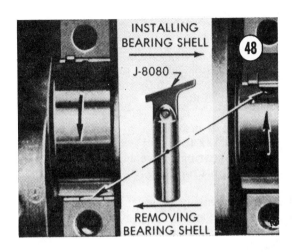

INSTALLING BEARING SHELL
J-8080
48
REMOVING BEARING SHELL

4

standard size bearings or regrind the crankshaft and fit with proper undersize bearings.

16. Use a micrometer to measure diameter of crankshaft pins and journals. Measure diameter at various points to determine wear, taper, and out-of-round condition.

17. Check dimensions against specifications. If the measurements indicate excessive wear, taper, or out-of-round condition, have the crankshaft reground to suit the nearest undersize bearings. Refer such service to an Opel dealer or automotive machine shop.

18. Use a suitable solvent to clean all parts of the cylinder block. If possible have the cylinder block "hot tanked" to remove all dirt and oil and to clean out water and oil passages.

19. To install, reverse the above steps and perform the following.

20. Lubricate all journal and bearing surfaces with clean engine oil.

21. On 1.5 and 1.9 engines, it is necessary to line up the thrust surfaces of the bearings before the cap bolts are tightened. To do this, move the crankshaft backward and forward several times. The last movement should be forward. Tighten the thrust bearing cap finger-tight during this operation. Rotate crankshaft and check for freedom of movement in the thrust bearing. If satisfactory, loosen cap bolts ½ turn and repeat above step for each bearing. After setting all bearings, torque cap bolts to specification.

22. Always replace rear main seals if the crankshaft is removed.

Rear Bearing Oil Seal
Removal/Installation

Removal of rear bearing oil seal requires removal of the transmission, clutch, pressure plate, and flywheel. See procedures earlier in this chapter and in Chapter Nine.

1. Remove transmission, pressure plate, clutch disc, and flywheel with the engine either removed or installed (depending on model).

2. Punch a hole into oil seal and screw in a sheet metal screw. Pull out the oil seal, as shown in **Figure 49**.

OIL SEAL PROTECTOR J-22928

REAR MAIN OIL SEAL

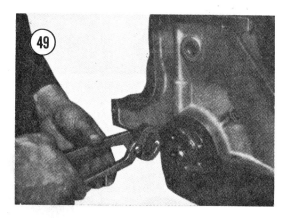

3. Thoroughly clean out oil seal seat in cylinder block. Check for burrs that might damage new seal during installation.

4. Lubricate seal with a suitable protective grease. Install seal on taper ring protector, as shown in **Figure 50**. Protector J-22928 is required for the 1.5 and 1.9 engines; protector J-21707-2 for the 1.1 engine. Rotate the seal to ensure lip of seal is not turned back.

5. See **Figure 51** (1.5, 1.9 engine) or **52** (1.1 engine). Drive in oil seal using appropriate installer. Be careful not to tilt seal so that it drives straight in and seats squarely.

6. Install flywheel, clutch disc, pressure plate, and transmission. Torque all bolts to specifications.

Crankshaft Distributor Drive Gear
(1.5, 1.9 Engines)

The crankshaft distributor drive gear can be removed and installed with the engine in or out of the car. The following steps are for when the engine is installed.

REAR MAIN BEARING SEAL

SEAL PROTECTOR J-22928

INSTALLER J-22928-2

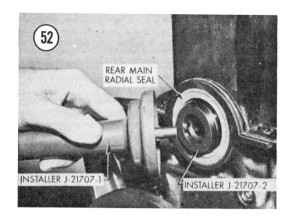

REAR MAIN RADIAL SEAL

INSTALLER J-21707-1

INSTALLER J-21707-2

1. Remove fan belt, as previously described.

2. Remove fuel pump. Plug end of fuel line to prevent loss of fuel.

3. Remove spark plug wires, distributor hold-down clamp, and distributor.

4. Turn the crankshaft so that the Woodruff key is on top.

5. Pry oil seal out of timing chain cover.

6. Insert screwdriver through fuel pump opening and push distributor drive gear out through oil seal opening in timing cover. The distributor drive gear is a push fit to the crankshaft and key.

7. Install new gear by reversing preceding steps. Make sure key fits into keyway. Always use new gaskets and seals.

ENGINE LUBRICATION SYSTEM

The engine is lubricated by a pressure-feed oil system. The gear-type oil pump is driven by a shaft that locks into the distributor drive shaft. **Figure 53** shows the oil distribution for 1.5 and 1.9 engines. The 1.1 engine oil distribution is similar except the oil pump is located inside the crankcase/oil pan rather than on the timing gear cover. Oil pump service in the 1.1 engine requires removal of the oil pan. On the 1.5 and 1.9 engines, the oil pump (except suction tube and screen) can be serviced without removing the oil pan.

As shown in the illustration, oil is sucked out of the oil pan through a filter screen into the gear-driven oil pump. Oil is pumped through a passage to the full flow oil filter, where it is filtered before being pumped into the engine oil passages. A pressure relief valve and bypass valve are built into the oil pump cover on the 1.5 and 1.9 engines and into the oil filter support on 1.1 engines. After being filtered, the oil is pumped through drillings (galleries) to the main bearings, connecting rod bearings, crankshaft, camshaft, timing chain, and cylinder head. The valve system and hydraulic lifters (if so equipped) are lubricated from the cylinder head oil passage. Oil returns to the oil pan through a passage at the rear of the cylinder block. Cylinder walls are lubricated through holes in the connecting rod big ends and by splash from the crankshaft.

The lubrication system consists of the following components:

a. Oil pan

b. Oil pump

c. Full-flow oil filter

d. Low pressure sending unit and warning lamp

e. Oil passages

f. Oil pressure relief valve

g. Oil filter bypass valve

OIL PAN

Removal/Installation

The oil-pan-to-engine mounting flanges should be inspected periodically for signs of oil leaks at the gaskets. The oil pan should only be removed to replace gaskets or to service the oil pump (1.1 engine) and oil screen, or during engine overhaul or major service. Removal of the oil pump requires lowering of the front suspension, as discussed in Chapter Ten.

1. Run the engine until normal operating temperature is reached. Drain engine oil as described in Chapter Two.

2. Jack up the car and place it on jackstands. Lower the front suspension to gain access to the oil pan.

3. Remove bolts and washers fixing oil pan to cylinder block.

4. Lower oil pan and remove from under car. Take care not to damage gaskets or seals. As a matter of good practice, replace gaskets and seals with new ones whenever the pan is removed.

5. Inspect condition of oil suction pipe screen. If the screen is plugged or restricted with oil sludge, remove it and clean in suitable solvent.

6. Use a suitable solvent to clean the inside and outside of the oil pan. Remove all traces of gasket and gasket sealing compound from the oil pan and crankcase mating surfaces.

7. Inspect the oil pan for cracks and dents. Repair by welding or replace if badly damaged or bent. Use a straightedge to check oil pan

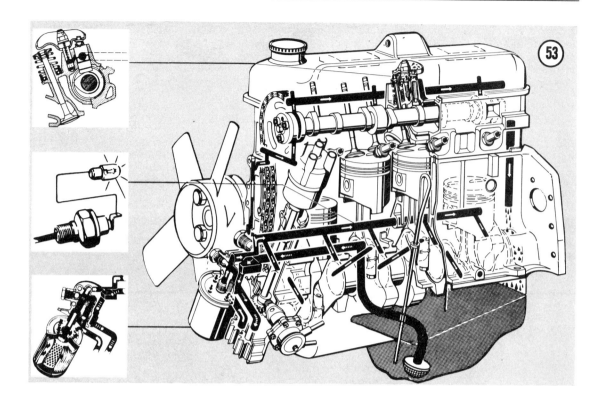

mating flanges for distortion or warpage. If defective, straighten or replace.

8. To install, reverse the above steps. During installation, coat all mating surfaces with a suitable gasket compound and install the gaskets.

9. Fit the oil pan to the crankcase and screw in fixing bolts and washers. Tighten the bolts equally and gradually, working from the center toward the ends to avoid distortion. Torque to 5 ft.-lb.

10. Fill the engine with oil as previously described, start the engine, and check for oil leaks.

OIL PUMP

Figure 54 shows the oil pump with the pan removed on the 1.1 engine; **Figure 55** shows the 1.5 and 1.9 engines.

The oil pump and filter screen should be serviced whenever the oil pan and/or timing gear cover are removed. The following provides information for removal, disassembly, inspection, repair or replacement, assembly, and installation.

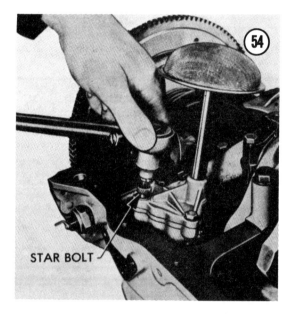

STAR BOLT

Servicing (1.1 Engine)

1. Remove oil pan as previously described.

2. See Figure 2. Use a wrench fitted with a serrated bit to remove 2 star bolts fixing oil pump to crankcase.

3. See **Figure 56**. Remove oil pump cover and screen assembly. Slide out pump gears.

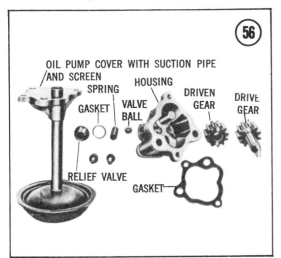

4. Remove pressure relief valve plug, gasket, relief valve, spring, and check ball.

5. Clean all parts in a suitable solvent. Thoroughly clean pickup screen and blow dry with compressed air.

6. Inspect all parts for wear and damage. Pay special attention to gear teeth and drive shaft-to-distributor drive surface. Check relief valve spring for wear and distortion. Replace any defective parts.

7. Install oil pump gears into housing. Use a feeler gauge to measure gear lash between gears.

Clearance must be 0.004 to 0.006 in. (0.101 to 0.152mm). See **Figure 57**.

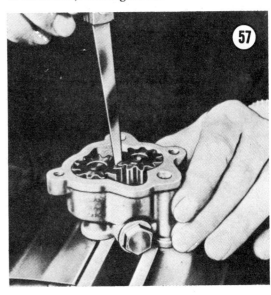

8. See **Figure 58**. Place a straightedge over gears. Clearance between straightedge and housing should be 0.001-0.004 in. (0.025-0.101mm).

9. Install ball, spring, relief valve gasket, and relief valve spring.

10. Install pump cover and screen assembly to oil pump body. Use a new gasket.

11. Check gears for smooth operation. Fill housing with engine oil. Using a new gasket, mount the housing to the crankcase.

12. Insert star bolts and torque to 15 ft.-lb.

13. Install oil pan and fill with oil. Connect front suspension, start engine, and check for oil leaks.

Servicing (1.5 and 1.9 Engines)

1. Remove bolts fixing oil pump cover assembly to timing chain cover.

2. Remove cover assembly and slide out gears.

3. See **Figure 59**. Remove bypass valve plug and remove gasket, spring, and bypass ball.

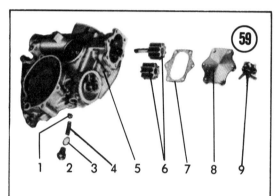

1. Bypass valve ball
2. Plug, bypass valve
3. Gasket
4. Spring
5. Timing case
6. Oil pump gears
7. Cover gasket
8. Cover
9. Cover attaching screws

4. Clean all parts in a suitable solvent. Inspect all parts for wear and damage. Pay special attention to gear teeth drive shaft-to-distributor drive surface. If teeth are defective, replace gear.

5. Check the pump cover for signs of wear from gear action. If wear is obvious, replace the cover. Check spring for distortion and ball for wear. Replace if defective.

6. See Figure 3. Use a straightedge to check clearance between gear faces and oil pump housing. Clearance must not exceed 0.004 in. (0.101mm).

7. Use a feeler gauge to check gear lash, as shown in **Figure 60**. Clearance must be 0.004 to 0.006 in. (0.101 to 0.152mm). If clearance is excessive, replace gears.

8. Install ball, spring, relief valve gasket, and relief valve spring. During installation, use a brass drift to tap ball lightly into its seat. Install bypass valve plug.

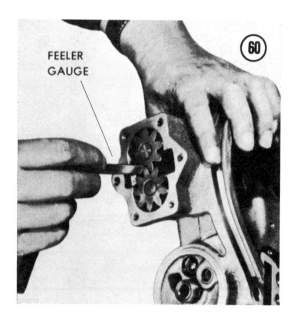

FEELER GAUGE

9. Lubricate spindles and gear teeth. Using a new gasket, install oil pump cover. Torque the bolts to 15 ft.-lb.

10. If the oil pan has been removed, remove bolts fixing pipe and screen assembly to crankcase, as shown in **Figure 61**. Clean the screen and pipe thoroughly in suitable solvent and blow dry with compressed air.

PIPE & SCREEN ASSEMBLY

OIL PRESSURE SENDING UNIT

The oil pressure sending unit is connected electrically to the warning indicator on the dashboard instrument panel. The lamp lights when the oil pressure falls to critically low levels.

If the lamp lights during normal operation, stop the engine immediately and find out why. Check the level of the engine oil first and replenish as required. If engine oil condition and level are normal, check the connections to the sending unit and the lamp. If normal, replace sending unit with new one. If this does not solve the problem, remove drain plug and drain engine oil. Install new oil filter and fill the pan with new oil. If abnormal condition persists, the problem is probably in the oil pump, oil pressure relief valve, or blocked oil line. If this is the case, service the oil pump and clean out oil passages, which requires engine removal and disassembly.

OIL PASSAGES/GALLERIES

Whenever the engine is disassembled for overhaul, special attention should be given to cleaning and clearing of all oil passages in the cylinder block, cylinder head, crankshaft, and connecting rods. If possible, the block and head should be "hot tanked" thoroughly to clean out the passages. Compressed air should be forced through the passages to make sure they are completely cleared of obstructions. The use of high-quality detergent oil will help eliminate blockages in the oil passages and galleries. It is extremely important to change engine oil every 3,000 miles, as recommended by the manufacturer.

ENGINE REASSEMBLY

To reassemble the engine, reverse the steps used during disassembly. Use new gaskets and seals. Torque all nuts and bolts to specification. If the engine has been overhauled and/or new rings or valves installed, use a high quality break-in oil and limit speed to a maximum of 65 mph during the first 100 miles with moderate stopping and starting. After the first 100 miles, increase speed gradually as the mileage accumulates. Avoid driving for extended periods at any one speed for the first 500 miles. After 500 miles, replace break-in oil with oil suitable for anticipated driving conditions and temperatures. Replace oil filter after first 500 miles to rid the engine of foreign material that might have been dislodged or caused by the overhaul procedures. Check and adjust valves to proper setting after 500 miles and retorque cylinder head bolts to specifications.

SPECIFICATIONS AND TORQUE TIGHTENING DATA

Tables 1 through 9 provide specifications and tightening torques for all 1.1-1.9 engines.

Table 1   ENGINE SPECIFICATIONS — 1.1 ENGINE

Type — No. of cylinders	In-line 4
Valve arrangement	Overhead valve
Bore and stroke	2.95 x 2.40
Piston displacement	65.8 cu. in.
Compression ratio	7.6:1
Horsepower (gross)	56 at 5,800 rpm
Horsepower (installed)	49 at 5,500 rpm
Torque (ft.-lbs.) (gross)	55 at 4,400 rpm
Torque (ft.-lbs.) (installed)	52 at 3,600 rpm
Octane requirement	Low lead content
Firing order	1-3-4-2
Cylinder block material	Cast iron
Cylinder liners	None
Crankshaft bearings number and type	3 replaceable liners
Material	Steel backed tri-metal babbitt
Piston material and surface	Aluminum alloy, cast
Treatment	Steel inserts
Piston pin offset (large dimension distributor)	.031 to right
Compression rings material and surface treatment:	
No. 1	Chrome-plated cast iron, squared
No. 2	Cast iron, tapered
Oil ring	Chrome plated steel
Location of all piston rings	Above piston pin
Camshaft type and material	Tempered castings
Camshaft drive	Chain-slack controlled by special tensioner
Number and type of camshaft bearings	3 steel backed babbitt
Valve lifter type	Solid
Valve spring type	Single helical
Oiling system type	Forced feed
Oil supplied to:	
Bearing surfaces, crankshaft, camshaft, connecting rods, and lifters	Full pressure
Piston, pins	Oil vapor
Cylinder walls	Splash
Rocker arms	Pressure
Oil reservoir capacity—quarts	2½ quarts (3 quarts with dry filter)
Oil filter make and type	AC 650352
Cooling system type	Pressure
Filler cap type—pressure	Bayonet type—10.4 - 12.4 psi
Water temperature control	Thermostat and bypass
Thermostat opens at	189°
Cooling system capacity	
Less heater	4½ quarts
With heater	5 quarts
Fan diameter—No. of blades	5 blades
Fan drive	Water pump shaft

Table 2   ENGINE DIMENSIONS AND TOLERANCES — 1.1 ENGINE

Crankshaft journal diameter	2.1260"
Crankshaft end play	.004"—.008"
Crankshaft journal to bearing clearance	.0004"—.0022"
Crankshaft thrust bearing effective length	1.1438"
Maximum permissible out-of-roundness of crankshaft bearing journal and crankpin	.0002"
Maximum permissible taper of crankshaft bearing journal and crankpin	.0004"
Crankpin journal diameter	1.77"
Connecting rod bearing to crankpin clearance	.0006"—.0025"
Connecting rod bearing length	.7165"—.7402"
Connecting rod end clearance on journal	.004"—.010"
Piston clearance in bore (on skirt bottom)	.0004"—.0012"
Maximum permissible cylinder bore out-of-roundness	.003"
Maximum permissible cylinder bore taper	.005"
Piston pin fit in connecting rod	Press
Compression ring clearance in grooves	
Top	.0024"—.0034"
Bottom	.0013"—.0025"
Oil ring clearance in groove	.0013"—.0025"
Piston ring gap	
Compression rings in bore	.012"—.018"
Oil ring in bore	.010"—.016"
Camshaft bearing journal diameter	
No. 1	1.613"
No. 2	1.594"
No. 3	1.574"
Camshaft journal clearance in bearings	.001"—.003"
Camshaft end play	.007"—.013"
Valve lifter clearance in crankcase	.0006"—.002"
Valve head diameter	
Inlet	1.259"
Exhaust	1.063"
Valve seat angle—inlet and exhaust	45°
Over cut of valve seat	25°
Valve face angle—inlet and exhaust	44°
Valve stem diameter	
Inlet—standard	28"
Exhaust—standard	28"
Valve stem bore in cylinder head—standard	.2766"—.2774"
Valve stem clearance in guide	
Inlet	.0006"—.0018"
Exhaust	.0014"—.0026"
Valve spring closed at length	33 lbs. at 1.28"
Valve spring open at length	99 lbs. at .91"
Valve clearance (hot lash)	
Intake	.006"
Exhaust	.010"
Fan belt adjustment	45 lbs. with gauge J-23600
Oil pump gear backlash	.004"—.008"
Oil pump gear to housing clearance	Gears must protrude .002"—.004"

4

Table 3   ENGINE SPECIFICATIONS — 1.5 AND 1.9 ENGINES (EARLY MODELS)

	1.5	1.9
Type—No. of cylinders	In-line 4	
Valve arrangement	In head	
Bore and stroke	3.25 x 2.75	3.66 x 2.75
Piston displacement cu. in.	91	115.8
Compression ratio	9.0:1	
Brake horsepower @ rpm	80 @ 5,100	102 @ 5,200
Torque @ rpm	87 @ 3,100-3,700	115 @ 2,800-3,400
Octane requirement	Premium	
Firing order	1-3-4-2	
Cylinder block material	Cast iron	
Crankshaft bearings number and type	5 removable steel backed in-metal babbitts	
Bearing which takes end thrust	5	
Connecting rod bearing material	Steel locked tri-metal babbitts	
Piston material and surface	Aluminum alloy, lead coated	
Piston pin offset	.032 in. to the right	
Compression rings material and surface treatment		
No. 1	Chrome-plated, cast iron—rectangular	
No. 2	Cast iron, tapered	
Oil ring	Cast iron	
Location of all piston rings	Above piston pin	
Camshaft material	Alloy cast iron	
Camshaft drive	Chain	
Number and type of camshaft bearings	3 steel backed babbitts	
Valve lifter type	Solid	
Oiling system type	Circulating high pressure	
Oil supplied to:		
Bearing surfaces, crankshaft, camshaft and connecting rods	Pressure	
Pistons, pins	Splash	
Cylinder walls	Splash	
Rocker arms	Low pressure	
Oil reservoir capacity quarts	(3) 3¼ with dry filter	
Oil filter—type	Throw-away element	
Cooling system type	Liquid cooling with circulating pump	
Filler cap type—pressure	10.2-12.2 psi	
Water temperature control	Thermostat and bypass	
Thermostat open at	190°F.	
Cooling system capacity	6	
Fan drive	Water pump shaft	

Table 4   ENGINE DIMENSIONS AND TOLERANCES — 1.5 AND 1.9 ENGINES (EARLY MODELS)

	1.5	1.9
Cylinder bore limits for standard size pistons, size 1	3.245-3.246 in.	3.659-3.660 in.
Cylinder bore limits for standard size pistons, size 2	3.247-3.249 in.	3.661-3.663 in.
Cylinder bore limits for standard size pistons, size 3	3.250-3.252 in.	3.664-3.668 in.
Cylinder bore limits, oversize pistons, .02 in. oversize	3.266-3.268 in.	3.679-3.681 in,
Cylinder bore limits, oversize pistons, .04 in. oversize	3.286-3.288 in.	——
Maximum permissive cylinder bore out-of-roundness	—— .0005 in. ——	
Maximum permissible cylinder bore taper	—— .0005 in. ——	
Piston clearance, nominal	—— .0012 in. ——	
No. 1 compression ring side clearance, piston groove	.0024-.0034 in.	
No. 2 compression ring side clearance, piston groove	.0013-.0024 in.	
Oil control ring side clearance in piston groove	.0013-.0024 in.	
Piston ring gap		
No. 1 compression ring	.0118-.0177 in.	.0118-.0216 in.
No. 2 compression ring	.0118-.0177 in.	.0118-.0216 in.
Oil control ring	.0098-.0157 in.	
Piston pin in piston	Press	
Valve spring pressure	Intake	Exhaust
Valve closed	1.634 in. = 72.75 lbs.	1.378 in. = 68.34 lbs.
Valve open	1.319 in. = 125.66 lbs.	1.063 in. = 131.61 lbs.
Valve dimensions	Intake	Exhaust
Stem diameter, standard size	.3538-.3543 in.	.3524-.3528 in.
Stem diameter, .003 in. oversize	.3567-.3572 in.	.3553-.3559 in.
Stem diameter, .0059 in. oversize	.3597-.3602 in.	.3583-.3588 in.
Stem diameter, .0118 in. oversize	.3656-.3661 ni.	.3642-.3647 in.
Total length, nominal	4.843 in.	5.021 in.
Valve head diameter		
Intake	1.496 in.	1.574 in.
Exhaust	1.259 in.	1.338 in.
Valve guide bores in cylinder head (intake & exhaust)		
Standard size	.3553-.3562 in.	
.003 in. oversize	.3582-.3592 in.	
.006 in. oversize	.3615-.3622 in.	
.0118 in. oversize	.3671-.3681 in.	
Valve stem clearance		
Intake	.001-.0025 in.	
Exhaust	.002-.0035 in.	
Maximum permissible head to stem runout		
Intake	.0032 in.	
Exhaust	.0019 in.	

(continued)

Table 4   ENGINE DIMENSIONS AND TOLERANCES — 1.5 AND 1.9 ENGINES
(EARLY MODELS) (continued)

Valve seat and correction angle in cylinder head	
Intake	
Valve seat angle	45°
Outer correction	30°
Exhaust	
Valve seat angle	45°
Outer correction	30°
Valve face angle	44°
Valve seat width in cylinder head	
Intake	.049-.059 in.
Exhaust	.063-.073 in.
Valve head contact area	Aim at centricity
Valve clearance at 176°F. coolant and 140°F. to	
176°F. oil temperature	
Intake and exhaust	.012 in.
Maximum permissible out-of-roundness of connect-	
ing rod bearing journals	.0002 in.
Maximum permissible taper of connecting rod and	
crankshaft bearing journals	.0004 in.
Maximum permissible radial runout of center main	
bearing journals when supported in end bearings	.0012 in.
Maximum permissible unparallelism of connecting	
rod bearing journals when crankshaft is placed	
in V-blocks so that main bearing journals next	
to each other are supported	.0005 in.
Maximum permissible runout of crankshaft to	
flywheel contact area	.0008 in.
Crankshaft end play	.0017-.0061 in.
Main bearing clearance	.0009-.0025 in.
Connecting rod bearing clearance	.0006-.0023 in.
Connecting rod end play on bearing journal	.0043-.0095 in.
Camshaft bearing clearance	.001-.003 in.
Camshaft end play	.004-.04 in.
Maximum permissible radial runout of camshaft center	
bearing—camshaft supported in outer bearing	.001 in.
Valve lifter clearance in cylinder head bore	.0003-.0013 in.

Table 5   ENGINE SPECIFICATIONS — 1.9 ENGINE (LATE MODELS)

Type—No. of cylinders	In-line 4
Valve arrangement	In head
Bore and stroke	3.66 x 2.75
Piston displacement cu. in.	115.8
Compression ratio	7.6:1
Octane requirement	Regular—low lead (1975, unleaded)
Firing order	1-3-4-2
Cylinder block material	Cast iron
Crankshaft bearings number and type in-metal babbitts	5 removable steel backed
Bearing which takes end thrust	5
Connecting rod bearing material	Steel backed tri-metal babbitts
Piston material and surface	Aluminum alloy, lead coated
Piston pin offset	.031 in. to the right
Compression rings material and surface treatment	
No. 1	Chrome-plated, cast iron—rectangular
No. 2	Cast iron—tapered
Oil ring	Chrome-plated, cast iron
Location of all piston rings	Above piston pin
Camshaft material	Alloy cast iron
Camshaft drive	Chain
Number and type of camshaft bearings	4 steel-backed babbitt
Valve lifter type	Hydraulic
Oiling system type	Circulating high pressure
Oil supplied to:	
Bearing surfaces, crankshaft, camshaft & connecting rods	Pressure
Piston, pins	Vapor
Cylinder walls	Nozzle spray
Rocker arms	Pressure
Oil reservoir capacity—quarts	3¼ with dry filter
Oil filter—type	Throw away element
Filler cap type—pressure	13.2-15.2 psi
Water temperature control	Thermostat and bypass
Thermostat open at	189°F (1975, 203°F)
Cooling system capacity	6 quarts (1975, 7 quarts)
Fan drive	Water pump shaft (1975, automatic fan clutch)

4

Table 6   ENGINE DIMENSIONS AND TOLERANCES — 1.9 ENGINE (LATE MODELS)

	Intake	Exhaust
Cylinder bore limits for standard size pistons:		
Size 1	3.659-3.660 in.	
Size 2	3.661-3.663 in.	
Size 3	3.664-3.668 in.	
Cylinder bore limits for oversize pistons, .02 in. oversize	3.679-3.681 in.	
Maximum permissible cylinder bore out-of-roundness	.0005 in.	
Maximum permissible cylinder bore taper	.0005 in.	
Piston clearance, nominal (on skirt bottom)	.0014 in.	
No. 1 compression ring side clearance in piston groove	.0024-.0034 in.	
No. 2 compression ring side clearance in piston groove	.0013-.0024 in.	
Oil control ring side clearance in piston groove	.0013-.0024 in.	
Piston ring gap:	.014-.022 in.	
No. 1 compression ring		
No. 2 compression ring	.014-.022 in.	
Oil control ring	.015-.055 in.	
Piston pin in connecting rod	Press fit	
	Intake	**Exhaust**
Valve spring pressure		
Valve closed	1.57 in at 93 lbs.	1.36 in. at 97 lbs.
Valve open	1.18 in. at 182 lbs.	.96 in. at 180 lbs.
Valve stem diameters		
Standard size	.3538-.3543 in.	.3524-.3528 in.
.003 in. oversize	.3567-.3572 in.	.3553-.3559 in.
.0059 in. oversize	.3597-.3602 in.	.3583-.3588 in.
.0118 in. oversize	.3656-.3661 in.	.3642-.3647 in.
Valve length, nominal	4.843 in.	4.92 in.
Valve head diameter	1.574 in.	1.34 in.
Valve guide bores in cylinder head (intake and exhaust)		
Standard size	.3553-.3562 in.	
.003 in. oversize	.3582-.3592 in.	
.006 in. oversize	.3615-.3622 in.	
.0118 in. oversize	.3671-.3681 in.	
Valve stem clearance		
Intake	.001-.0029 in.	
Exhaust	.0039 in.	
Maximum permissible head to stem runout		
Intake	.0016 in.	
Exhaust	.0019 in.	
Valve seat and correction angle in cylinder head		
Intake		
Valve seat angle	45°	
Outer correction	30°	
Exhaust		
Valve seat angle	45°	
Outer correction	30°	
Valve face angle	44°	

(continued)

Table 6   ENGINE DIMENSIONS AND TOLERANCES — 1.9 ENGINE
(LATE MODELS) (continued)

Valve seat width in cylinder head	
Intake	.049-.059 in.
Exhaust	.063-.073 in.
Valve head contact area	Aim at centricity
Valve clearance at 176°F. coolant and 140 to 176°F. oil temperature	
Intake and exhaust	Zero plus one turn
Max. permissible out-of-roundness of connecting rod bearing journals	.0002 in.
Max. permissible taper of connecting rod and crankshaft bearing journals	.0004 in.
Max. permissible radial runout of center main bearing journals when supported in end bearings	.0012 in.
Max. permissible unparallelism of connecting rod bearing journals when crankshaft is placed in V-blocks so that main bearing journals next to each other are supported	.0005 in.
Max. permissible runout of crankshaft to flywheel contact area	.0008 in
Crankshaft end play	.0017-.0061 in.
Main bearing clearance	.0009-.0025 in.
Connecting rod bearing clearance	.0006-.0025 in.
Connecting rod end play on bearing journal	.0043-.0095 in.
Connecting rod bearing length	.7785-.7992 in.
Crankshaft thrust bearing length	1.08 in.
Camshaft bearing clearance	.001-.003 in.
Camshaft end play	.004-.008 in.
Max. permissible radial runout of camshaft center bearing—camshaft supported in outer bearings	.001 in.
Valve lifter clearance in cylinder head bore	.0003-.0013 in.
Oil pump gear backlash	.004-.008 in.
Oil pump gear end play in housing not more than .004 in.	Gears protruding over edge
Clearance of spindle in bore of oil pump driven gear	.0003-.0015 in.
Clearance between oil pump drive gear and bushing	.00035-.0015 in.
Oil pump relief valve spring pressure at a spring length of .8 in.	.44-.66 lbs.

4

Table 7   TORQUE TIGHTENING SPECIFICATIONS — 1.1 ENGINE

Part	Torque Ft.-Lbs.
Connecting rod bolts	20
Crankshaft main bearing bolts	45
Engine mount bolts	30
Flywheel to crankshaft attaching bolts	25
Cylinder head attaching bolts	35
Sprocket to camshaft attaching bolts	30
Oil pump cover bolts	15
Oil pan bolts	5
Pulley to crankshaft attaching bolts	30
Rocker arm cover bolts	5
Spark plugs	30
Water pump bolts	11
Unless otherwise noted:	
10mm bolt (15mm head)	30
8mm bolt (13mm head)	15
6mm bolt (11mm head)	60 in.-lbs.

Table 8   TORQUE TIGHTENING SPECIFICATIONS — 1.5 AND 1.9 ENGINES
(EARLY MODELS)

Part	Torque Ft.-Lbs.
Connecting rod bolts	36
Crankshaft main bearing bolts	72
Flywheel to crankshaft attaching bolts	43
Cylinder head attaching bolts	72 cold
	58 warm
Camshaft sprocket attaching bolt(s)	18
Generator bracket to cylinder block attaching bolts	29
Generator bracket to timing case attaching bolts	29
Crankshaft pulley attaching bolts	54
Rocker arm stud in cylinder head	29
Spark plugs	29
Clutch housing to cylinder block attaching bolts	36
Timing case to cylinder block attaching bolts	14
Water pump to timing case attaching bolts	11
Engine support to cylinder block attaching bolts	40
Rear engine suspension to transmission rear bearing retainer bolts	22
Transmission to clutch housing attaching bolts	29
Starter to clutch housing attaching bolts	40
Support to starter attaching nut	4
Intake and exhaust manifold to cylinder head attaching bolts	33

Table 9   TORQUE TIGHTENING SPECIFICATIONS — 1.9 ENGINE
(LATE MODELS)

Part	Torque Ft.-Lb.	
	Through 1974	1975
Connecting rod bolts	36	33
Crankshaft main bearing bolts	72	73
Flywheel to crankshaft attaching bolts	43	43
Cylinder head attaching bolts	72 cold	72 cold
	58 warm	58 warm
Camshaft sprocket attaching bolts	18	18
Generator bracket to cylinder block attaching bolts	29	29
Generator bracket to timing case attaching bolts	29	29
Crankshaft pulley attaching bolts	72	72
Rocker arm stud in cylinder head	29	25
Spark plugs	30	29
Clutch housing to cylinder block attaching bolts	36	36
Timing case to cylinder block attaching bolts	14	11
Water pump to timing case attaching bolts	11	11
Engine support to cylinder block attaching bolts	40	33
Rear engine suspension to transmission rear bearing retainer bolts	22	22
Transmission to clutch housing attaching bolts	29	29
Starter to clutch housing attaching bolts	40	57
Support to starter attaching nut	4	3
Intake and exhaust manifold to cylinder head attaching bolts	33	29
Unless otherwise noted:		
10mm bolt (15mm head)	30	30
8mm bolt (13mm head)	15	15
6mm bolt (10mm head)	30 in.-lb.	30 in.-lb.

4

CHAPTER FIVE

FUEL AND EXHAUST SYSTEMS

The fuel and exhaust systems consists of the fuel tank, fuel lines, fuel pump, carburetor(s) or fuel injection system, intake/exhaust manifolds, mufflers, exhaust pipes, and air cleaner. Fuel is sucked from the fuel tank through the fuel lines by the fuel pump. It is then supplied to the carburetor(s) or fuel injection system where it is mixed with air and fed to the combustion chambers through the intake manifold. After combustion, exhaust gases are expelled from the combustion chambers through the exhaust manifold to the exhaust pipes and mufflers and, ultimately, out through the tailpipes.

WARNING
Exercise extreme care when servicing the various parts of the fuel system to minimize the danger of fire or explosion. Before servicing the fuel tank or lines, make certain the fuel is completely drained into a suitable sealed container. Residual gases in the fuel tank should be expelled by filling the tank completely with an inert gas or, as a last resort, water. Soldering or welding the tank should be done with it full of inert gas or water. If water is used, be certain to dry the inside of the tank thoroughly before refilling with fuel.

NOTE: *This chapter applied to 1966-1975 models. See the* Supplement *section, Chapter Five, at back of this manual, for 1976 and later models.*

FUEL TANK

Removal/Installation (1900, Manta)

Figure 1 shows the details of the fuel tank and associated parts.

1. Use a pinch clamp to close the fuel hose between the fuel line and fuel tank, as shown in **Figure 2**. Loosen hose clamp and pull hose off the fuel line. Disconnect the fuel gauge electrical connectors.

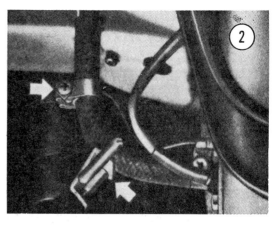

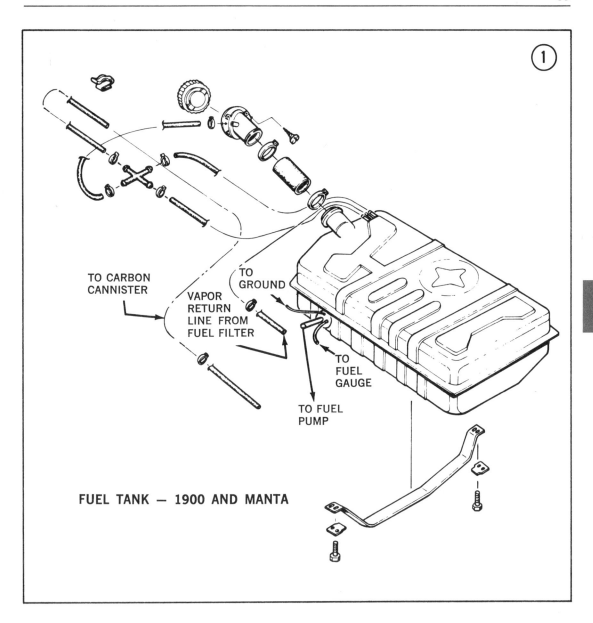

TO CARBON
CANNISTER

TO
GROUND

VAPOR
RETURN
LINE FROM
FUEL FILTER

TO
FUEL
GAUGE

TO FUEL
PUMP

FUEL TANK — 1900 AND MANTA

2. Remove filler cap. Remove screws fixing filler neck to side panel.

3. Pull off fuel tank hose and plug connecting tubes on tank.

4. See **Figure 3**. With a jack and suitable block of wood, support fuel tank.

5. Remove bolts from both ends of fuel tank strap and remove strap.

6. Lower the jack and remove the fuel tank from under car.

7. To install, reverse preceding steps. Be careful not to kink fuel lines or hoses.

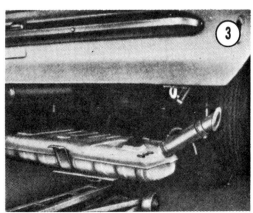

Removal/Installation (GT)

Figure 4 shows the details of the fuel tank and associated parts.

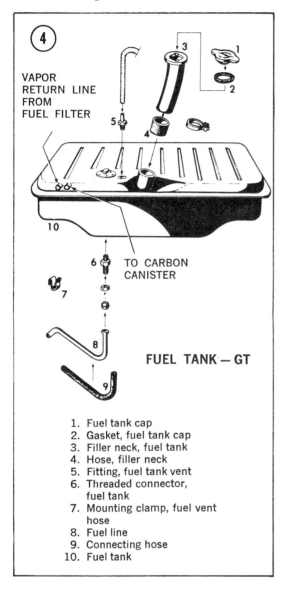

VAPOR RETURN LINE FROM FUEL FILTER

TO CARBON CANISTER

FUEL TANK — GT

1. Fuel tank cap
2. Gasket, fuel tank cap
3. Filler neck, fuel tank
4. Hose, filler neck
5. Fitting, fuel tank vent
6. Threaded connector, fuel tank
7. Mounting clamp, fuel vent hose
8. Fuel line
9. Connecting hose
10. Fuel tank

SPARE TIRE SUPPORT BRACKETS

JACK ASSEMBLY

GAS TANK COVER   6C-9

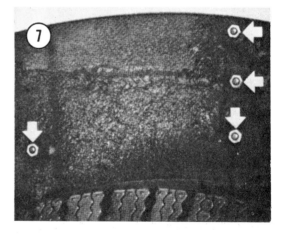

1. Disconnect battery.

2. Remove rubber cap, unscrew fuel line from tank, and drain fuel into suitable container. See **Figure 5**.

3. Remove spare tire and jack.

4. See **Figure 6**. Remove spare tire hold-down and brackets. Remove spare tire support panel.

5. See **Figure 7**. Remove spare tire support attaching brackets. The spare tire hold-down and support attaching brackets are attached to the rear wheel housing panel and are covered with sound deadening compound.

6. Remove fuel tank vent hose and filler hose. Disconnect lines from carbon canister and vapor return line from fuel filter.

7. Disconnect electrical connections from gas tank gauge sending unit.

8. Remove fuel tank attaching bolts and lift it up and out of trunk.

9. To install, reverse the above steps.

FUEL FILTER

Late models are equipped with an in-line fuel filter. **Figure 8** shows a typical installation. Inspect the fuel filter periodically for foreign material. If the filter becomes dirty, disconnect all lines and replace it with a new unit.

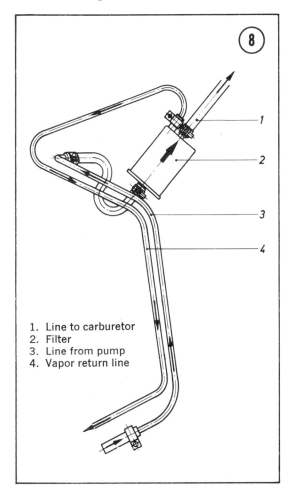

1. Line to carburetor
2. Filter
3. Line from pump
4. Vapor return line

FUEL LINES

On late models, all fuel lines are made of plastic. Earlier models used a combination of plastic, rubber, and metal lines. Periodically inspect all fuel lines and connectors for signs of damage, deterioration, and kinks. Defective fuel lines are non-repairable and must be replaced. When replacing plastic lines, place the new line in hot water to make it flexible. Use the old line as a pattern to form the new line, permit it to cool, and dry thoroughly before installation. Make certain that fuel lines are attached to all clips and led through all grommets during installation to prevent rubbing and wear.

FUEL GAUGE TANK SENDING UNITS

The fuel gauge inside the passenger compartment is connected electrically to the fuel gauge tank sending unit to indicate fuel level in the tank. If the gauge does not register fuel level properly, check the electrical connections at the instrument panel and at the sending unit. If the connections are satisfactory, remove the sending unit and replace with new one.

MECHANICAL FUEL PUMP

Removal/Installation (1.1 Engine)

The fuel pump used on the 1.1 engine is of the conventional rocker arm type. **Figure 9** shows the fuel pump installed. To remove, disassemble, assemble, and install, proceed as follows.

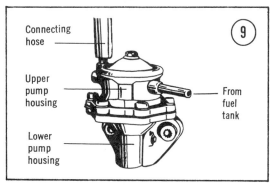

Connecting hose

Upper pump housing

Lower pump housing

From fuel tank

1. Disconnect lines from fuel tank and to carburetor at fuel pump.

2. Plug end of intake line to prevent loss of fuel from fuel tank.

3. Use a serrated-bit type wrench to remove bolts fixing fuel pump to engine.

4. Remove fuel pump and gasket from engine.

5. Clean outside of fuel pump thoroughly with suitable solvent.

6. Remove bolt from center of upper housing. Separate cover and gasket from upper housing. Remove filter screen from inside housing.

7. Inspect filter screen for damage and foreign material. Clean thoroughly with suitable solvent.

8. Mark position of upper housing relative to lower pump housing for later assembly.

9. Remove 6 screws fixing upper housing to lower housing. Separate the 2 housings. Be careful not to damage diaphragm.

10. See **Figure 10**. Inspect condition of upper housing inlet and outlet valves. If the valves are defective, the entire upper housing must be replaced.

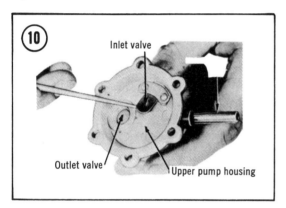

11. See **Figure 11**. Remove spring from fuel pump rocker arm. Remove one retainer from rocker arm pin and drive out pin.

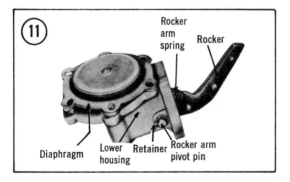

12. Lift rocker arm and pump diaphragm assembly out of lower housing. **Figure 12** shows the lower housing disassembled.

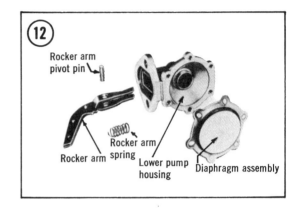

13. Work rubber oil seal off diaphragm operating rod and slide off seal retainer and spring. **Figure 13** shows the diaphragm assembly.

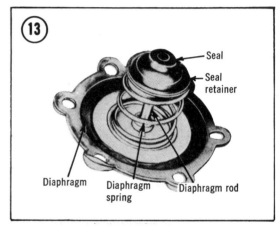

14. Clean and inspect all parts. Replace defective parts. Pay special attention to condition of diaphragm and seal. The diaphragm must be free of cracks, hardness, or deterioration.

15. To assemble, reverse disassembly steps. Make certain the diaphragm is installed so that the outer lip is not distorted or ripped.

16. After assembly and before installation to the engine, connect the inlet fuel line to the upper housing and move the rocker arm up and down until fuel flows out of the outlet valve. Fuel flow should be strong with each stroke and without air bubbles.

**Fuel Pump Filter Cleaning
(1.1 Engine)**

1. Remove inlet fuel line from fuel pump. Plug end of fuel line to prevent loss of fuel.

2. Remove bolt from center of upper housing cover. Remove cover and gasket.

3. Remove plastic filter screen.

4. Cover center opening in sediment bowl with finger and blow out sediment bowl with compressed air. Be careful not to let foreign material enter outlet line or valve.

5. Wash filter in solvent. If filter does not clean up or is damaged, replace with new strainer.

6. To install, reverse preceding steps. Always install a new cover gasket and seal under the center bolt.

7. Reconnect the fuel line, start the engine, and check for fuel leaks at gasket, seal, and fuel line connections.

Removal/Servicing (1.5, 1.9 Engines)

The fuel pumps used on the 1.5 and 1.9 engines are of the pushrod type. The pushrod is operated by an eccentric on the distributor drive shaft. **Figure 14** shows installation of the fuel pump.

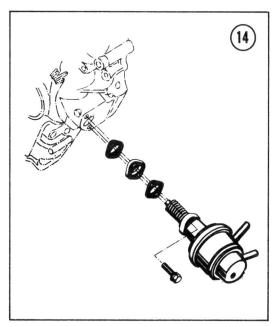

1. Disconnect inlet and outlet fuel lines from fuel pump. Plug end of inlet line to prevent loss of fuel.

2. Remove bolts fixing fuel pump to engine. Clean outside of fuel pump with suitable solvent.

3. Remove center bolt and bolt seal from upper housing cover. **Figure 15** shows the details of the fuel pump.

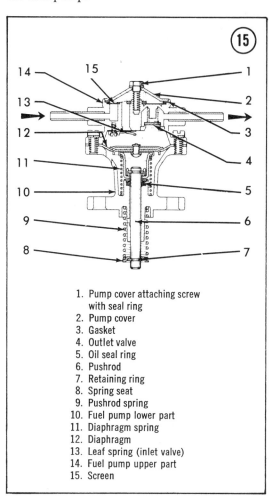

1. Pump cover attaching screw with seal ring
2. Pump cover
3. Gasket
4. Outlet valve
5. Oil seal ring
6. Pushrod
7. Retaining ring
8. Spring seat
9. Pushrod spring
10. Fuel pump lower part
11. Diaphragm spring
12. Diaphragm
13. Leaf spring (inlet valve)
14. Fuel pump upper part
15. Screen

4. Remove and inspect filter inside upper housing. Replace if defective. Clean thoroughly before installation.

5. Remove screws fixing upper housing to lower housing. Remove upper housing. Take care not to damage diaphragm. Clean thoroughly and inspect inlet and outlet valves. You should be able to blow air in through the inlet valve, but not suck it out. On the outlet valve, you should be able to suck air out but not blow in. If valves are defective, replace upper housing assembly.

6. At bottom of pushrod, remove pushrod spring seat. Remove pushrod spring.

7. Push the pushrod and diaphragm assembly upward and out of the lower housing.

8. Clean all parts in solvent and inspect for wear or damage. Pay special attention to condition of diaphragm and oil seal ring. Replace defective parts.

9. To assemble and install, reverse the above steps. Before installation, connect inlet fuel line to inlet side of pump and move pushrod in and out by hand. Fuel flow out of the outlet should be strong with no bubbles.

Fuel Pump Filter Cleaning (1.5, 1.9 Engines)

Cleaning of the fuel pump filter for the 1.5 and 1.9 engines is the same as described earlier for the 1.1 engine.

ELECTRICAL FUEL PUMP

The mechanical fuel pump has been replaced by an electric fuel pump for 1975, located near the left front corner of the gas tank.

Removal/Installation

1. Disconnect fuel pump electrical connector.

2. Remove the fuel pump lower bracket bolt with a 10mm socket.

3. Open the fuel pump bracket and remove the fuel pump and fuel pump insulator.

4. Loosen the fuel hose clamps. Remove the fuel hoses.

> CAUTION
> *Fuel is under pressure. When fuel hoses are disconnected some fuel will be lost. Plug the fuel lines until a new fuel pump is installed.*

5. Remove the fuel pump insulator from the fuel pump.

6. To install, reverse the above steps. Check for fuel leaks with the engine running.

Fuel Pump Filter Replacement

The fuel pump filter should be replaced every 15,000 miles, as follows.

1. Remove the fuel filter bracket bolt.

2. Open the fuel filter bracket and remove the fuel filter and fuel filter insulator.

3. Loosen the 2 hose clamps and remove the fuel hoses.

> CAUTION
> *Fuel is under pressure. When fuel hose is removed, some fuel will be lost.*

4. Remove the insulator from the fuel filter.

5. Install the new fuel filter by reversing the previous steps. Check for fuel leaks with the engine running.

CARBURETORS

All 1966-1974 Opels are equipped with Solex carburetors. Several different models have been used over the years, depending on engine performance specifications and emission control requirements. **Table 1** lists the number of carburetors, numbers of barrels, and choke type by model year, model, and engine type.

Due to the differences in the carburetors, always order replacement parts by model, model year, engine number, and chassis number.

Figures 16 and 17 are exploded views of carburetors used on early 1.1 engines; **Figure 18** late model dual carburetor 1.1 engines.

Figure 19 is an exploded view of the carburetor used on 1.5 and 1.9 engine models; **Figure 20** is a sectional view of late 1.9 engine models.

A carburetor in good operating condition will deliver the proper gasoline and air ratios for all engine running speeds. A gradual decline in smoothness, response, and power will occur as the carburetor slips from adjustment and its delicate parts become dirty or worn.

Accurate calibration of passages and discharge holes requires that extreme care be taken in disassembly, cleaning, and reassembly. Never use wire or pointed instruments for cleaning; calibration of the carburetor will be affected.

Removal/Installation (Early 1.1 Engine)

1. Remove air cleaner.

2. See **Figure 21**. Disconnect fuel and vacuum hose from carburetor.

3. Loosen bowden control cable clamp and setscrew. Disconnect cable.

4. Unhook throttle linkage by removing cotter pin and 2 washers.

Table 1   CARBURETOR USAGE

Year	Engine	Number of Carburetors	Barrels	Choke
1966-1967	1.1	1	1	Manual
	1.1 Rallye	2	1	Manual
1968	1.1	1	2	Manual
	1.5	1	2	Manual
	1.9	1	2	Automatic
1969	1.1	1 (AIR)*	1	Manual
	1.1R	2 (OECS)*	1	Manual
	1.1SR	2 (OECS)*	1	Manual
	1.9	1	2	Automatic
1970	1.1R	2 (OECS)*	1	Manual
	1.1SR	2 (OECS)*	1	Manual
	1.9	1	2	Automatic
1971	1.1	2	1	Automatic
	1.9	1	2	Automatic
1972-1974	1.9	1	2	Automatic

* AIR = Air Injection Reactor system. OECS = Opel Emission Control System.
See Chapter Seven for description.

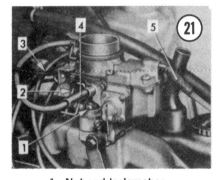

1. Nut and lockwasher
2. Throttle rod
3. Choke wire
4. Vacuum advance hose
5. Fuel hose

5. Remove nuts and lockwashers fixing carburetors to intake manifold.

6. Lift up and remove carburetor and gasket clear of intake manifold studs.

7. To install, reverse preceding steps. Always use new gaskets at bottom of carburetor. Adjust engine idle speed and mixture, as required.

Removal/Installation (Late 1.1 Engine)

Removal and installation procedures are essentially the same as those for early 1.1 engines except for number of nuts and washers holding carburetors to intake manifold. Unless absolutely essential, do not disconnect linkages between carburetors because of possible misadjustment. If they must be separated, mark all linkage locations and positions before disassembly.

Removal/Installation
(Early 1.5, 1.9 Engines)

1. Remove air cleaner.

2. Disconnect the fuel and vacuum hoses from the carburetor.

3. Disconnect 2 hoses from water-heated automatic choke (if so equipped). Plug holes to prevent loss of coolant.

4. Disconnect throttle linkage by unsnapping ball socket from ball on end of throttle shaft.

5. On manual choke models, disconnect bowden wire cable from carburetor.

6. Remove nuts and lockwashers fixing carburetor to intake manifold.

7. Remove the carburetor and gasket from the intake manifold.

8. To install, reverse Steps 1-7. On automatic choke, check that choke housing is set to proper index mark and that choke valve is nearly closed

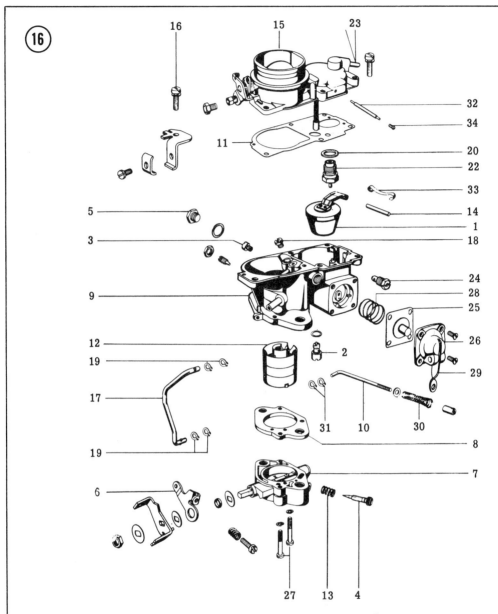

EARLY MODEL 1.1 CARBURETOR

1. Float
2. Power valve
3. Main metering jet
4. Idle mixture screw
5. Plug with seal ring for main jet
6. Throttle lever
7. Throttle body
8. Insulating flange gasket
9. Float bowl
10. Pump rod
11. Air horn gasket
12. Main venturi
13. Thrust spring for idle adjustment screw
14. Float pivot
15. Air horn
16. Carburetor cover attaching screw
17. Throttle rod
18. High speed bleeder
19. Clip
20. Seal ring for float needle valve
21. Vacuum piston
22. Float needle valve
23. Fuel inlet
24. Idle jet
25. Pump diaphragm
26. Pump cover
27. Throttle body to float bowl attaching screw
28. Diaphragm return spring
29. Pump lever
30. Duration spring
31. Clip
32. Filler pin
33. Leaf spring
34. Plug for filler pin

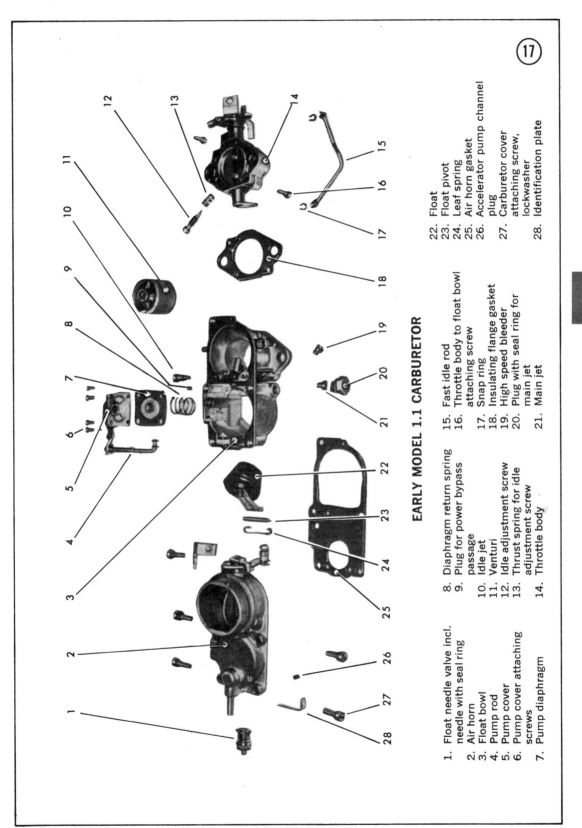

EARLY MODEL 1.1 CARBURETOR

1. Float needle valve incl. needle with seal ring
2. Air horn
3. Float bowl
4. Pump rod
5. Pump cover
6. Pump cover attaching screws
7. Pump diaphragm
8. Diaphragm return spring
9. Plug for power bypass passage
10. Idle jet
11. Venturi
12. Idle adjustment screw
13. Thrust spring for idle adjustment screw
14. Throttle body
15. Fast idle rod
16. Throttle body to float bowl attaching screw
17. Snap ring
18. Insulating flange gasket
19. High speed bleeder
20. Plug with seal ring for main jet
21. Main jet
22. Float
23. Float pivot
24. Leaf spring
25. Air horn gasket
26. Accelerator pump channel plug
27. Carburetor cover attaching screw, lockwasher
28. Identification plate

5

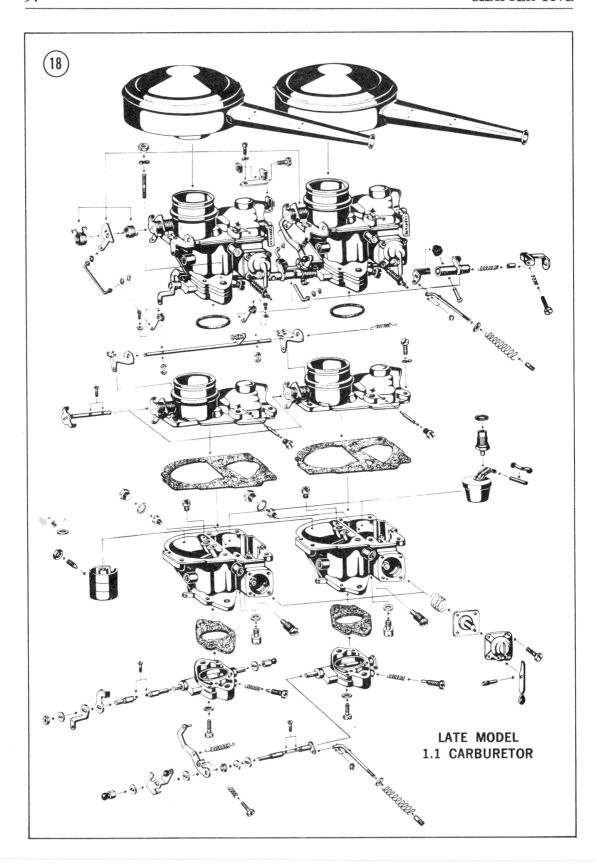

LATE MODEL
1.1 CARBURETOR

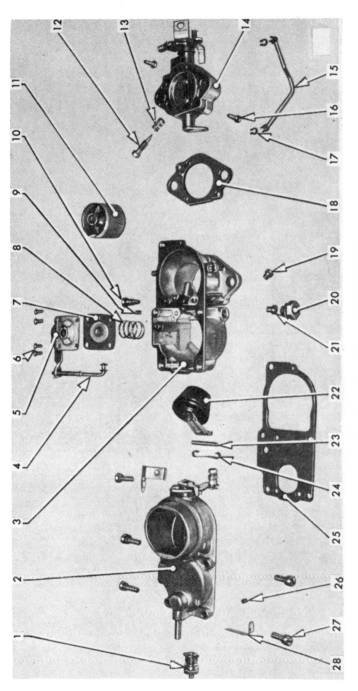

(19)

5

1.5 AND EARLY 1.9 CARBURETOR

1. Float needle valve incl. needle with seal ring
2. Air horn
3. Float bowl
4. Pump rod
5. Pump cover
6. Pump cover attaching screws
7. Pump diaphragm
8. Diaphragm return spring
9. Plug for power bypass passage
10. Idle jet
11. Venturi
12. Idle adjustment screw
13. Thrust spring for idle adjustment screw
14. Throttle body
15. Fast idle rod
16. Throttle body to float bowl attaching screw
17. Snap ring
18. Insulating flange gasket
19. High speed bleeder
20. Plug with seal ring for main jet
21. Main jet
22. Float
23. Float pivot
24. Leaf spring
25. Air horn gasket
26. Accelerator pump channel plug
27. Carburetor cover attaching screw, lockwasher
28. Identification plate

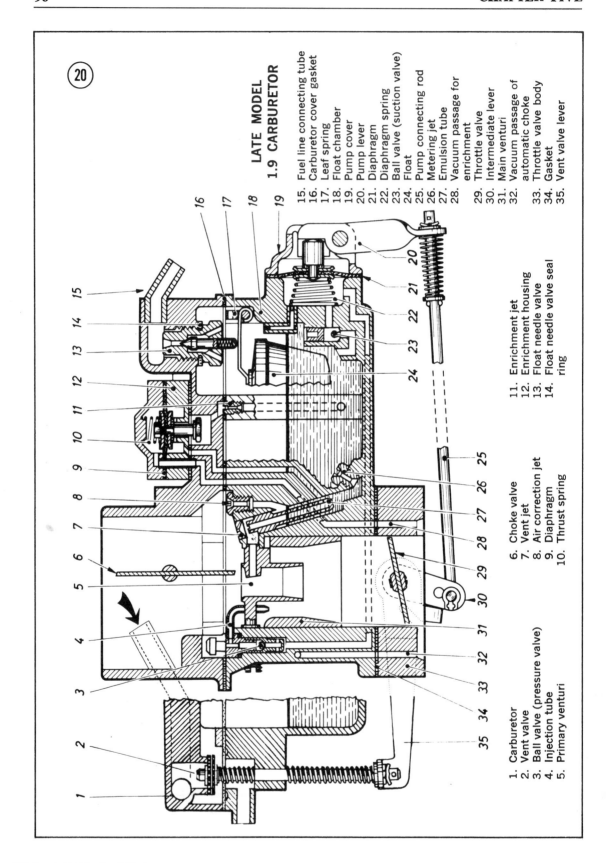

LATE MODEL 1.9 CARBURETOR

1. Carburetor
2. Vent valve
3. Ball valve (pressure valve)
4. Injection tube
5. Primary venturi
6. Choke valve
7. Vent jet
8. Air correction jet
9. Diaphragm
10. Thrust spring
11. Enrichment jet
12. Enrichment housing
13. Float needle valve
14. Float needle valve seal ring
15. Fuel line connecting tube
16. Carburetor cover gasket
17. Leaf spring
18. Float chamber
19. Pump cover
20. Pump lever
21. Diaphragm
22. Diaphragm spring
23. Ball valve (suction valve)
24. Float
25. Pump connecting rod
26. Metering jet
27. Emulsion tube
28. Vacuum passage for enrichment
29. Throttle valve
30. Intermediate lever
31. Main venturi
32. Vacuum passage of automatic choke
33. Throttle valve body
34. Gasket
35. Vent valve lever

at 70°F. Adjust engine idle speed and mixture. Always use new gasket between intake manifold and carburetor.

Removal/Installation (Late 1.5, 1.9 Engines)

Removal and installation procedures are essentially the same as those for early 1.5 and 1.9 engines. Proper indexing of the automatic choke is shown in **Figure 22**. Check that choke valve has freedom of movement in all positions.

CARBURETOR IDLE MIXTURE ADJUSTMENT

Before adjusting carburetor(s), adjust ignition point gap, dwell angle, spark plug gap, ignition timing, and valve clearance to specification. Warm the engine to normal operating temperature, check that choke valve(s) are in full open position, and connect tachometer according to manufacturer's instructions.

The procedures given below are typical for the carburetors shown in Figures 16 through 21. Dual carburetor installations are covered, as required.

Early 1.1 Engines

Refer to Figures 16 and 17.

1. See **Figure 23**, which shows the location of the throttle stop screw and the idle mixture adjustment screw.

2. Adjust the engine to 700-800 rpm by turning the throttle stop screw.

3. Adjust idle mixture screw until the highest tachometer reading is obtained.

4. If idle rpm is too fast, back off throttle stop screw and readjust idle mixture screw.

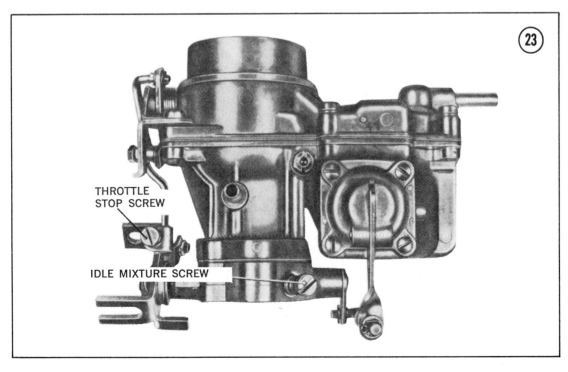

THROTTLE STOP SCREW

IDLE MIXTURE SCREW

Early 1.1 Engines (Dual)

1. See **Figure 24**, which shows a typical installation of the dual carburetors.

2. Remove air cleaners.

3. Loosen coupling screw until there is clearance between the screw end and pickup lever.

4. Carefully close both idle mixture screws until they are just closed. Do not tighten so tightly that the screw end or orifice is damaged.

5. On the rear carburetor, back out the idle mixture screw ¾ turn.

6. On the front carburetor, back out throttle idle speed screw so engine is running on rear carburetor only.

7. Adjust rear carburetor idle speed screw until engine runs at 700 rpm. Adjust rear carburetor idle mixture screw until smoothest operation at 700 rpm is achieved. Readjustment of both screws may be necessary.

8. Slowly bring front carburetor into operation with a basic adjustment of ¾ turn on idle mixture screw while closing rear carburetor idle mixture screw. Count the turns on the rear screw as you close it.

9. Close the idle speed screw on the rear carburetor by backing the screw out until it is clear of the throttle valve arm. The throttle valve must be closed on rear carburetor while making mixture adjustment on front carburetor.

10. Adjust front carburetor idle mixture screw and idle speed screw to obtain smoothest operation at 700 rpm.

11. Back out the idle mixture screw on the rear carburetor the number of turns counted in Step 8. Increase the idle speed by adjusting the idle speed screw on rear carburetor until the engine runs at 1,000 rpm.

12. Final idle speed is 950 to 1,000 rpm. Make minor adjustments to both carburetors until the proper idle speed with smoothest operation is obtained.

13. To check that both carburetors are carrying an equal share of the load, back off the idle speed screw of front carburetor and check idle. Bring idle back to 1,000 rpm and repeat on the rear carburetor.

NOTE: *Each carburetor should read the same rpm with either throttle valve closed (approximately 600 to 700 rpm). Differences greater than 100 rpm should be divided between both carburetors by splitting the difference with the lower-reading carburetor's idle speed screw only.*

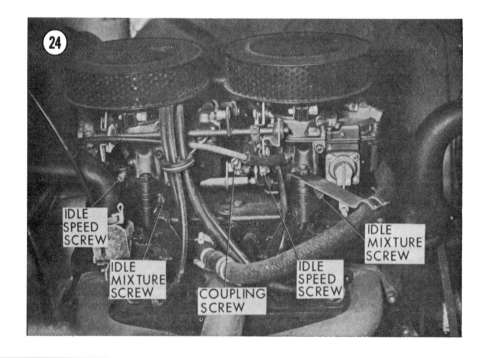

14. When idle speed and mixture are correct, tighten coupling screw between carburetors. Set the screw so that there is a 0.006 in. (0.152mm) clearance between screw and pickup lever.

15. Install air cleaners and road test car.

Early 1.5, 1.9 Engines

Refer to Figure 19.

1. See **Figure 25**, which shows the location of the idle air (speed) adjusting screw and idle mixture needle screw.

> NOTE: *Do not attempt carburetor adjustment by changing position of throttle stop screw or idle jet. They have been calibrated and set at the factory for best operation to meet emission control requirements.*

2. Adjust idle air (speed) adjusting screw until engine speed is 750 to 800 rpm.

3. Adjust idle mixture needle screw to obtain highest tachometer reading. If speed exceeds 800 rpm, reduce speed to 770 to 800 rpm with idle air adjusting screw.

4. Readjust the idle mixture needle to obtain smoothest operation at 770-800 rpm.

5. Lean the mixture slightly by turning in idle mixture needle screw until speed is reduced by 20 rpm. This slight leanness is necessary to reduce engine "flare" on AIR system cars (emission controlled) or to enable non-AIR cars to comply with emission control requirements.

Late 1.9 Engines

Refer to Figure 20. The following procedure applies to models through 1971. Carburetor service and adjustment for 1972 to 1974 models should be referred to your Opel dealer or carburetor specialist due to the need for special tools and knowledge necessary to meet emission control requirements.

1. See Figure 25. Do not remove air cleaner.

2. Disconnect distributor advance vacuum line

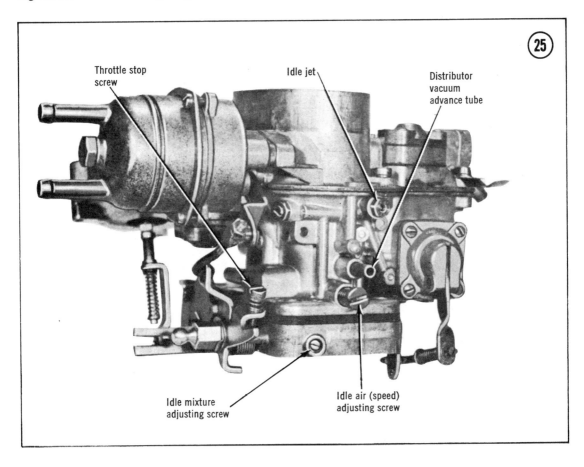

Figure 25

Throttle stop screw
Idle jet
Distributor vacuum advance tube
Idle mixture adjusting screw
Idle air (speed) adjusting screw

from carburetor. Install vacuum gauge to carburetor vacuum connector.

3. Carefully close idle air speed adjusting screw by screwing it in. It may be necessary to adjust idle mixture screw to keep the engine at idle.

4. Plug the charcoal canister vent tube at the rear of the carburetor.

5. If so equipped, close and block hot idle compensator with a large screwdriver placed against the plug to cover the port.

6. Adjust throttle stop screw to obtain 1/16 to 1/2 in. mercury on vacuum gauge.

7. Adjust the idle mixture screw to obtain the smoothest idle at 400 to 600 rpm.

8. Open idle air speed screw approximately 2 turns. At the same time, adjust the idle mixture screw to obtain smoothest idle at 870 to 920 rpm (manual transmission) or 820 to 870 rpm (automatic transmission).

9. If idle speed is excessive, reduce by turning in idle air speed screw. Make minor adjustment of idle mixture screw to obtain smoothest idle at specified rpm.

10. Close idle mixture screw until idle speed drops 20 rpm. Final idle speed should be 850 to 900 rpm (manual transmission) or 800 to 850 rpm (automatic transmission).

11. Remove the test equipment and reconnect vacuum advance and charcoal canister vent hoses. Unblock hot idle compensator.

CARBURETOR OVERHAUL

Complete disassembly and overhaul is rarely required because of the small number of moving parts. Before complete disassembly, check condition of float, float valve, accelerator pump, and choke assembly. These parts are most often the cause of carburetor trouble because they are subject to wear and deterioration. If engine operation is not satisfactory, check out general engine condition and efficiency of ignition system until trouble is isolated to the carburetor and its internal parts.

To prevent carburetor trouble, always use clean, high-quality fuel and always make certain the fuel tank cap is firmly in place so that foreign material cannot enter fuel system. Check in-line fuel filter frequently (if equipped) and replace if dirty. As a preventive measure, the periodic addition of a good commercial carburetor cleaner to the fuel tank will help prevent buildup of varnish and foreign material on delicate carburetor parts.

Should overhaul of the carburetor be absolutely necessary, proceed as follows.

1. Remove air cleaner from carburetor.

2. Disconnect all fuel lines and hoses attached to carburetor.

3. Remove carburetor from intake manifold, as previously described.

4. Thoroughly clean the outside of the carburetor with suitable solvent.

5. Refer to the appropriate carburetor exploded diagram for your car.

6. Disassemble carburetor sufficiently to gain access to all jets, valves, and adjusting screws. Make certain to note the exact location of all parts. Draw a diagram and note location of all jets and their size. The jets are normally stamped to show orifice size.

7. Use a high quality carburetor cleaner to soak and clean parts. After soaking and cleaning, wash all parts in clean fuel and dry with compressed air. Do not use sharp objects to clean jets and passages. Inspect all parts for wear. Visible wear is sufficient cause to replace a part.

8. Assemble the carburetor by reversing steps used during disassembly. Always use new gaskets and rubber or plastic parts. Use all parts in the overhaul kit. Do not tighten needle valve adjusting screws tightly into orifices; seat them lightly so that damage and miscalibration will not occur.

9. After assembly and installation, follow the idle speed/mixture adjusting procedures given earlier for basic adjustment.

FUEL INJECTION

All 1975 Opels are equipped with the Bosch L-Jetronic Fuel Injection System, a pulse time manifold injection system that injects metered fuel into the intake manifold near the intake valves by electronically controlled injection valves.

Various components of the EFI system electronically monitor a wide range of driving factors which are fed into a control unit. The control unit uses the information it receives from the various components to continuously compute the desired air/fuel ratio under all operating conditions. The control unit continuously calculates the proper air/fuel ratio and controls the pulse time of the fuel injectors to achieve this ratio.

Opel strongly recommends that owners not attempt their own work on the fuel injection system, other than normal servicing of the air cleaner system (change every 24 months or 30,000 miles, whichever comes first).

AIR CLEANER

Carburetor Models

The air cleaner is located on top of the carburetor and, in most cases, contains the air filter that should be replaced on a periodic basis, as noted in Chapter Two. Some models, as shown in Figure 24, have the air filter held in place by a cover and hold-down nut, rather than encased in the air cleaner housing.

Late models equipped with emission control systems use the air cleaner housing to control the heat of the air entering the carburetor and to feed crankcase, exhaust, and fuel vapors to the carburetor for combustion. Details of this system are given in Chapter Seven.

Maintenance to the air cleaner normally requires replacement of the air filter as well as checking that flaps operate freely and that valves operate satisfactorily.

Periodically inspect all hoses and lines attached to the air cleaner for signs of damage or deterioration and replace if defective.

Fuel Injection Models

Unhook spring clamps on the air cleaner housing and loosen attaching nut at the air flow meter. Lift upper part of air cleaner housing, remove old element, clean any foreign material from lower housing, and install new element. Rehook spring clamps and retighten attaching nut at air flow meter. Air filter replacement is recommended every 30,000 miles.

INTAKE MANIFOLD

Maintenance to the intake manifold is not normally required, but it should be inspected for cracks and distortion whenever the carburetor is removed or the engine is disassembled. Always replace gaskets when intake manifold is removed from engine.

EXHAUST SYSTEM

The exhaust system consists of pipes, brackets, connectors, and mufflers. **Figure 26** shows a typical exhaust system used on models other than the GT, which is shown in **Figure 27**. All parts are replaceable, but a cutting torch and welding device are usually required for removal of the mufflers from the exhaust pipes. Such service is usually done faster by a specialist in exhaust systems.

Periodically inspect all parts of the exhaust system for signs of damage and deterioration. With the engine running, check for holes and seam leaks. Exhaust gases not properly expelled through the tailpipe might enter the inside of the car and be hazardous to driver and passengers.

Whenever the exhaust manifold is removed from engine or exhaust pipe separated from exhaust manifold, replace gaskets with new ones.

GAS PEDAL AND LINKAGES

Periodically inspect, clean, and lubricate all linkages and connections on the gas pedal and carburetor. Inspect bushings and rubber parts for wear and deterioration. Disassemble and replace if defective.

5

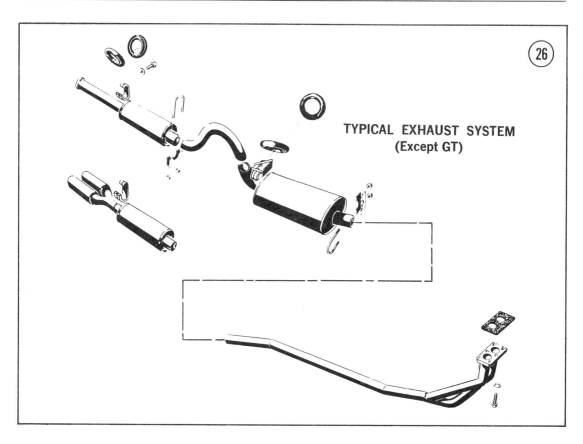

TYPICAL EXHAUST SYSTEM
(Except GT)

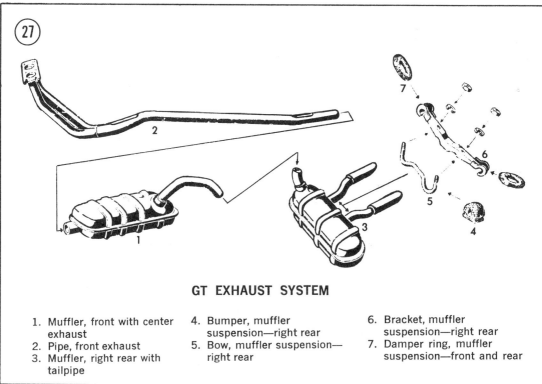

GT EXHAUST SYSTEM

1. Muffler, front with center
   exhaust
2. Pipe, front exhaust
3. Muffler, right rear with
   tailpipe
4. Bumper, muffler
   suspension—right rear
5. Bow, muffler suspension—
   right rear
6. Bracket, muffler
   suspension—right rear
7. Damper ring, muffler
   suspension—front and rear

CHAPTER SIX

COOLING AND HEATING SYSTEMS

The cooling system consists of a pressurized radiator, thermostat, radiator cap, centrifugal-type water pump, fan, and necessary hoses.

> NOTE: *For 1976 and later models, refer to* Supplement *section, Chapter Six, at the back of this manual.*

Figure 1 shows the radiator and hoses on the 1.1 engine; **Figure 2** the 1.5 and 1.9 engines. On the 1.1 engine, the fan and water pump are attached directly to the front of the engine block and the thermostat is located within the housing that is part of the water pump. On 1.5 and 1.9 engines, the water pump and fan are attached as part of the timing gear cover. The thermostat is located in the housing on the top, right-hand side of the cylinder head. In both cases, the upper radiator hose is connected to the thermostat housing.

The water pump circulates the coolant through the block and cylinder head until the engine reaches normal operating temperature.

If the heater controls are turned on, water is also circulated through the heater for use until the engine is warm. When the engine coolant temperature is normal (180-189°F), the thermostat opens and then the coolant is circulated through the radiator as well as the engine. **Figure 3** shows typical coolant circulation through heater core.

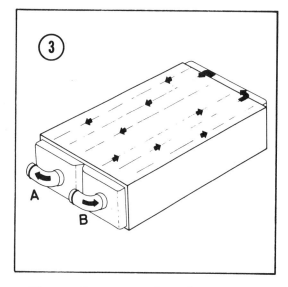

The cooling system has changed slightly for 1975 in that a bypass regulation thermostat is used inside a new thermostat housing.

With the thermostat in the bypass mode (engine not yet at operating temperature) the coolant is drawn by the water pump from the cylinder head through the thermostat housing, and finally forced into the engine block. The thermostat is closed in the flow direction from the radiator, and the flow direction from the cylinder head is fully opened.

The thermostat goes into the bypass regulation mode as the coolant temperature in the engine begins to warm up. The thermostat begins to close off hot coolant flow from the cylinder head into the thermostat housing. At the same time the thermostat begins to close off hot coolant flow, it also opens cold coolant flow from the radiator into the thermostat housing. This mixture of hot and cold coolant then passes through the water pump and on into the engine block.

The bypass regulation thermostat closes the housing inlet from the cylinder head at the same rate it opens the housing inlet from the radiator.

The thermostat normal operating temperature mode is in effect as the coolant temperature reaches normal operating temperature and the passage from the cylinder head to the thermostat housing closes. The hot coolant from the cylinder head is now flowing through the upper radiator hose. The passage from the lower radiator hose to the thermostat housing is now fully open and coolant flow is as follows: The hot coolant from the cylinder head flows through the upper radiator hose into the radiator, where it is cooled, then into the lower radiator hose, to the thermostat housing and the water pump, then into the cylinder block and back to the cylinder head.

The 1975 thermostat is not interchangeable with any other model or model years.

DRAINING COOLING SYSTEM

1. Set heater control lever to full heat position.
2. Remove radiator cap.

WARNING
Use care when removing radiator cap on a warm or hot engine. Hot water under pressure can boil out when pressure is released and cause severe scalding or burns. Loosen radiator cap to first notch and wait for pressure to escape before removing cap entirely.

3. Loosen hose clamp fixing lower radiator hose to radiator.
4. Remove drain plug on right side of cylinder block and pull off lower radiator hose from radiator. The radiator is not fitted with a drain plug.
5. Allow the coolant to drain from the cylinder block and radiator. If the coolant is to be reused, drain it into suitable container.

FILLING COOLING SYSTEM

1. Install drain plug and connect lower radiator hose to radiator. Tighten hose clamp on lower radiator hose.
2. Set heater control valve to full heat position.
3. Fill radiator with anti-freeze solution.

4. Start the engine. Warm up engine until normal operating temperature is reached and the thermostat has opened.

5. Remove radiator cap and check coolant level; replenish as required.

6. Install and tighten radiator cap.

7. Check all hoses and connections for leaks.

> NOTE: *The manufacturer recommends that a mixture of water and inhibited ethylene glycol be used as a year-round coolant. Mix the water and ethylene glycol in the proper proportion according to degree of protection desired, according to manufacturer's instructions.*

THERMOSTAT

The thermostat should be removed, inspected, and replaced as required if the engine runs hotter than normal or if it takes too long to warm up. Overheating may indicate that the thermostat is stuck in the closed position. Failure of the engine to warm up in a normal time may mean the thermostat is stuck in the open position.

Location of thermostat is described earlier in this chapter.

Removal/Installation (through 1974 Models)

1. Remove radiator cap and drain coolant below level of thermostat by removing lower radiator hose or removing drain plug from cylinder block.

2. Loosen hose clamp on hose connected to thermostat housing. Pull off radiator hose.

3. Remove bolts fixing upper thermostat housing to water pump (1.1 engine) or cylinder head (1.5 and 1.9 engines).

4. Pull up and remove upper housing and gasket.

5. Remove thermostat from water pump housing or cylinder head housing. Note carefully the direction it was installed for later installation.

6. During installation, use a new gasket and place thermostat in housing correctly.

Removal/Installation (1975 Models)

1. Remove air flow meter and air cleaner assembly.

2. Remove throttle lever spring.

3. Disconnect accelerator linkage springs.

4. Disconnect EGR pipe from throttle body housing.

5. Disconnect accelerator linkage at throttle body housing.

6. Remove thermostat.

7. To install, reverse preceding steps. Be sure to use a new gasket.

RADIATOR

Removal/Installation (1.1 Engine)

1. Drain radiator, as previously described.

2. Loosen clamp on upper radiator hose at radiator. Pull off hose.

3. Loosen and remove bolts fixing radiator to radiator support.

4. Pull up and remove radiator from engine compartment.

5. To install, reverse the above steps.

Removal/Installation (1.5 and 1.9 Engines)

1. Drain radiator, as previously described.

2. Loosen clamp on upper radiator hose at radiator. Pull off hose.

3. Disconnect air filter breather hose (if so equipped) at front cowl. Push the hose aside so that it is out of the way.

4. Remove screws fixing radiator shroud and radiator to support on each side of radiator. Be careful not to lose screw clips from support.

5. Pull up on radiator and shroud and remove from engine compartment.

6. To install, reverse Steps 1-5. Make certain the radiator is held firmly by rubber vibration pads on both sides of radiator.

WATER PUMP

Defective water pumps are not repairable because the impeller shaft and bearings are heated

6

and press fitted into the housing. Replace the pump if defective.

Removal/Installation (through 1974 Models)

1. Drain coolant, as previously described.

2. Remove radiator and radiator shroud (if so equipped), as previously described.

3. Remove fan belt, as previously described.

4. Remove upper and lower water hoses.

5. Loosen and remove bolts and washers fixing fan pulley to water pump drive shaft hub. Remove fan pulley. It may be necessary to use a puller.

6. Remove bolts fixing water pump to engine block (1.1 engine) or timing gear housing (1.5 and 1.9 engines).

7. Remove water pump and gasket.

8. Check pump shaft bearing for end-play and roughness by pushing the shaft back and forth and by rotating the shaft. If defective, replace water pump assembly.

9. Clean away all rust and corrosion from inside water pump housing and impeller blades. Remove all gasket material from water pump/timing gear cover/engine block mating surfaces. Use a straightedge to check mating surfaces for flatness and signs of distortion.

10. To install, reverse removal procedures. Use a new gasket. Torque bolts to 11 ft.-lb.

Removal/Installation (1975 Models)

1. Drain coolant as previously described. (If equipped with air conditioning, splash shield must be removed to gain access to lower radiator hose.)

2. Remove fan shroud and radiator mounting screws.

3. Disconnect upper radiator hose at radiator and radiator overflow hose.

4. Remove radiator first, then fan shroud.

5. Remove fan clutch assembly (the hold-down bolt for the fan clutch is a left-hand thread).

6. Loosen fan belt.

7. Disconnect thermostat housing hose and heat hose at water pump.

8. Remove water pump (water pump and pulley are serviced as an assembly).

9. Install the water pump by reversing the removal procedure, using a new water pump gasket.

AUTOMATIC FAN CLUTCH

All 1975 Opels are equipped with a Visco-Fluid fan clutch. The fan clutch, located on the water pump shaft, functions to improve cooling at idle while reducing the noise level at high speeds.

Removal/Installation

Follow Steps 1 through 5 under *Water Pump, Removal/Installation (1975 Models),* preceding.

FAN BELT

Removal/Installation

1. Loosen the alternator (generator) bracket mounting bolt and pivot bolt.

2. Push the alternator (generator) toward the engine block until the belt is slack.

3. Remove the belt from crankshaft pulley, water pump pulley, and alternator (generator) pulley.

4. Manipulate belt over fan blades and remove from engine.

5. To install, reverse preceding steps.

6. After installation, check fan belt tension by pushing in on the belt with your thumb midway between the alternator and water pump. The belt should push in approximately ½ inch. If tension is not correct, loosen alternator (generator) fixing bolts and move alternator (generator) until tension is correct. Tighten bolts.

WATER HOSES

Periodically inspect all water hoses, including heater hoses, for signs of leaks, cracks, or weakness. Replace defective hoses at the earliest signs of deterioration.

HEATER

The following instructions are given for removal and installation of the heater used in standard Opel, GT, and 1900 models, respectively. Normally, the heater need not be removed unless the blower fan or heater core is known to be defective. If the blower doesn't work, always check first to see if a fuse has blown and that all electrical connections are properly made. A defective heater core is usually indicated whenever water (coolant) leaks are found in the passenger compartment. Always check heater hoses and connections for defects before removal of heater.

Opel (Standard Models)

Figure 4 shows the heater system used on standard Opel models.

1. Drain coolant from heater and engine, as previously described.

2. See **Figure 5**. Loosen heater hose clamps and remove hoses.

3. Remove screws fixing heater housing to dashboard. Remove housing.

4. Remove heater core.

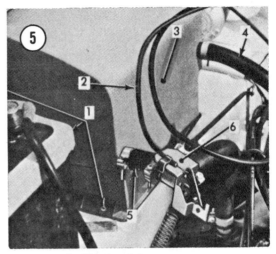

1. Sheet metal screws
2. Temperature control valve bowden wire
3. Heater housing
4. Heater house, to water pipe
5. Heater hose, to temperature control valve
6. Temperature control valve

6

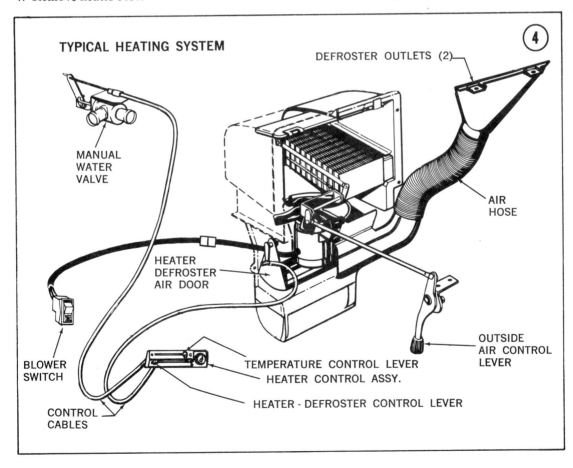

TYPICAL HEATING SYSTEM

DEFROSTER OUTLETS (2)

4

MANUAL WATER VALVE

AIR HOSE

HEATER DEFROSTER AIR DOOR

BLOWER SWITCH

OUTSIDE AIR CONTROL LEVER

TEMPERATURE CONTROL LEVER
HEATER CONTROL ASSY.

HEATER - DEFROSTER CONTROL LEVER

CONTROL CABLES

NOTE: *To remove air distributor housing and blower motor, perform the following steps:*

5. See **Figure 6**. Disconnect the blower switch wire (4).

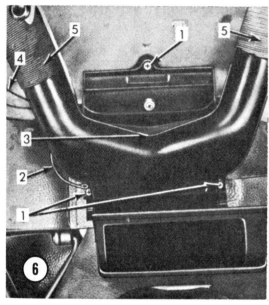

1. Sheet metal screws
2. Heater-defroster control valve
3. Air distributor housing
4. Wire to blower switch
5. Hose to defroster control jet

6. Disconnect the control cable (2) from the air distributor door.

7. Remove screws (1) fixing air distributor housing to dashboard.

8. Remove air hoses (5) from air distributor housing (3) and remove housing.

9. Remove screws securing blower motor to air distributor housing and remove motor.

10. To install, reverse the above steps.

Opel GT

Figure 7 shows the heater system used on GT models.

1. Drain coolant from heater and engine, as previously described.

2. Loosen hose clamps and pull off heater hoses from heater.

3. Disconnect hood lock control cable and retaining clip from hood release latch.

4. Remove ash tray. Unscrew and remove 2 screws under ash tray.

5. Remove retaining screw from headlamp lever handle and remove handle.

6. The console cover is held in place by 4 push-button type studs. Unsnap studs by prying cover up and work cover upwards over shift lever and rubber shift lever boot.

7. See **Figure 8**. Remove left cover and right plug in instrument panel cover. Through openings (A, B) remove the instrument panel fixing screws.

8. Lower the steering column, as discussed in Chapter Ten.

9. Disconnect multiple wire plug connectors from steering column harness.

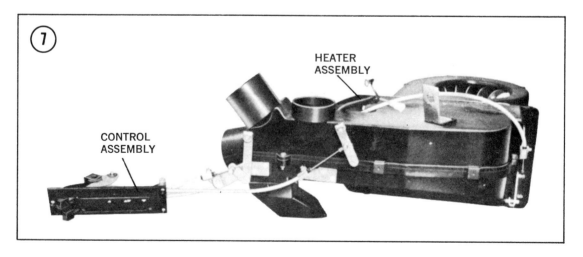

HEATER ASSEMBLY

CONTROL ASSEMBLY

10. Detach speedometer cable. Unplug and remove turn signal flasher.

11. Disconnect 5 multiple wire plug connectors below left side of instrument panel.

12. Remove sheet metal screws from both sides of radio face. Remove nut from bracket on lower left side of instrument housing.

13. Remove housing by pulling on top side of instrument panel and unsnapping pushbutton retainers.

14. Detach and mark ammeter wire (if so equipped).

15. Remove screws from heater control panel. Remove nuts and disconnect support bracket from back side of control panel.

16. Disconnect heater and defroster duct hoses from instrument panel.

17. Remove all screws fixing instrument panel padding. Remove the padding from the instrument panel.

18. Remove one bolt on top of heater blower case and 2 nuts from bottom of case. Remove heater blower and case assembly.

19. Check and mark relative position of mixed air door so that hand control levers can be properly installed and adjusted.

20. To install, reverse the preceding steps.

Model 1900

1. See **Figure 9**. Remove bolts fixing hood lock and ground wire (if so equipped) to fire wall.

2. Unscrew and remove screws fixing heater housing cover, as shown in **Figure 10**.

3. Pull windshield washer system hose off jet and remove jet from housing cover.

4. Disconnect bowden cable control wire from heater valve.

5. Unscrew heater housing from dashboard and pull it off carefully.

6. Disconnect and remove heater hoses from heater core by loosening hose clamps.

7. Pull heater core out of heater housing.

To remove motor proceed as follows:

8. See **Figure 11**. Remove shroud cover fixing screws. Carefully remove cover.

9. Disconnect wires to heater motor by disconnecting multiple plug connection on left side of shroud.

10. Remove screws fixing the heater motor to the housing (**Figure 12**) and withdraw motor from housing.

11. To install, reverse the preceding steps. During installation use a sealing compound to seal shrouds.

CHAPTER SEVEN

EMISSION CONTROL SYSTEMS

This chapter provides information for models from 1966 through 1975. For 1976 and later models, refer to *Supplement* section, Chapter Seven, at back of this manual.

The 1968 and 1969 Opels were equipped with an Air Injection Reactor system (AIR). The AIR system uses an engine-driven pump to compress, distribute, and inject clean, filtered air into each exhaust port. Exhaust gases at this point are close to combustion temperature and injection of excess oxygen continues the burning action. This "afterburning" limits the amount of unburned hydrocarbons and changes most of the carbon monoxide to carbon dioxide. At high speed and loads, the pressure relief valve opens to reduce excessive pressure in the system and to prevent high exhaust temperatures.

A slightly leaner carburetor is used for operation during normal engine running. At idle, an external vent opens to permit normal idle. The anti-backfire valve prevents backfire after hard acceleration and sudden deceleration. The check valve prevents backflow of exhaust gases into the injection lines. See **Figure 1**.

The 1970 through 1973 models used an Emission Control System (OECS). The basic features of the OECS are leaned out carburetion,

heated air to carburetor (except GT), and tuned spark timing.

The carburetor idle system incorporates emission control adjustments in addition to the idle mixture adjustments manufactured into the carburetor. All such adjustments should be referred to an Opel dealer.

The heated air system consists of a heat stove, a corrugated paper heated air pipe, and an air cleaner that contains a temperature controlled door operated by vacuum through a temperature sensor. **Figure 2** shows the parts of the air system and direction of air flow.

Additionally, an Exhaust Gas Recirculation system (EGR) made its debut on the 1973 models and is still used on the latest (1975) Opels. The EGR system consists of a pipe connected to the center of the front exhaust pipe, an EGR valve, a short pipe from the valve to the intake manifold, and a short vacuum hose from the EGR valve to the base of the carburetor. The system does not receive sufficient vacuum at idle to operate, but will operate during acceleration and part throttle providing sufficient intake manifold vacuum is present.

The 1974 Opels featured a Controlled Combustion System (CCS) which is essentially the

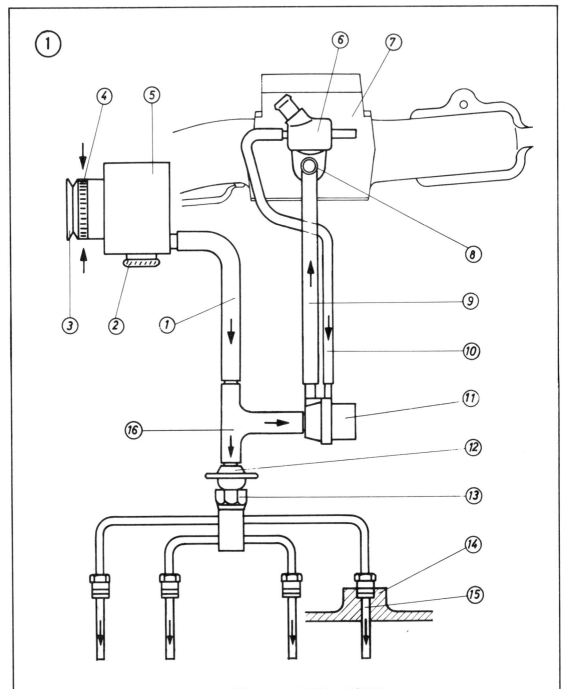

AIR INJECTION REACTOR SYSTEM

1. Airhose from 5 to
   11 and 12
2. Pressure relief valve
3. Drive belt pulley
4. Air intake filter fan
5. Air pump
6. Vacuum control connector
7. Intake manifold
8. Air bleeder pipe
9. Air bleeder line from
   11 to 8
10. Vacuum line for
    control valve
11. Control valve
12. Check valve
13. Air distributor assy.
14. Exhaust manifold
15. Air injection nozzles
16. Rubber hose fitting

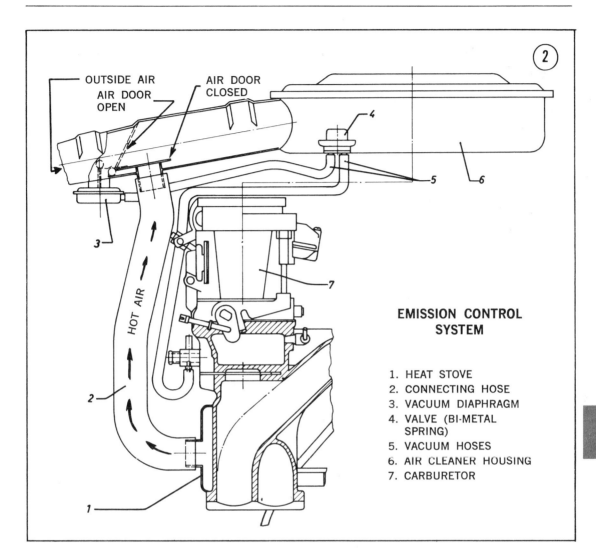

OUTSIDE AIR
AIR DOOR OPEN

AIR DOOR CLOSED

HOT AIR

EMISSION CONTROL SYSTEM

1. HEAT STOVE
2. CONNECTING HOSE
3. VACUUM DIAPHRAGM
4. VALVE (BI-METAL SPRING)
5. VACUUM HOSES
6. AIR CLEANER HOUSING
7. CARBURETOR

same as the 1973 OECS system except 2 versions of the Exhaust Gas Recirculation system (EGR) are used—one for California, the other for the rest of the United States. The non-California version is the same as the 1973 EGR system (see **Figures 3 and 4**). The California version (**Figure 5**) is controlled by 2 in-line connected valves. The first valve is a control valve operating from ported vacuum which varies with throttle opening. The second valve is a regulating valve and is operated by manifold vacuum which varies with engine load. The result of having 2 valves is that at idle speed there is no exhaust gas recirculation, and at low partial load, a small amount of exhaust gas recirculation is present, and at higher partial load, a maximum amount of exhaust gas recirculation is obtained.

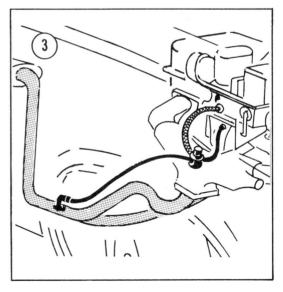

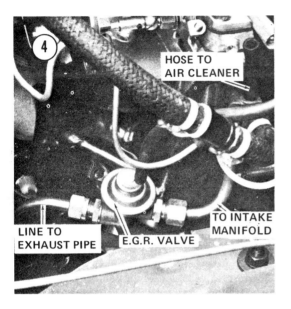

HOSE TO
AIR CLEANER

LINE TO
EXHAUST PIPE   E.G.R. VALVE

TO INTAKE
MANIFOLD

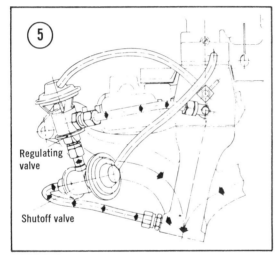

Regulating
valve

Shutoff valve

In addition, 1974 Opels sold in California and equipped with a manual transmission featured a dashpot, which prevented the throttle valve from closing at a high rate during deceleration, thereby reducing the formation of exhaust emissions. See **Figure 6**.

The 1975 Opels feature fuel injection and the EGR system. In addition, California cars (only) utilize a catalytic converter, an emission control device added to the exhaust system (see **Figure 7**) to reduce hydrocarbon and carbon monoxide pollutants from the exhaust gas stream. The converter contains beads which are coated with a catalytic material containing platinum and palladium.

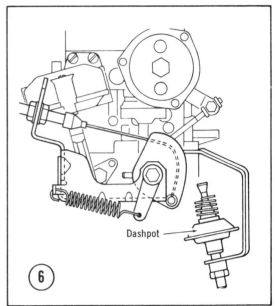

Dashpot

Details of all of the preceding systems are given in this chapter.

AIR INJECTION
REACTOR SYSTEM (AIR)

All parts of the AIR system are non-repairable and must be replaced if defective. **Figures 8 and 9** show air pump installation on the 1.1 and 1.9 engines, respectively.

1. Air hose
2. Pump support bracket
3. Fan belt adjuster rail
4. Air pump
5. Pressure relief valve
6. Air pump drive belt

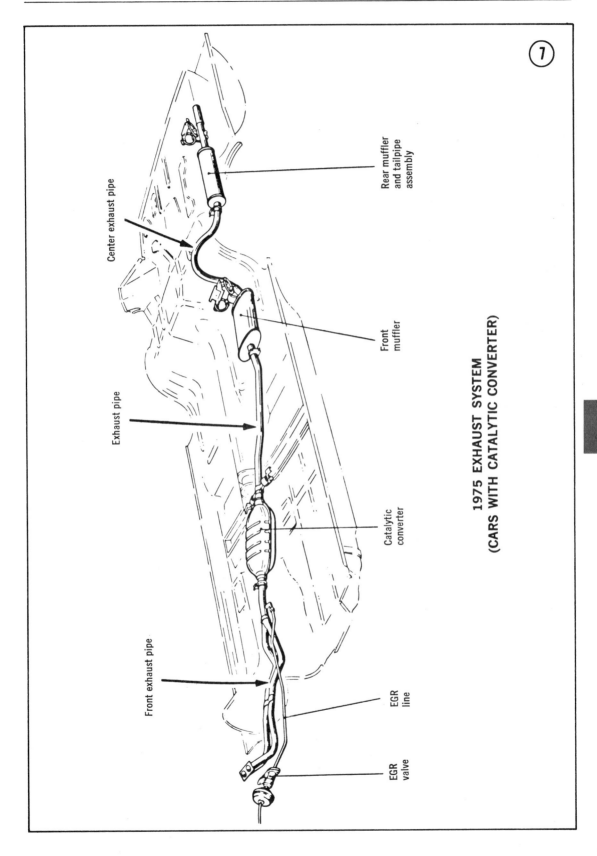

7

Center exhaust pipe

Exhaust pipe

Front exhaust pipe

Rear muffler and tailpipe assembly

Front muffler

Catalytic converter

EGR line

EGR valve

**1975 EXHAUST SYSTEM
(CARS WITH CATALYTIC CONVERTER)**

⑨
1. Air pump support bracket
2. Air hose
3. Pressure relief valve
4. Air pump
5. Air pump pulley and filter fan
6. Air pump drive belt
7. Twin-pulley on crankshaft

⑩
1. Air distributor pipes
2. Air distributor housing
3. Check valve
4. Air bleeder line
5. Vacuum line
6. Rubber hose connector
7. Air pump hose
8. Control valve

Air Pump Removal/Installation

1. Disconnect hose at air pump.

2. Remove bracket-to-pump mounting bolts.

3. Remove drive belt from pump and remove pump from engine.

4. To install, reverse Steps 1-3. Make sure belt tension is correct, as described in the next procedure.

AIR Drive Belt Removal/Installation (1.1 Engine)

Refer to **Figure 10**.

1. Loosen air pump mounting bolts.

2. Push the pump toward the engine.

3. Remove the belt from around the air pump, water pump, and crankshaft pulleys.

4. To install, reverse Steps 1-3. Adjust position of pump so that drive belt will deflect approximately ½ inch when pushed in midway between crankshaft and pump pulleys.

AIR Drive Belt Removal/Installation (1.9 Engine)

Refer to **Figure 11**.

1. Loosen the generator adjusting bracket mounting bolts.

⑪
1. Air distributor pipes
2. Air distributor housing
3. Check valve
4. Rubber hose connector
5. Control valve
6. Air bleeder line
7. Air pump line
8. Vacuum line
9. Vacuum control connector

2. Push generator toward engine to loosen fan belt tension.

3. Remove belt from around generator and crankshaft pulleys.

4. Loosen air pump mounting bolts and push pump toward engine.

5. Remove belt from around crankshaft, water pump, and air pump pulleys.

6. To install, reverse Steps 1-5. Adjust generator and air pump belts so that they will deflect approximately ½ inch when pushed in by thumb pressure midway between 2 pulleys.

AIR Check Valve Removal/Installation

Figures 10 and 11 show check valve installation for the 1.1 and 1.9 engines, respectively.

1. Remove carburetor air cleaner.

2. Detach rubber hose from check valve after loosening hose clamp.

3. Unscrew check valve from distributor housing. On the 1.9 engine, it may be necessary to remove the control valve to gain access to the check valve.

4. To install, reverse Steps 1-3.

AIR Control Valve Removal/Installation

1. Remove carburetor air cleaner.

2. Detach rubber hose, air bleeder line, and vacuum line from control valve.

3. Remove the bolts fixing the control valve to the mounting bracket.

4. Remove control valve from bracket.

5. To install, reverse Steps 1-4.

AIR Distributor/Nozzle Assembly Removal/Installation

1. Disconnect battery cables at battery.

2. Remove air cleaner.

3. Disconnect fuel and vacuum hoses from carburetor.

4. Disconnect vacuum hose from intake manifold. Release pressure in cooling system before disconnecting hose.

5. *1.9 Engine*—Disconnect and plug 2 hoses from water-heated automatic choke.

6. Remove positive crankcase ventilation hose at intake manifold.

7. Disconnect throttle linkage from carburetor.

8. Remove carburetor.

9. Detach rubber hose from check valve. Unscrew and remove check valve.

10. Remove bolt fixing control valve to intake manifold.

11. Remove bolts holding intake manifold to cylinder block.

12. Remove star bolts securing intake manifold to exhaust manifold.

13. Remove intake manifold from engine.

14. Unscrew AIR distributor pipe fittings from exhaust manifold and remove air distributor assembly.

15. To install, reverse preceding steps. Lubricate pipe fittings and pipe ends. Always use new intake, exhaust, and carburetor gaskets.

Air Pump Troubleshooting

Under normal conditions, the air pump is not completely noiseless because of the bearings and vanes rubbing inside the housing. If noise becomes excessive, remove the drive belt and rotate the drive pulley by hand. If it rotates freely without noise, the belt may have been too tight. A "chirping" or squeaking noise usually is associated with the vanes rubbing against the housing, which is normal. If the noise is excessive, the vanes may be worn and the air pump must be replaced.

Bearing noise is usually distinguishable by a rolling sound at all speeds. Bearing noises are usually continuous, but vane noise may be intermittent. If noise becomes excessive, replace the air pump because the bearings are lubricated for life. Failure of the rear bearing is distinguishable by a heavy knocking noise.

Check all hoses periodically for signs of deterioration or leaky connections. Feel the hoses by hand for air leaks. Put soapy water on hose connections to check for air leaks. Check mounting bolts and brackets for tightness.

Check the air pump relief valve. If air is escaping from the valve during idle, the valve is defective and the air pump must be replaced.

CAUTION
There is a filter behind the centrifugal fan which is behind the pulley. If the engine is to be steam cleaned or pressure cleaned with detergent, be sure to cover the front of the air pump so the filter is not damaged.

7

Control Valve Troubleshooting

Explosion-like noises, especially when the engine is cold, indicate that the control valve may be defective. To check the control valve, proceed as follows.

1. Remove air cleaner.

2. Remove hose from top of control valve.

3. Start engine and run at idle.

4. Using a flashlight, look at the white valve inside the control valve.

5. Pull hose from manifold vacuum connector.

6. Count 5 seconds. Put hose back onto manifold vacuum connector.

7. The white valve should have moved upward for 1 to 3 seconds. If white valve stays up for more than 5 seconds or doesn't move at all, the valve is defective and must be replaced.

Check Valve Troubleshooting

A good field test for testing the one-way check valve has not been found. However, a good indication that the check valve is defective is when the connecting hose is brittle, excessively hot when touched, or has a burned appearance. Remove air cleaner and hose and check inside of valve with flashlight. If black rubber is burned away or partially burned, remove the valve and replace it. If the check valve is found to be defective, check air pump for possible damage.

OPEL EMISSION CONTROL SYSTEM (OECS) AND CONTROLLED COMBUSTION SYSTEM (CCS)

Troubleshooting the OECS or CCS system should be referred to an Opel dealer. However, the following procedures can be used if a part is known to be defective.

Damper Door

The damper door is non-repairable. If it is defective, the air cleaner assembly must be replaced.

Vacuum Motor Removal/Installation

1. See **Figure 12**. Remove vacuum motor retainer spring. Disconnect vacuum hose.

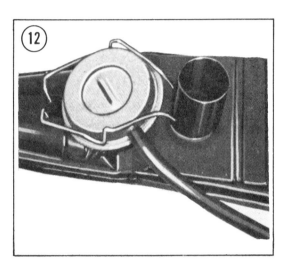

2. Lift vacuum motor, cock it to one side to unhook linkage at control door, and remove the motor.

3. To install, reverse these steps.

Air Cleaner Sensor Removal/Installation

1. See **Figure 13**. Disconnect and remove air cleaner from carburetor.

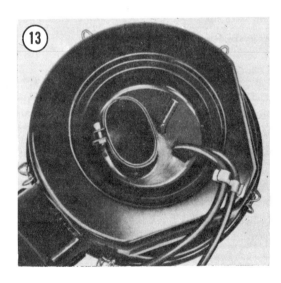

2. Remove sensor retaining clips by prying.

3. Pull vacuum hoses off sensor.

4. Note position of sensor so that you can install new sensor in same position. Remove sensor.

Exhaust Gas Recirculation (EGR) Valve Removal/Installation

1. Remove air flow meter and air cleaner assembly.

2. Remove EGR valve.

3. Clean the exhaust gas recirculation valve (or valves) and fitting with a piece of stiff wire, removing all exhaust deposits. Install EGR valve by reversing Steps 1 and 2, using new gaskets.

DASHPOT

A quick operational check and adjustment of the dashpot on 1974 Opels with manual transmissions for sale in California (only) can be accomplished with the engine idling normally. The carburetor throttle stop screw should be seated on the throttle stop.

1. Loosen the nut on the lower end of the dashpot. Revolve the dashpot in the bracket downward until the stem comes free of throttle lever.

2. Bring the dashpot upward again until the stem just touches the throttle lever.

3. Make 3 additional revolutions of the dashpot against the throttle lever. Fasten the nut at the lower end of the dashpot to prevent it from turning in the bracket.

4. The stem of the dashpot should move freely in the housing when an external force is applied. The stem should be able to be moved away from the throttle lever by 1/16 in. minimum.

5. If the throttle valve is opened, the stem of the dashpot must move outward about ⅛ in.

6. If the dashpot does not work as described above, replace with a new one.

CATALYTIC CONVERTER

Due to the need for special equipment it is recommended that any work on the catalytic converter be referred to your Opel dealer.

FUEL EVAPORATION CONTROL SYSTEM

Late models are equipped with a carbon canister that absorbs the fuel vapors developed in the fuel tank, especially when the car is parked, due to atmospheric pressure and temperature conditions. The carbon canister releases these vapors through the carburetor during car operation. If the carbon canister is suspected of being defective, refer service to your Opel dealer. If lines to the carbon canister are disconnected, make sure to mark them for correct installation.

POSITIVE CRANKCASE VENTILATION SYSTEM

7

The PCV system consists of a one-way (PC) valve and necessary hoses to vent the crankcase gases to the intake manifold for burning. Every 10,000 miles, disconnect the hose and remove the valve. Clean it thoroughly in solvent and dry with compressed air. Shake the valve back and forth and listen for a sliding and clicking sound. Air should be able to be blown through in one direction but not sucked through in the other direction. If the valve is defective, replace it.

CHAPTER EIGHT

ELECTRICAL SYSTEM

All models have a 12-volt negative ground electrical system. Overload protection is supplied by fuses and, on later models, fusible links that protect the wiring harnesses.

> NOTE: *This chapter provides information on 1966-1975 models. Turn to the* Supplement *section, Chapter Eight, at back of this manual, for 1976 and later models.*

Several electrical testing devices are required for complete diagnosis and adjustment of the charging and starting circuits. However, preliminary diagnosis of these circuits, and most work on the rest of the electrical system, can be done with a voltmeter, ohmmeter, and 12-volt test lamp. Electrical parts can be removed and taken to an automotive electrical shop for testing, adjusting, and repair. This is especially true of the generator (alternator), regulator, and starter motor. Unless you are experienced and have proper equipment for testing, adjustment, and overhaul, refer necessary service to your Opel dealer or automotive electrical shop.

BATTERY

Typically, the battery is mounted within a holder on the left side of engine compartment.

Inspection

1. Inspect the battery frequently for signs of corrosion on top of the battery and on the case. Use a solution of water and baking soda to neutralize any corrosion. Rinse with water and wipe the battery clean.

2. After cleaning, coat battery terminals lightly with Vaseline.

3. Inspect the battery connections and battery cables for tightness and corrosion damage. Replace if defective.

4. Check battery condition with a hydrometer, as discussed in Chapter Two. If any of the cells are weak, recharge the battery. If recharging does not return the battery to satisfactory condition, replace it before trouble starts.

When batteries are being charged, highly explosive hydrogen gas forms in each cell. Some of this gas escapes through the filler openings and may form an explosive atmosphere around the battery. This explosive atmosphere may exist for several hours. Sparks, open flame, or a lighted cigarette can ignite this gas, causing an internal explosion and possible serious personal injury. The following precautions should be taken to prevent an explosion.

1. Do not smoke or permit any open flame near

any battery being charged or which has been recently charged.

2. Do not disconnect live circuits at battery terminals, because a spark usually occurs where a live circuit is broken. Care must always be taken when connecting or disconnecting any battery charger; be sure its power switch is off before making or breaking connections. Poor connections are a common cause of electrical arcs which cause explosions.

Replacement

1. Disconnect battery cables from battery terminals by loosening the nuts and spreading the connectors.

> NOTE: *Always remove the negative cable first to prevent possible shorts. Do not twist the cable around the battery poles as damage to the poles or insulation may occur.*

2. Remove nuts and battery hold-down bracket.

3. Remove battery from battery holder. Make certain to note which cable connects to the positive terminal and which connects to the negative terminal.

4. Install new battery, battery holder, and cables. Tighten all connections securely. Make certain the battery is full of electrolyte.

5. Coat battery terminals and cable connections with Vaseline.

IGNITION/STARTER SWITCH

Maintenance of the ignition/starter switch is not required. A defective switch must be replaced.

STARTER MOTOR

Figure 1 shows installation of the starter motor on the 1.1 engine; **Figure 2** the 1.5 and 1.9 engines.

Removal/Installation (1.1 Engine)

1. Disconnect battery. Remove air cleaner. Disconnect choke control cable.

2. Jack up the front of the car and support it with jackstands.

3. Disconnect right engine mount from body, as discussed in Chapter Four.

4. Disconnect tailpipe at rear of car.

5. Loosen bolts at left engine mount. Remove one bolt only.

6. With a hoist, raise engine on starter side and remove the engine mount bracket-to-crankcase bolts.

7. Remove bracket to gain access to starter.

8. Disconnect all wires leading to starter. Mark wire positions for later installation.

9. Remove the bolts fixing starter to flywheel housing.

10. Remove starter from engine.

11. To install, reverse the preceding steps. During installation, use a sealer on engine mount bracket bolts to prevent leaks.

Removal/Installation (1.5, 1.9 Engines)

1. See **Figure 3**. Disconnect all wires leading to starter. Mark wire positions for later installation.

2. Remove bolts and washers fixing support bracket to starter motor and engine block.

3. Remove support bracket.

4. Remove bolts, nuts, and washers fixing starter to flywheel housing.

5. See **Figure 4**. Use a soft hammer to drive out stud. Remove starter.

6. To install, reverse Steps 1-5.

Disassembly (1.1 Engine)

1. Remove field frame cover band.

2. Remove field lead connecting nut from motor terminal on the solenoid.

3. Remove screws holding solenoid to the drive housing. Remove the solenoid and gasket.

4. Remove screws fixing 4 brushes to holders. Remove brushes.

5. Remove the 2 thru-bolts and nuts. Remove commutator end frame and field frame assembly.

6. Remove solenoid shift lever fulcrum bolt, nut, and lockwasher. Withdraw armature and drive assembly with shift lever from the drive housing.

7. Remove the drive assembly from the armature by placing a ½-inch pipe coupling over the end of the shaft so that it bears against the pinion stop retainer. Tap the retainer toward the arma-

ture to uncover the snap ring. Remove snap ring from groove in shaft and slide the retainer and the pinion drive assembly from the shaft. Remove assist spring.

8. Clean all parts thoroughly with clean rags. Do not use a solvent on the armature field coils or the drive assembly. Inspect all parts for wear and damage. Repair or replace as required.

9. To assemble, reverse the preceding steps. Lubricate the armature shaft, drive housing bushing, shift lever linkage, and commutator end frame bushing during assembly.

Disassembly (1.5, 1.9 Engines)

Figure 5 is an exploded diagram of the starter.

1. Place the starter in a vise equipped with soft jaws, as shown in **Figure 6**. Mark end frame and field frame for later assembly.

2. Remove starter thru-bolts and field coil end from solenoid switch lower threaded bolt.

3. Remove end frame from field frame. Pull insluating tubes out of field frame.

4. See **Figure 7**. Place a socket over commutator

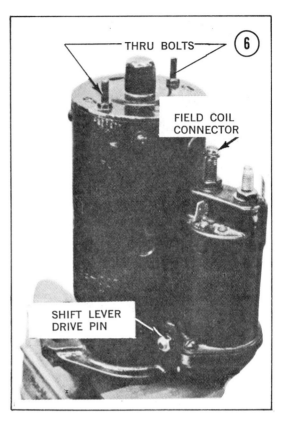

THRU BOLTS ⑥

FIELD COIL CONNECTOR

SHIFT LEVER DRIVE PIN

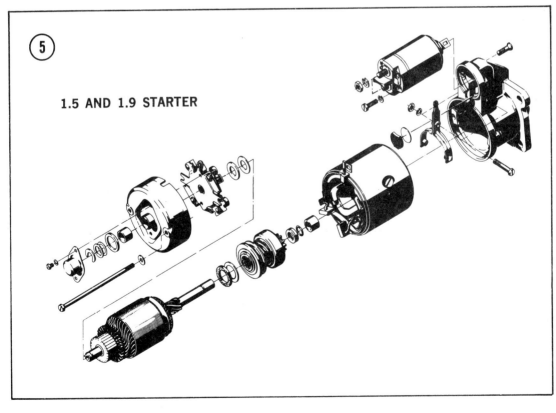

⑤

1.5 AND 1.9 STARTER

8

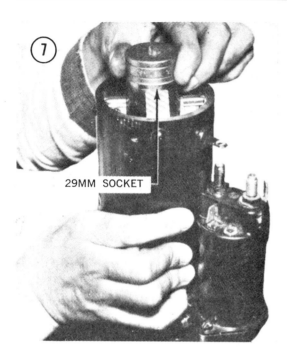

29MM SOCKET

and lift up on the field frame. The brushes will be held in place by the socket.

5. Remove 2 solenoid attaching screws and remove solenoid and spring.

6. Remove shift lever shaft. Withdraw armature and shift lever assembly.

7. See **Figure 8**. Drive back retaining ring on armature shaft.

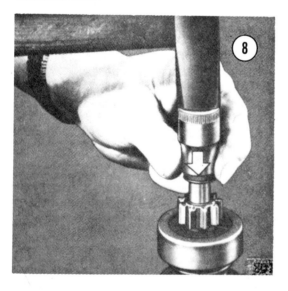

8. Remove lock ring, retaining ring, and overrunning clutch and pinion from armature shaft.

9. To assemble, reverse the preceding steps. Lubricate the armature shaft and drive housing bushing during assembly. Use a sealer between solenoid and frame, as shown in **Figure 9**.

APPLY SEALER IN THIS AREA

DISTRIBUTOR

The distributor is the heart of the ignition system, which consists of the distributor, contact breaker points, condenser, coil, high and low tension circuit parts. The low tension (primary) circuit consists of the power source (battery), contact breaker points, condenser, and ignition coil primary winding. The high tension (secondary) circuit consists of ignition coil secondary winding, rotor arm, distributor cap electrical contacts, high tension cables, and spark plugs.

The combination vacuum advance-retard unit as used on previous model distributors has been replaced by a single function vacuum unit on the 1975 models. The location of the contact points and the vacuum unit attachment on the breaker plate have changed to provide a means for vacuum retard instead of vacuum advance.

Removal and installation of the distributor no longer requires removal and installation of the fuel pump on the 1975 models.

Mechanically, the distributor is driven by a gear on the camshaft on the 1.1 engines and by a gear on the crankshaft on the 1.5 and 1.9 engines. **Figure 10** is a cutaway view of the distributor drive.

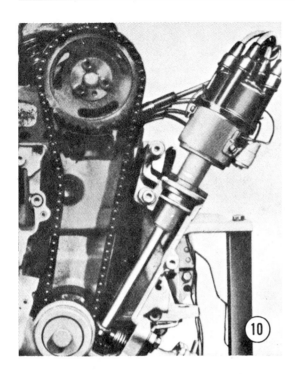

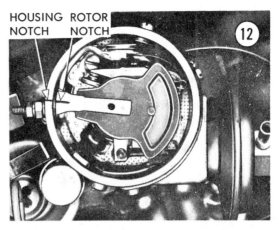

HOUSING ROTOR
NOTCH   NOTCH

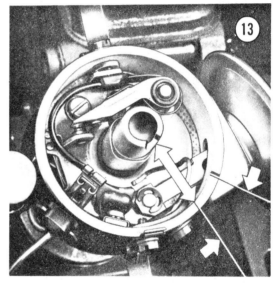

Most of the trouble encountered in the distributor will be in the cap, rotor, contact points, condenser, or wiring. The distributor should not make any noise while the engine is running. If noises are apparent, either the bearings or gears are worn and should be replaced. Unless it is essential to remove the distributor from the engine for disassembly and part replacement, all services can be performed with the distributor in place. The contact points should be serviced and replaced periodically, as specified in Chapter Two. Replace the rotor and condenser whenever the contact points are replaced.

Figure 11 is an exploded view of the distributor used on the 1.5 and 1.9 engines. The distributor used on the 1.1 engine is similar.

Contact Point Adjustment

Figure 12 shows the inside of the distributor on the 1.1 engine with the distributor cap removed; **Figure 13** shows the distributor on the 1.5 and 1.9 engines. The illustrations show the rotor, driveshaft, and body alignment marks positioned when No. 1 cylinder is at TDC on the compression stroke.

1. Unsnap the distributor cap.

2. Remove rotor by pulling it off the distributor shaft. Once the rotor is removed, the contact point assembly can be adjusted.

> NOTE: *Some late models are equipped with an insulator between the rotor and distributor contact point assembly to prevent contamination of the point assembly. After removing rotor, lift up and remove insulator.*

3. Rotate distributor drive shaft cam by turning crankshaft pulley until the moving contact (rubbing arm) is positioned at the highest point on the cam lobe. The contact points should be separated (open).

> NOTE: *Removal of the spark plugs will make it easier to turn crankshaft pulley.*

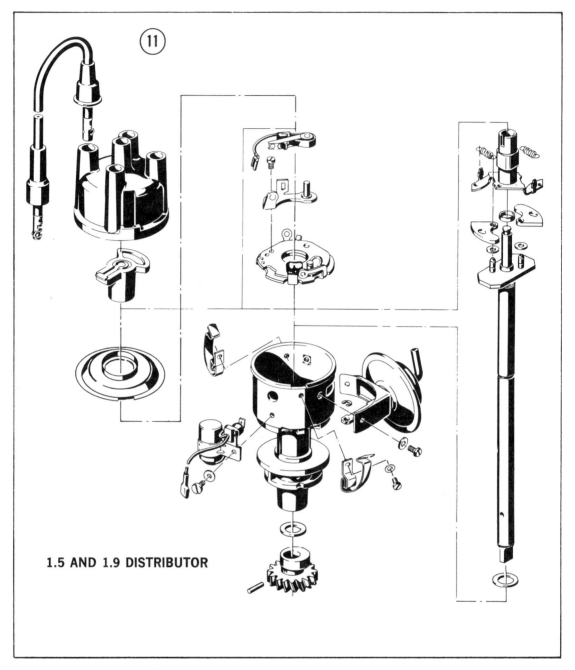

1.5 AND 1.9 DISTRIBUTOR

4. Use a feeler gauge to measure the gap between the moveable and stationary contact points. For correct gap, refer to Chapter Two.

5. Loosen screw fixing contact breaker assembly to breaker plate.

6. Move the stationary point until the correct gap is achieved. Tighten the screw. The feeler gauge should have a slight drag as the gauge is moved back and forth, but you should not be able to see the moveable point move. Recheck gap after tightening screw. If incorrect, readjust.

NOTE: *The contact point mating surfaces should have a grey frosted appearance and mate to each other exactly. If the surfaces are partly worn, clean with a point file as required. If excessively worn, pitted, or burned, replace them.*

Contact Point Replacement

1. Unsnap the distributor cap clamps, remove distributor cap, remove rotor, and remove insulating plate (if so equipped).

2. Disconnect breaker point wire by pulling it off of connector (1.5, 1.9 engines) or by loosening screw fixing it to contact post (1.1 engine).

3. Remove screw fixing contact point assembly to breaker plate. Pull up and remove breaker point assembly.

4. Discard old points and install new points by reversing above steps. Make certain the pivot shaft at the spring end of the assembly fits into the guide hole in the breaker plate.

5. See **Figure 14**. Lightly lubricate with oil the sliding parts of breaker plate (B) and felt in drive shaft (C). Apply a thin coating of high-melting-point grease to the cam (A).

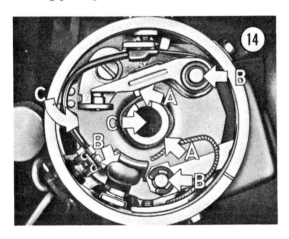

6. Adjust the points as described above. Make certain the points mate exactly. If not, bend the moveable arm until they do.

Condenser Replacement

1. Remove the screw fixing the condenser to the distributor body.

2. Disconnect the condenser wire and remove the condenser.

3. To replace, reverse Steps 1-2.

Distributor Removal/Installation (1.1 Engine)

1. Disconnect spark plug wires and high tension coil wire from distributor cap. Mark each wire's

position for later installation. Remove the distributor cap.

2. Rotate crankshaft pulley until No. 1 cylinder is at TDC on the compression stroke. Check that alignment marks of distributor body and rotor line up and that timing marks on crankshaft pulley and stationary pointer are aligned.

3. Disconnect vacuum line from vacuum advance unit.

4. Disconnect primary ignition wire leading from coil to distributor.

5. Mark position of distributor relative to mounting pedestal.

6. Remove bolt from hold-down clamp at base of distributor. Remove hold-down clamp.

7. Pull up on distributor and remove from engine.

8. To install, reverse the preceding steps. Inspect paper gasket on distributor housing and replace if defective.

9. See **Figure 15**. When inserting distributor into engine, rotate it to the position shown. As the teeth on the drive shaft mesh with the teeth on the camshaft, the distributor will rotate to the proper position, as shown in Figure 12.

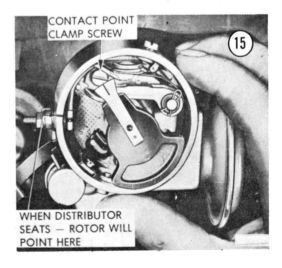

CONTACT POINT CLAMP SCREW

WHEN DISTRIBUTOR SEATS — ROTOR WILL POINT HERE

Distributor Removal/Installation (1.5, 1.9 Engines)

1. Disconnect spark plug wires and high-tension wire from distributor cap. Mark each wire's position for later installation. Remove distributor cap, insulator, and rotor.

8

2. Rotate crankshaft pulley until No. 1 cylinder is at TDC on the compression stroke. Check that alignment mark on distributor housing and notch in drive shaft line up, as shown in Figure 13.

3. Check that alignment of timing ball in flywheel and stationary pointer coincide.

4. Remove the fuel pump, as described in Chapter Five. (This step is not necessary on 1975 models.)

5. Disconnect vacuum line from vacuum unit(s).

6. Disconnect primary ignition wire leading from coil to distributor.

7. Mark the position of distributor relative to mounting pedestal.

8. Remove bolt from hold-down clamp at base of distributor. Remove hold-down clamp.

9. Pull up on distributor and remove from timing cover.

10. To install, reverse the above steps. Inspect paper gasket on distributor housing and replace if defective.

11. See **Figure 16**. When inserting distributor into timing cover, rotate it to the position shown. As the teeth on the drive shaft mesh with the teeth on the crankshaft, the distributor will rotate to the proper position, as shown in Figure 13.

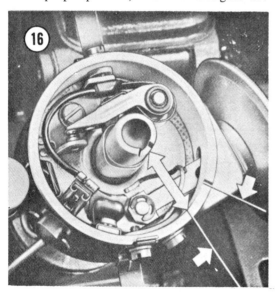

Distributor Overhaul

The following discussion applies specifically to the 1.9 engine. The procedures can be used

as guides for the 1.1 and 1.5 engine models. See Figure 11 for an exploded view of the distributor.

1. Remove distributor, as previously described.

2. Remove screws fixing distributor cap clamps and remove clamps.

3. Disconnect and remove the vacuum control unit(s).

4. See **Figure 17**. Remove retaining ring from groove in distributor shaft.

5. Push up on distributor shaft. Remove breaker plate from distributor.

6. Remove the breaker point assembly from the breaker plate.

7. Disassemble breaker plate by unscrewing ball thrust spring screw, as shown in **Figure 18**. Remove spring and ball.

8. Further disassembly is not recommended. If drive gear, cam lobes, bushings, or shaft are defective, install new distributor.

9. Inspect all parts for wear and damage. Pay special attention to condition of springs, cam lobes, drive shaft, centrifugal weights, and distributor cap. Visible wear or damage is sufficient cause to replace a part.

10. Partly pull distributor shaft and centrifugal advance mechanism out of distributor housing to clean. Do not disassemble the advance mechanism.

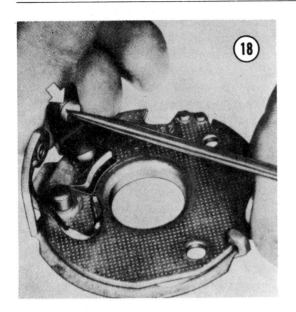

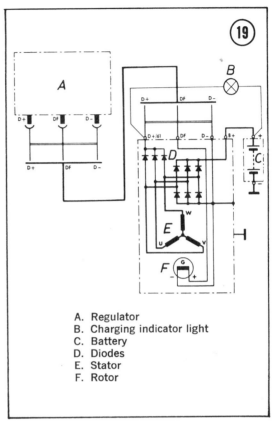

A. Regulator
B. Charging indicator light
C. Battery
D. Diodes
E. Stator
F. Rotor

11. To assemble, reverse Steps 1-10. Lubricate centrifugal advance mechanism and other parts as described in Chapter Two.

ALTERNATOR

The alternator is a continuous-output, diode rectified electrical generator. The rotor, which carries the field winding, is mounted in ball bearings at both ends. The ball bearings are lubricated for life. Two brushes and slip rings are used. One brush conducts the current provided by the voltage regulator to one end of the field coil. The other brush conducts the current from the other end of the rotating field to ground.

The 3-phase stator windings are assembled on the inside of a laminated core that forms the center section of the alternator frame. Nine rectifier diodes are connected to the stator windings (3 to each phase lead). The diodes change the alternator AC voltages to DC voltage coming out of the B positive and the D positive alternator terminals. **Figure 19** is a schematic diagram of the alternator circuit.

When servicing the alternator, always follow these general precautions.

1. Disconnect the leads between the battery, alternator, and regulator only when the ignition switch is turned off.

2. If the battery is to be charged in the car, disconnect battery positive and negative leads.

3. If arc welding is to be done to any part of the car, connect the arc welder ground terminal directly to the car body.

Removal/Installation

Figure 20 shows alternator installation parts.

1. Disconnect battery ground strap.

2. Unplug wiring connector from alternator.

3. Disconnect the alternator battery and the ground leads.

4. Remove adjusting brace, bolt, lockwasher, plain washer, and nut.

5. Loosen pivot bolt. Push alternator inward and remove belt from pulley.

6. Drop alternator down and remove pivot bolt, nut, lockwasher, and plain washer.

7. Remove alternator from engine.

8. To install, reverse the above steps. Adjust the alternator position so that the belt pushes in (deflects) under thumb pressure to approximately ½ inch.

8

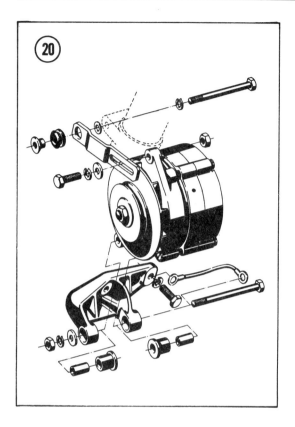

an exploded view of the early type alternator; **Figure 22** of the later type.

GENERATOR

The direct current generator is a conventional type with an externally completed field circuit. The armature is supported by a ball bearing at the drive end and a bronze bushing at the commutator end. To lubricate the bushing, it is necessary to remove the plastic plug in the end frame to gain access to the bushing area.

Once the generator has been in operation, a residual magnetism remains to induce voltage as the armature is rotated. The strength of the magentic field increases rapidly as voltage is induced. As speed and magnetic field strength are increased, voltage is increased. After the generator has reached cut-in speed, the voltage regulator keeps the voltage within specified limits.

Figure 23 shows a typical installation on the 1.1 engine; **Figure 24** the 1.5 and 1.9 engines.

Removal/Installation

1. Disconnect battery cables from battery.

2. Disconnect 3 wires from generator.

3. See **Figure 25**. Remove adjusting brace bolt, lockwasher, and plain washer. **Figure 26** shows the generator parts clearly.

Overhaul

General overhaul of the alternator, especially the diode assembly, is not recommended because special knowledge and tools are required. Refer such service to your Opel dealer. **Figure 21** is

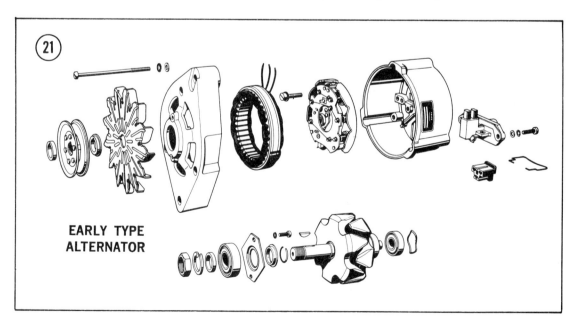

EARLY TYPE ALTERNATOR

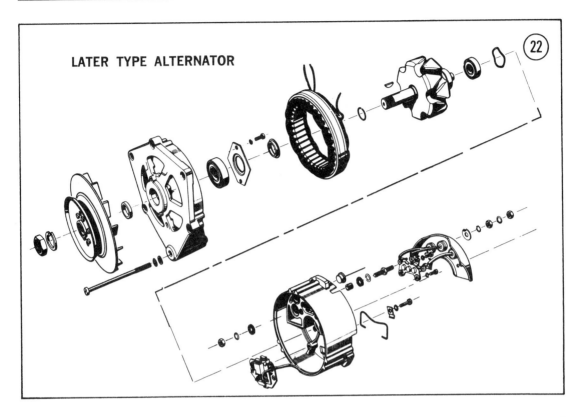

LATER TYPE ALTERNATOR

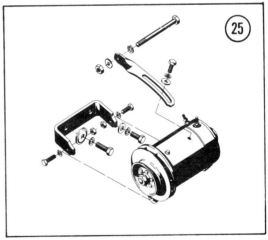

8

4. Loosen 2 pivot bolts. Push generator inward and remove belt from pulley.

5. Drop generator down and remove 2 pivot bolts, nuts, and lockwashers.

6. Remove the generator from engine.

7. To install, reverse Steps 1-6. Adjust the generator position so that the belt pushes in (deflects) under thumb pressure to approximately ½ inch.

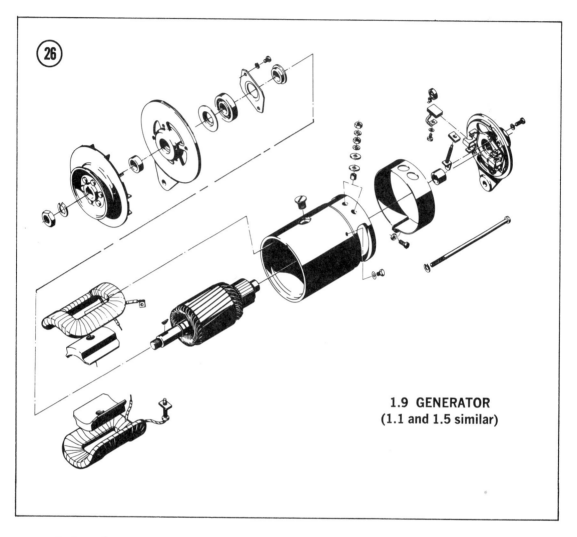

㉖

1.9 GENERATOR
(1.1 and 1.5 similar)

GENERATOR/ALTERNATOR VOLTAGE REGULATOR

Due to the critical adjustment procedures and tolerances necessary in repairing the regulator, procedures are not given here. If trouble is suspected in the regulator, refer service to an Opel dealer or automotive electrical shop or replace the unit with a new one.

IGNITION COIL

The ignition coil is connected to the distributor with high and low tension wires and to the car's wiring system. If faults are isolated to a defective coil, the coil must be replaced. To remove and install, disconnect wires leading to coil, unscrew and remove fixing screws, and install new coil. When installing, make certain the harness wire and distributor low tension wire are connected to the proper terminals.

SPARK PLUGS

The spark plugs should be removed periodically and cleaned or replaced depending on condition. Refer to Chapter Two for tune-up and adjustment specifications.

IGNITION CABLES

The high-tension ignition cables should be disconnected from the spark plugs, distributor, and ignition coil periodically and inspected for general condition. Inspect for cracks in the insulation, corroded terminals, and broken wires. If defective, replace wtih new cables.

LIGHT BULBS

Bulb replacement usually only requires removal of lens covers and lenses to gain access to defective bulbs. Visual inspection of light bulb filament(s) will usually indicate whether or not a bulb is defective. Other than the headlight sealed-beam units, all bulbs are easily removed by pushing in on the bulb and turning it counterclockwise.

FUSIBLE LINKS

Most Opels have fusible links between the starter motor post and voltage regulator. These links are the weakest point in the car's electrical system. Consisting of a short section of light-gauge wire soldered into a heavier wire, fusible links are intended to burn out if an overload occurs. This protects the wiring harness. Individual accessories are protected by fuses or circuit breakers.

The fusible links are located in the engine compartment, in position where fire is unlikely if they become overheated.

Figure 27 is a typical fusible link installation.

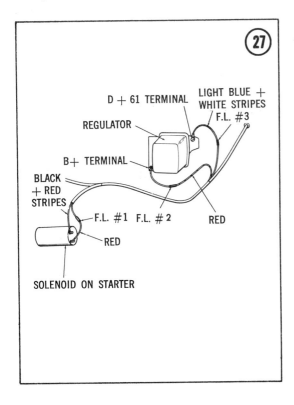

Fusible Link Removal/Installation

1. Disconnect battery cable from battery.

2. Disconnect the connector eye on the end of the fusible link.

3. Cut off other end of burned-out link, along with soldered joint.

4. Strip insulation from end of new fusible link and from end of wiring harness so that each will slide into soldering sleeve.

5. Crimp the new link in soldering sleeve and solder carefully.

6. Cover the new connection tightly with electrical tape.

7. Install new link connector eye on other end of fusible link.

NOTE: *A burned-out fusible link connected to the starter solenoid is usually indicated if all electrical accessories are dead or if the starter solenoid will not even click when the ignition switch is turned to start. The only other possible cause is a completely dead battery.*

FUSES

Whenever a failure occurs in any part of the electrical system, always check the fusible links, as shown in Figure 27, and then the fuses. A blown fuse is indicated by blackening or by a break of the metal element within the fuse. Usually the trouble that caused the fuse to blow is a short-circuit in the wiring. This may be caused by a worn-through insulation or by a wire that works its way loose at a connection and shorts to ground. Carry several spare fuses of proper amperage rating in the car.

Before replacing a fuse, determine what caused it to blow and correct the trouble. Never replace a fuse with one of a higher amperage rating than originally used. Never use tinfoil or other material to jump across fuse terminals. Failure to follow these basic rules could result in fire or damage to major parts. By following the wiring diagrams at the end of this chapter, the circuits protected by each fuse can be determined. The amperage rating is marked on each fuse.

8

CHAPTER NINE

CLUTCH, TRANSMISSION, AND DRIVE SHAFT

This chapter covers the clutch, 4-speed manual transmission, and drive shaft. Automatic transmission adjustments are given as appropriate for the average owner/mechanic. Transmission service and overhaul should be referred to an Opel dealer or transmission specialist.

> NOTE: *This chapter provides information on 1966-1975 models. Turn to the* Supplement *section, Chapter Nine, at back of this manual, for 1976 and later models.*

CLUTCH ASSEMBLY

Figure 1 illustrates the clutch assembly used with all 1.1, 1.5, and 1.9 liter engines. The clutch assembly is enclosed in the bell housing. On 1.1 engines, this housing and the transmission housing are one unit. The bell housing is a separate unit on 1.5 and 1.9 engines. See **Figures 2 and 3**.

The clutch release bearing and release fork are of conventional design; the fork pivots on a ball stud located opposite the control cable attaching point. The bearing flange fits over 2 vertical pins that are riveted to and extend into the eye of the yoke. The clutch pressure plate is of the radially slotted diaphragm spring type.

The clutch disc is a single dry plate type with torsional damper springs and spring leaves between facings to cushion application. The damper springs are preloaded.

Whenever the clutch is disassembled due to defective clutch disc, pressure plate, or release bearing, it is recommended that all of these parts be replaced at the same time. All parts are non-repairable; repair is by replacement.

Clutch Pedal Mechanism

Figure 4 shows a typical clutch pedal mechanism for the 1.1 engine. **Figure 5** is typical for all 1.5 and 1.9 engines except for GT models, which are shown in **Figure 6**.

Clutch Adjustment (1.1 Engine)

Pedal free-play (pedal lash) must be adjusted occasionally to compensate for normal wear of the clutch disc facings. As the facings wear thinner, pedal free-play decreases. The free-play shown in Figure 4 applies to 1970 and 1971 models. Free-play for 1966 through 1968 models should be ¾ in. to 1 in.; 1969 models should be ½ in. to 1 in. To adjust, proceed as follows.

1. Loosen locknut on ball stud end of cable.

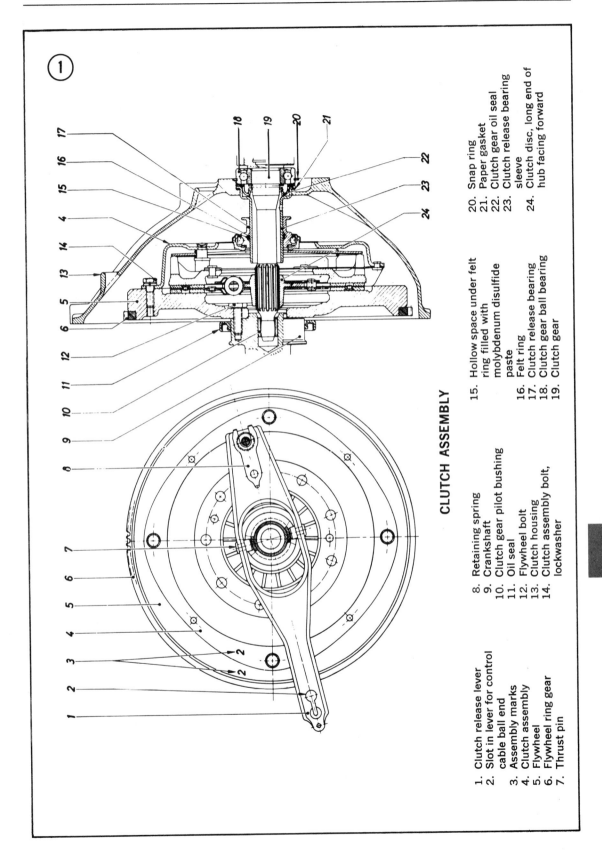

CLUTCH ASSEMBLY

1. Clutch release lever
2. Slot in lever for control cable ball end
3. Assembly marks
4. Clutch assembly
5. Flywheel
6. Flywheel ring gear
7. Thrust pin
8. Retaining spring
9. Crankshaft
10. Clutch gear pilot bushing
11. Oil seal
12. Flywheel bolt
13. Clutch housing
14. Clutch assembly bolt, lockwasher
15. Hollow space under felt ring filled with molybdenum disulfide paste
16. Felt ring
17. Clutch release bearing
18. Clutch gear ball bearing
19. Clutch gear
20. Snap ring
21. Paper gasket
22. Clutch gear oil seal
23. Clutch release bearing sleeve
24. Clutch disc, long end of hub facing forward

9

CLUTCH HOUSING (1.5 AND 1.9)

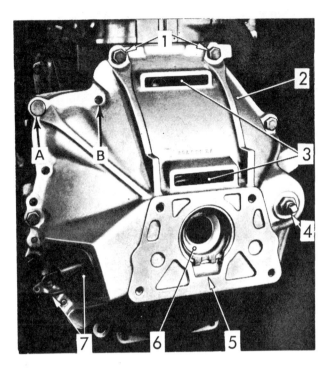

1.5, 1.9 BELL HOUSING

1. Upper attaching bolts
2. Flywheel housing
3. Vent holes
4. Clutch release lever ball stud and locknut
5. Recess in flywheel housing
6. Clutch release bearing sleeve
7. Clutch release lever and boot

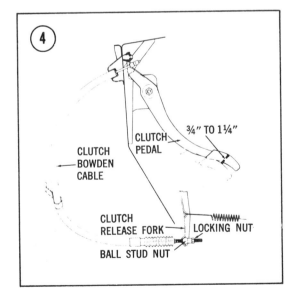

stops and then push it down until resistance is felt. Pedal travel should be as specified.

3. Tighten locknut against ball stud nut.

Clutch Adjustment (1.5, 1.9 Engines)

Clutch adjustment for early cars and all GT's is as given previously for the 1.1 engine. Pedal play should be ¾ in. to 1 in. On 1969 models, pedal play should be ½ in. to 1 in.

On late models, clutch actuation works without clutch pedal free-play. Readjustment of the clutch is required if the indicator lamp on the instrument panel lights up. If the indicator lights up, make certain the emergency brake is disengaged. If it is and the indicator is still on, the clutch must be adjusted as follows.

1. See Figure 5. Loosen ball stud locknut.

2. Adjust ball stud until the distance between clutch housing contacting surface and clutch release lever is 4¼ in.

2. Adjust ball stud nut to obtain proper pedal lash and free-play. Lift up on the pedal until it

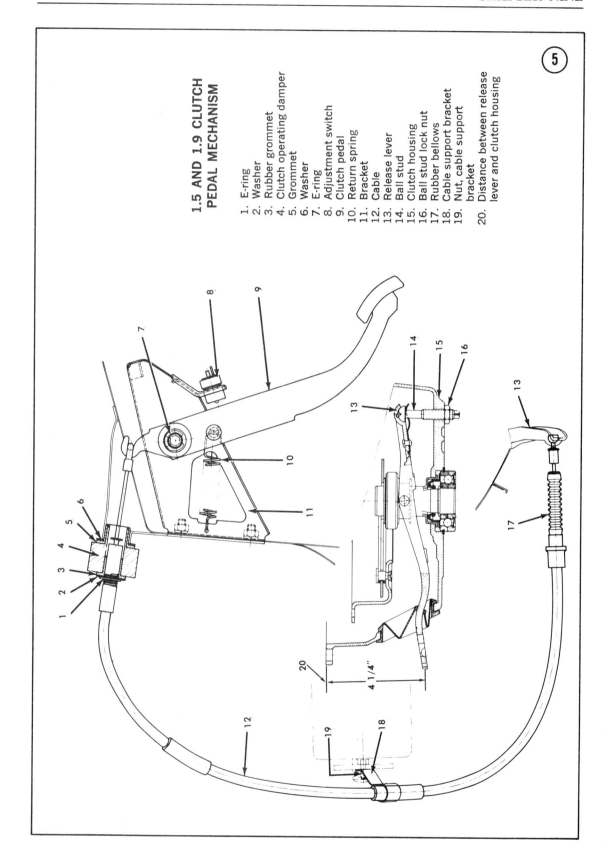

1.5 AND 1.9 CLUTCH PEDAL MECHANISM

1. E-ring
2. Washer
3. Rubber grommet
4. Clutch operating damper
5. Grommet
6. Washer
7. E-ring
8. Adjustment switch
9. Clutch pedal
10. Return spring
11. Bracket
12. Cable
13. Release lever
14. Ball stud
15. Clutch housing
16. Ball stud lock nut
17. Rubber bellows
18. Cable support bracket
19. Nut, cable support bracket
20. Distance between release lever and clutch housing

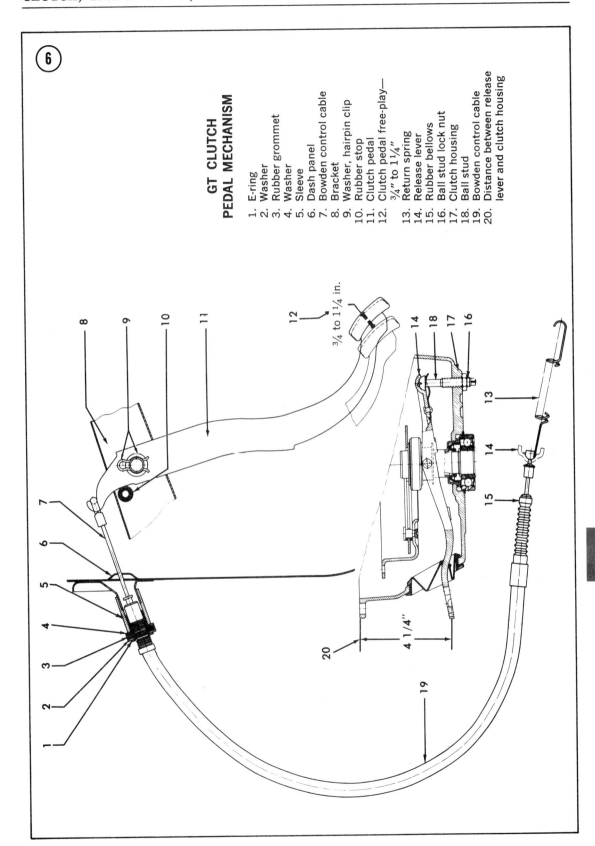

GT CLUTCH PEDAL MECHANISM

1. E-ring
2. Washer
3. Rubber grommet
4. Washer
5. Sleeve
6. Dash panel
7. Bowden control cable
8. Bracket
9. Washer, hairpin clip
10. Rubber stop
11. Clutch pedal
12. Clutch pedal free-play—3/4" to 1 1/4"
13. Return spring
14. Release lever
15. Rubber bellows
16. Ball stud lock nut
17. Clutch housing
18. Ball stud
19. Bowden control cable
20. Distance between release lever and clutch housing

3. Tighten ball stud locknut. Check to make certain the indicator is not on.

Clutch Removal

1. Remove transmission, as discussed later in this chapter.

2. Check for assembly alignment marks at the clutch cover flange and flywheel rim. If no marks are visible, mark both parts for reassembly.

3. Remove clutch pressure plate retaining bolts. Loosen gradually and alternately so that pressure plate cover is not distorted.

4. Remove pressure plate and clutch disc. Be careful not to get dirt or grease on clutch disc facings if the disc is to be reused.

5. Check friction surfaces of flywheel and pressure plate for burns (blue-tinted areas) and scoring. If the flywheel is badly scored, remove it from crankshaft and have it resurfaced. Minor damage or burns can sometimes be removed with fine emery cloth. On the pressure plate, check ends of release fingers for wear. If defective, replace pressure plate.

6. Check clutch disc facings for wear and contamination. Check condition of springs. If defective or badly worn, replace with new clutch disc.

7. If the clutch disc appears in good condition, use a dial gauge to check lateral runout. Lateral runout must not exceed 0.016 in. (0.406mm).

8. Check clutch disc hub for general condition and easy slip fit onto transmission shaft drive splines. Do not lubricate. If defective, replace clutch disc.

9. Check release bearing for wear, binding, and roughness. If defective, remove and replace. Do not use solvent to clean release bearing or clutch disc.

10. Check pilot bearing surface on transmission drive shaft and pilot bearing in rear of crankshaft. If the pilot bearing is defective, use a remover and slide hammer as shown in **Figure 7** to withdraw the bearing from the crankshaft.

11. Install new bearing as shown in **Figure 8**. Do not damage rear main bearing seal ring.

12. To assemble and install, reverse steps used during removal and disassembly. During installation, use a pilot tool, as shown in **Figure 9**,

1. Flywheel
2. Clutch assembly
3. Assembly marks
4. Clutch aligning arbor J-22934

to properly align clutch disc before tightening pressure plate fixing bolts. The clutch disc must be centered exactly so that splines on transmission drive shaft will slide through the clutch disc and the end will be in proper contact with pilot bearing in crankshaft. Gradually tighten pressure plate fixing bolts to 15 ft.-lb. Make certain pressure plate and flywheel marks are properly aligned.

Release Bearing/Yoke Removal

1. See Figure 4. Disconnect clutch return spring at transmission and remove yoke boot from transmission case.

2. Slip yoke from ball stud and bearing flange. Slide ball stud and bearing flange forward over spline shaft.

3. Check release bearing for wear and smoothness of operation. Check for loss of lubricant. If release bearing is defective, replace it.

4. To assemble and install, reverse Steps 1-3. Pack a small amount of wheel bearing grease in both inner and outer grooves of release bearing. Lightly lubricate ball stud and yoke socket with graphite grease.

MANUAL TRANSMISSION

The manual transmission used in the Opel is a 4-forward and one-reverse gear unit. All forward gears are synchronized. Two models have been used; one with the 1.1 engine and the other with the 1.5 and 1.9 engines. Details of both units are given in the following discussion.

Figure 10 shows a cutaway view of the 1.1 engine model; Figure 11 the 1.5 and 1.9 engine model. On the 1.1 engine model, the clutch housing is part of the transmission case. On the 1.5 and 1.9 engine model, the clutch housing is separate from the cast iron main transmission case.

Several special tools are required to disassemble the transmission. For this reason, it may be quicker and cheaper to refer major overhaul to a transmission specialist or Opel dealer after the transmission has been removed from the car. The following sections show the special tools in actual use.

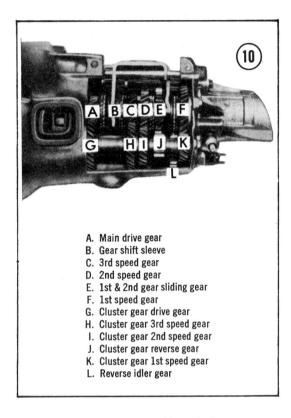

A. Main drive gear
B. Gear shift sleeve
C. 3rd speed gear
D. 2nd speed gear
E. 1st & 2nd gear sliding gear
F. 1st speed gear
G. Cluster gear drive gear
H. Cluster gear 3rd speed gear
I. Cluster gear 2nd speed gear
J. Cluster gear reverse gear
K. Cluster gear 1st speed gear
L. Reverse idler gear

Gearshift Lever Removal/Installation

Several types of gearshift levers have been used including standard, sport, and 1900 versions. Refer to appropriate steps for your model.

Standard/Sport Type

1. See **Figure 12**. Remove retaining ring (2) and pull gearshift lever upper part from lower part.

2. Press upper and lower snap ring out of groove in gearshift lever lower part (1). Remove and disassemble parts.

> NOTE: *On sport gearshift lever, snap ring (3) secures the lower end of the lever.*

3. To install, reverse above steps. On standard lever, use tool J-21709 to secure lock cap, as shown in **Figure 13**.

Model 1900

1. See **Figure 14**. Unscrew console from floor panel by removing attaching screws. Small consoles use 3 screws. Large consoles use 4. The

9

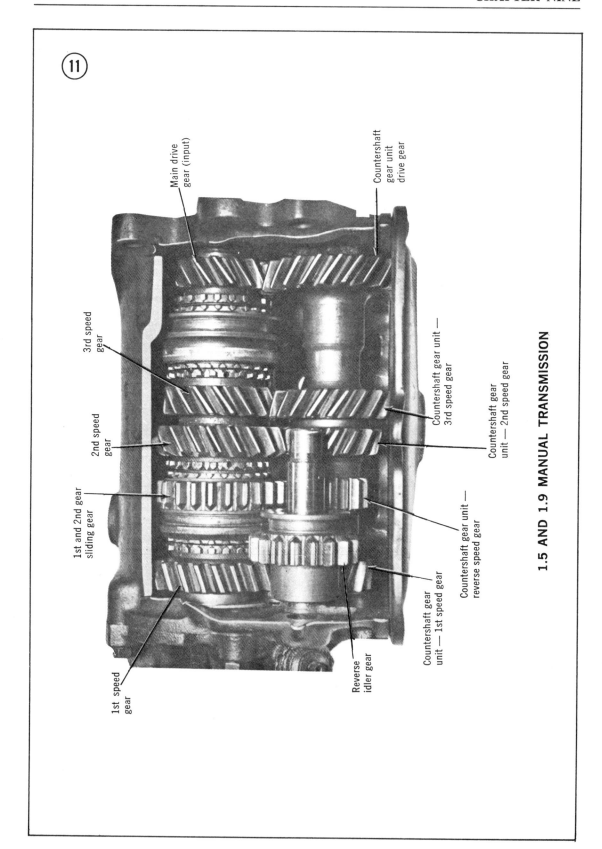

⑪

Main drive gear (input)

Countershaft gear unit drive gear

3rd speed gear

2nd speed gear

1st and 2nd gear sliding gear

1st speed gear

Reverse idler gear

Countershaft gear unit — 1st speed gear

Countershaft gear unit — reverse speed gear

Countershaft gear unit — 3rd speed gear

Countershaft gear unit — 2nd speed gear

1.5 AND 1.9 MANUAL TRANSMISSION

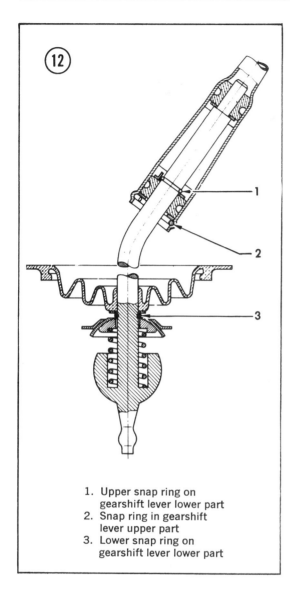

1. Upper snap ring on
   gearshift lever lower part
2. Snap ring in gearshift
   lever upper part
3. Lower snap ring on
   gearshift lever lower part

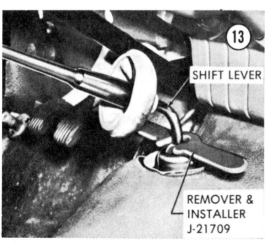

SHIFT LEVER

REMOVER &
INSTALLER
J-21709

fourth screw can be removed after removal of
the ashtray.

2. Remove rubber bellows from cover plate.
From under the car, loosen protective cap from
around intermediate shift lever.

3. See **Figure 15**. Unhook gearshift lever tension
spring and remove retaining washer. Push pivot
pin out of intermediate shift lever and remove
gearshift lever.

4. To install, reverse Steps 1-3. During installation, lubricate support and spherical end of shift
finger with grease.

5. See **Figure 16**. After installation, check that
pull ring can be lifted up from 0.04 to 0.08 in.
(1.016 to 2.032mm). This is distance B in the

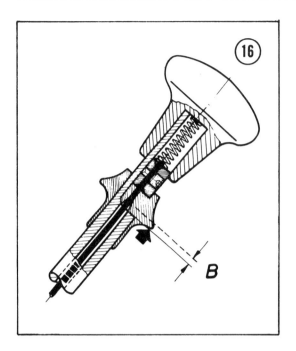

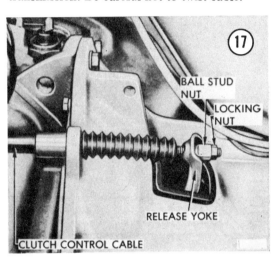

illustration. The stop sleeve must rest against the intermediate shift lever. If not, loosen control wire attachment threaded pin and adjust distance B by lifting up pull ring and retightening the threaded pin.

Transmission Removal/Installation (1.1 Engine)

1. Remove air cleaner and disconnect throttle rod from carburetor and rear support. Disconnect battery cables from battery.

2. Jack up the car and support it securely with jackstands.

> #### WARNING
> *Never get under a car supported by a jack only. Should the jack fail, serious injury or death could result.*

3. Loosen bolts fixing front exhaust pipe to exhaust manifold.

4. Remove gearshift lever on standard models with tool shown in Figure 13. Place tool around lower shift lever, then push down on lock cap with tool and turn counterclockwise until cap unlocks.

5. On the sport model, remove 3 cover plate sheet metal screws and pull rubber boot on gearshift lever upwards. Remove snap ring from groove in shift housing.

6. See **Figure 17**. Remove clutch cable-to-fork locknut and adjusting nut. Remove cable from transmission. Be careful not to twist cable.

7. Disconnect both wires from the back-up lamp switch.

8. Remove 3 cap screws from flywheel cover plate between the transmission and oil pan. Remove the cover plate.

9. Disconnect speedometer cable from speedometer gear housing.

10. See **Figure 18**. Unhook parking brake cable return spring and remove cable adjusting nut, equalizer, and spacer.

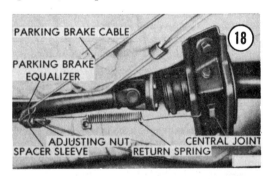

11. See **Figure 19**. Remove one bolt attaching speedometer gear housing and rear of transmission to underbody. Loosen the other bolt but do not remove.

12. Disconnect drive shaft at central joint. Make match marks on U-joint and drive pinion extension flange so they can be reassembled in the same relative positions. Loosen bolt locks and

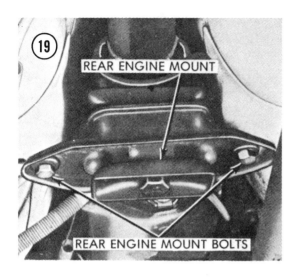

remove bolts or nuts. Move drive shaft forward, lower rear end of shaft, and slide assembly toward the rear. Remove thrust spring.

13. Install a plug in the rear of the transmission to prevent loss of lubricant.

14. See **Figure 20**. Remove lower bolt on each side fixing transmission case to crankcase. Install guide pins J-21722 to prevent warping of clutch disc. Support rear of transmission and loosen 4 remaining bolts.

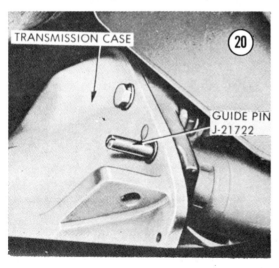

15. Place jack under lower front generator-to-block bracket. Remove right engine mount-to-crossmember bracket bolts.

16. Raise engine until sufficient clearance is acquired for transmission removal. As the engine is raised, the transmission will lower.

17. Remove remaining transmission case-to-crankcase bolts. Support transmission with a jack equipped with wheels. Slide transmission backward off guide pins and clutch disc splines until the pressure plate is clear. Be careful not to damage clutch splines or transmission drive shaft.

18. Lower transmission jack and pull transmission out from under car.

19. To install, reverse these steps. Make certain the clutch disc is exactly centered so the transmission drive shaft indexes with clutch disc splines. If the clutch disc has been moved, center it with a centering tool or a junk transmission drive shaft (main shaft) removed from another transmission. Torque mounting bolts as specified at the end of this chapter.

Transmission Removal/Installation (1.5, 1.9 Engines)

The procedures for removal and installation of the transmission are essentially the same as described for the 1.1 engine, with the following exceptions.

1. Disconnect the drive shaft from the transmission flange.

2. Remove one bolt attaching rear engine mount (transmission case extension housing) to underbody. Loosen other bolt but do not remove.

3. Remove transmission case-to-clutch housing attaching bolts. Remove transmission as previously described. It is not necessary to jack up the engine to lower transmission as described for the 1.1 engine.

4. For installation, reverse the preceding steps.

AUTOMATIC TRANSMISSION

Maintenance and repair of the automatic transmission is complex and should be referred to your dealer or transmission specialist. The following checks and adjustments should help prevent costly repairs. **Figure 21** is a cutaway view of the 3-speed automatic transmission.

Checking and Adding Fluid

Check the fluid level every 3,000 miles and at each oil change. The FULL and ADD marks on

9

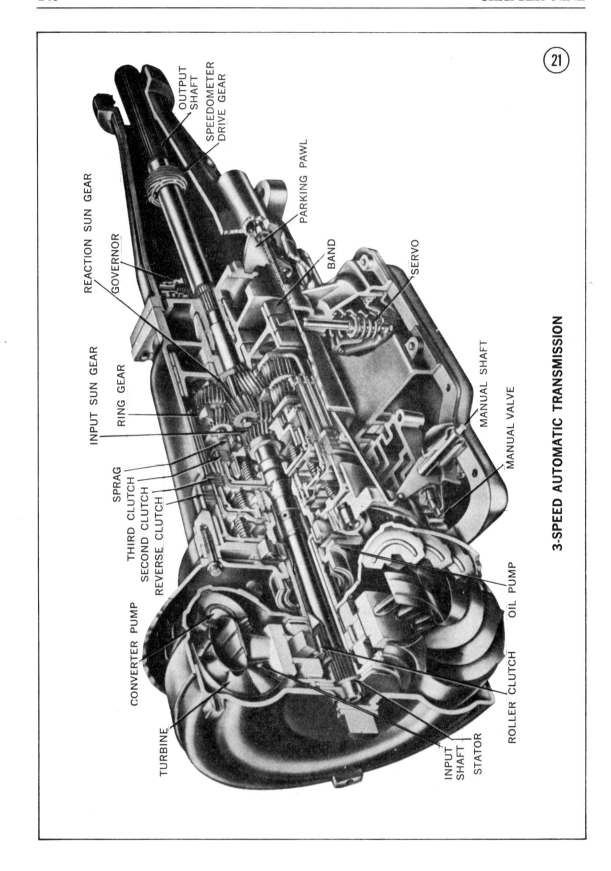

㉑

REACTION SUN GEAR

OUTPUT SHAFT

SPEEDOMETER DRIVE GEAR

GOVERNOR

PARKING PAWL

BAND

SERVO

INPUT SUN GEAR

RING GEAR

MANUAL SHAFT

MANUAL VALVE

SPRAG

THIRD CLUTCH

SECOND CLUTCH

REVERSE CLUTCH

OIL PUMP

CONVERTER PUMP

TURBINE

INPUT SHAFT

STATOR

ROLLER CLUTCH

3-SPEED AUTOMATIC TRANSMISSION

the transmission dipstick indicate one pint difference. To determine fluid level, proceed as follows.

1. Start the engine and drive the car until normal operating temperature is reached. The transmission oil temperature should be 180°F.

2. Place gearshift in PARK position and start engine. Do not race engine. Move gearshift lever through all driving ranges, including reverse. Return gearshift lever to PARK position.

3. Make certain car is on level surface. Remove dipstick from transmission and clean it with lint-free cloth or paper. Insert dipstick into transmission and remove. Look at level shown on dipstick while the engine is running.

4. If the fluid level is not at the full mark, replenish with high quality automatic transmission fluid, such as Dexron. Do not overfill as foaming, loss of fluid, or transmission damage may result.

Draining Oil Pan and Replacing Strainer Assembly

1. Raise car on hoist or jack up and support with jackstands. Have a container handy to collect draining fluid.

2. Remove oil pan and discard gasket.

3. Drain fluid from oil pan. Clean pan with suitable solvent and dry thoroughly.

4. Remove strainer assembly and gasket. Discard both.

5. Install new oil strainer gasket and strainer assembly.

6. Fit new gasket to oil pan and install pan. Tighten bolts to 10 ft.-lb. Do not overtighten as leaks may result.

7. Lower car and add approximately 3 pints of transmission fluid through filler tube.

8. Check fluid level as previously described. With engine and transmission cold, the level should be approximately ¼ in. below add mark on dipstick. Replenish as necessary. Do not overfill.

9. Drive the car until normal operating temperature is reached. Recheck fluid level, as previously described.

Oil Leakage Check

Abnormal oil usage usually indicates leaks that should be stopped before severe damage is done. To inspect for oil leaks, proceed as follows.

1. Raise car on hoist or jack up and place on jackstands.

2. Clean outside of transmission case with suitable solvent to remove dirt and oil accumulation.

3. Start engine and warm it to normal operating temperature.

4. Move gearshift lever to drive to increase oil pressure and circulation within transmission.

5. Inspect all outside surfaces for signs of leaks. Leakage of transmission fluid is distinguishable by its reddish color.

6. If leaks are detected, refer service and repair to transmission specialist.

Detent Cable Adjustment

1. See **Figure 22**. Adjustment is done with the adjuster nut. Loosen or tighten adjuster nut so that the ball is positioned against the lever as discussed below.

2. Move accelerator control cable to full throttle. The detent cable ball must rest firmly against the lever, as shown in **Figure 23**. Adjust with adjuster nut, as required.

3. To check the adjustment, pull the linkage to full throttle position, as shown in **Figure 24**.

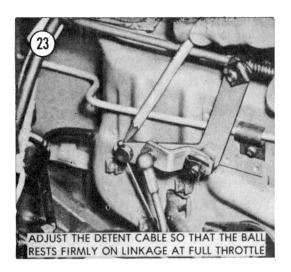

ADJUST THE DETENT CABLE SO THAT THE BALL RESTS FIRMLY ON LINKAGE AT FULL THROTTLE

3/8"

Pull detent cable through detent. If an approximate ⅜ in. travel is obtained between slide linkage and stops on linkage rod with noticeable resistance due to detent valve being opened, the adjustment is correct. If not, readjust.

DRIVE SHAFT

Figure 25 shows the drive shaft used on the 1.1 engine models; **Figure 26** the 1.5 and 1.9 engine models.

Removal

1. Jack up rear of car and support on jackstands at rear jack brackets.

2. Disconnect parking brake cable equalizer from rod.

3. Unhook the parking brake cable from the floor panel (1.5 and 1.9 engines).

4. Loosen rear engine mount bolts and remove only one of them (1.1 engine).

5. Make match marks on U-joint and drive pinion extension shaft flange so they can be installed in the same relative positions.

6. Loosen bolt locks and remove bolts or nuts.

7. Work drive shaft slightly forward. Lower rear end of drive shaft and slide assembly toward rear. Lower drive shaft and remove from under car. Remove thrust spring.

8. Install plug in transmission or extension housing to prevent loss of lubricant.

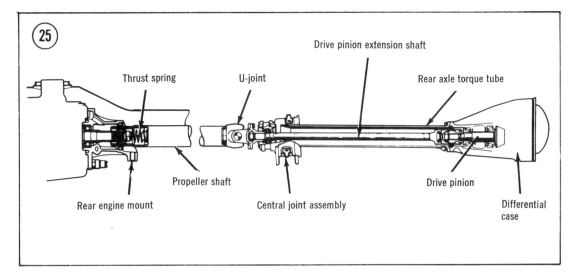

Thrust spring — U-joint — Drive pinion extension shaft — Rear axle torque tube — Rear engine mount — Propeller shaft — Central joint assembly — Drive pinion — Differential case

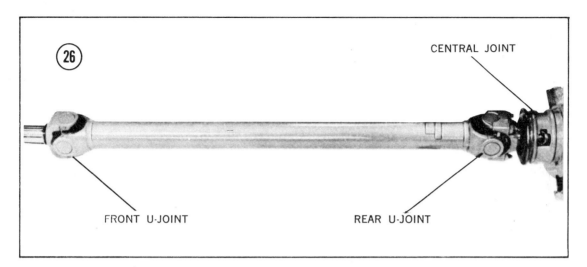

CENTRAL JOINT

FRONT U-JOINT   REAR U-JOINT

Installation

To install, reverse the removal procedure and perform the following.

1. On 1.1 engine models, affix small end of thrust spring on end of transmission output shaft and slide drive shaft through the oil seal and onto the barrel spline. Do not damage oil seal.

2. On 1.5 and 1.9 engine models, slide thrust spring onto transmission output shaft and slide drive shaft through oil seal and onto transmission output shaft. Do not damage oil seal.

3. Align rear universal joint and pinion flange match marks. Install fixing bolts, nuts, and lock plates. Tighten bolts to 18 ft.-lb. on 1.1 models and 11 ft.-lb. on 1.5 and 1.9 models.

4. Bend back tangs on lock plates to secure bolts and nuts in place.

5. On 1.1 engine models, install rear engine mounting bolt and torque bolts to 30 ft.-lb.

Central Joint Disassembly/Assembly

Disassembly and assembly require special tools and knowledge. Refer service to your Opel dealer.

9

CHAPTER TEN

FRONT SUSPENSION, WHEELS,
AND STEERING

This chapter covers the front suspension, wheels, and steering assemblies. The front suspension and steering are designed to be maintenance-free. Periodically, inspect the components for looseness, wear, or damage, and replace if necessary.

The average owner/mechanic should refer major overhaul and/or adjustment of suspension or steering to an Opel dealer.

NOTE: *This chapter provides information on 1966-1975 models. Refer to the* Supplement *section, Chapter Ten, at back of this manual, for 1976 and later models.*

FRONT SUSPENSION

Several different front suspension systems have been used. **Figure 1** shows the suspension system used on most early models equipped with drum brakes. **Figure 2** applies to GT's equipped with front disc brakes and **Figure 3** applies to late 1900 and Manta models.

Opel and GT

The Opel and GT have unequal length control arms with transverse leaf springs. Models with the 1.1 engine have 2 transverse leaf

springs; GT's and early 1.5-1.9 models have 3. The entire front suspension is attached to the front crossmember and can be removed as a complete unit if required.

The GT engines are not supported by mounting brackets but rest on a separate crossmember. The front suspension crossmember of all 3 engines is reinforced at point of attachment to the frame. A damper plate is installed between the crossmember and frame. Ball-joints provide the pivoting points between the control arms and steering knuckles. Upward movement of the control arms is limited by 2 large rubber bumpers attached to the crossmember.

Road shock is dampened by the double, direct-acting shock absorbers and the transverse double or triple steel band springs. The shock absorbers limit the downward travel of the control arms.

Model 1900 and Manta

The late model 1900 and Manta suspension is shown in Figure 3.

The front suspension has independent coil springs and control arms of different length. The stabilizer acts as a tie strut. The end of the stabilizer is supported in a rubber bushing that is located in a piece of tubing welded into the longer control arm. The horizontal shafts of the

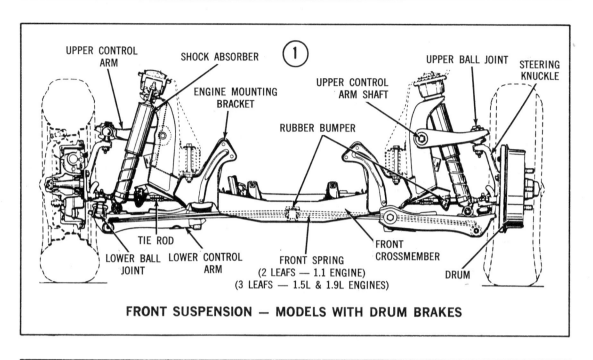

FRONT SUSPENSION — MODELS WITH DRUM BRAKES

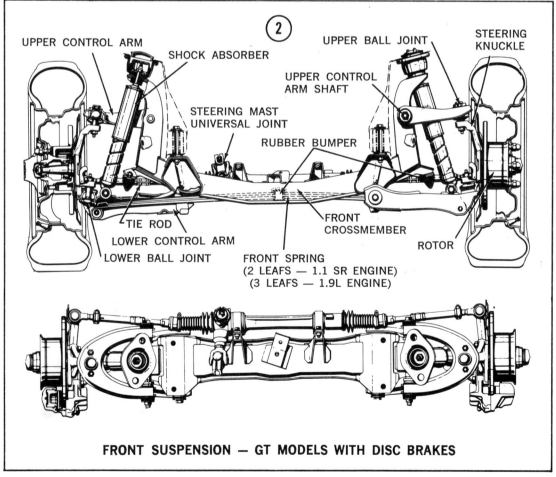

FRONT SUSPENSION — GT MODELS WITH DISC BRAKES

10

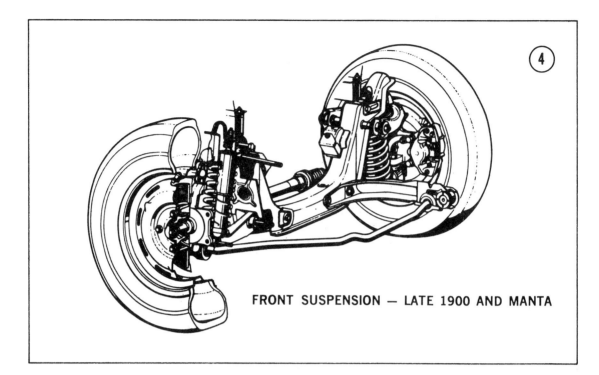

FRONT SUSPENSION — LATE 1900 AND MANTA

upper and lower control arm are not in parallel, which minimizes brake torque and provides an anti-dive effect. Each lower control arm is connected to its steering knuckle by a ball-joint.

The 2 crossmember-to-body supports are attached to the horizontal part of the crossmember with 2 bolts. The outer bolt is the support for the lower control arm. Since the bolt is inserted from the front, the crossmember-to-body support can be removed without the lower control arm. The inner bolt attaches to the steering. The engine damper blocks are bolted to the inside of the crossmember.

Removal (Opel, GT)

1. Set parking brake and block rear wheels.

2. Jack up the front of the car and support with jackstands at the jacking brackets.

3. Place a jackstand at the rear of the engine to support the engine/transmission assemblies.

4. *(Opel)* See Figure 5 in Chapter Four. Remove steering mast clamp bolt. Mark location of shaft to flange.

5. Remove steering mast guide sleeve stop bolt from mast jacket bracket as shown in Figure 6, Chapter Four.

6. *(GT)* See **Figure 4**. Loosen steering mast at lower universal joint. Loosen and remove clamp bolt. Loosen clamp at upper universal joint and lift steering mast upwards until it is free at the lower universal joint.

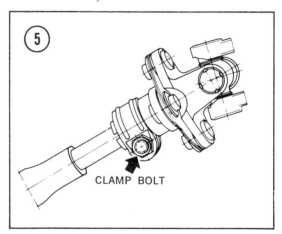

CLAMP BOLT

7. Disconnect brake lines at brake hose. Plug end of hose to prevent loss of brake fluid.

8. Disconnect shock absorber mountings at upper shock mounting bolts. On GT models, remove air cleaner first.

9. *(GT)* Detach radiator from support on crossmember.

10. Loosen and remove engine mounting nuts.

11. Remove front suspension crossmember attaching nuts and lower the crossmember. Remove front suspension from car.

Installation (Opel, GT)

To install, reverse preceding steps and perform the following:

1. Attach crossmember to front frame rail. Tighten to 36 ft.-lb.

2. Push steering column downward until a ⅛ in. (3.175mm) clearance exists between steering wheel hub and switch cover.

3. *(Opel)* Center steering wheel in straight-ahead position and make certain wheels are facing straight ahead. Tighten steering mast clamp bolt to 15 ft.-lb.

4. *(GT)* Center steering wheel and wheels in straight-ahead position. Tighten clamp bolt at the lower universal joint to 22 ft.-lb. Tighten clamp at the upper universal joint to 14 ft.-lb.

5. Install mast guide sleeve stop bolt. Always use new lock plate.

6. Remove jackstands and lower car. Have wheel alignment checked and adjusted as required.

Removal (Model 1900, Manta)

1. Set parking brake and block rear wheels.

2. See **Figure 5**. Install hooks J-23697 to assure the proper loading of the suspension bushings and mounts.

3. Raise front of car and support with jackstands below front frame.

4. Remove front wheels. Remove guard plate, as shown in **Figure 6**.

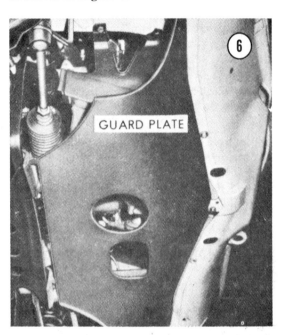

5. Remove brake line retainers on both sides of car. Unscrew brake calipers (Chapter Twelve) and suspend them in wheel house. It is necessary to unscrew upper control arm ball-joint. Do not turn upper control arm ball-joint flange, as camber will be affected.

6. Suspend the engine with a suitable support such as that shown in **Figure 7**.

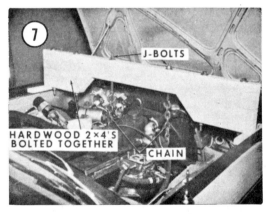

7. See **Figure 8**. Unscrew lower steering mast clamp bolt from pinion flange.

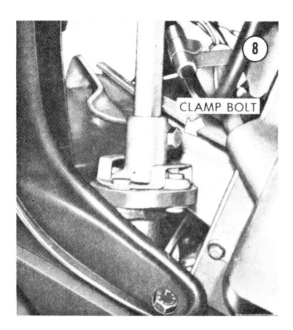

8. Detach front left and right engine mounts from damper block.

9. See **Figure 9**. On top and rear, detach front suspension assembly from frame at the cross-member-to-body support and lower suspension with a jack.

Installation (Model 1900, Manta)

To install, reverse removal procedure and perform the following:

1. With jack, lift front suspension assembly so that attaching points coincide. At the same time, insert lower steering mast into pinion flange, as shown in **Figure 10**. Bolt rear crossmember-to-body support to frame. Tighten to 51 ft.-lb. Use a suitable tool to hold damper bushing so that it does not turn. It may be necessary to detach heat deflector plate on right side to hold bushing.

2. Install bolts holding front suspension assembly to frame. Tighten to 40 ft.-lb.

3. Tighten lower steering mast to pinion flange to 22 ft.-lb.

4. Install upper control arm ball-joints. Tighten to 20 ft.-lb. Always use new self-locking nuts.

5. Install guard plate and front wheels. Tighten wheel nuts to 65 ft.-lb.

Inspection/Replacement

Inspect all parts for wear, damage, and loss of lubricant. Disassembly and replacement of defective parts requires special tools and knowledge. Refer such service to your dealer.

SHOCK ABSORBERS

Removal/Installation

The following steps generally apply to all models. Some models have a plastic cap installed over the upper end attachment in the engine compartment. Remove the plastic cap, if so equipped. On GT models, remove air cleaner to gain access to upper attachment. On models with coil springs around the shock absorbers, it is necessary to compress and retain the coil spring so that the shock absorber can be removed.

1. Jack up front end of car and support it with jackstands.

2. See **Figure 11**. Remove nut from shock absorber stud at upper end.

3. Remove attaching nut, lockwasher, and bolt from lower end of shock absorber.

4. Compress the shock absorber and remove it from the car.

5. Inspect shock absorber for damage and seal leaks. Defective shock absorbers must be replaced. Always replace upper and lower rubber grommets when replacing a shock absorber.

6. To install, reverse Steps 1-5. Tighten lower bolt and nut to 30 ft.-lb.

7. Install nut on upper stud. Tighten nut until distance from top of nut to top of stud is approximately ½ in.

FRONT WHEEL BEARINGS

Adjustment

1. Jack up front of car and support it with jackstands.

2. Remove hub caps.

3. Pry off grease cap. Straighten, remove, and discard cotter pin.

4. Loosen and remove spindle nut from steering knuckle.

5. Clean spindle nut and steering knuckle threads thoroughly with suitable solvent.

6. Lightly lubricate spindle nut and steering knuckle threads with light oil.

7. Thread nut onto steering knuckle. Tighten to 18 ft.-lb. while rotating wheel.

8. Back off nut ¼ turn. If slot and cotter pin hole do not align, back nut off ½ turn or until the slot and hole align. Do not tighten.

9. Install new cotter pin; bend over both legs.

10. Check that there is a small amount of end-play in the wheel and that the nut is loose. These conditions indicate a properly adjusted wheel bearing.

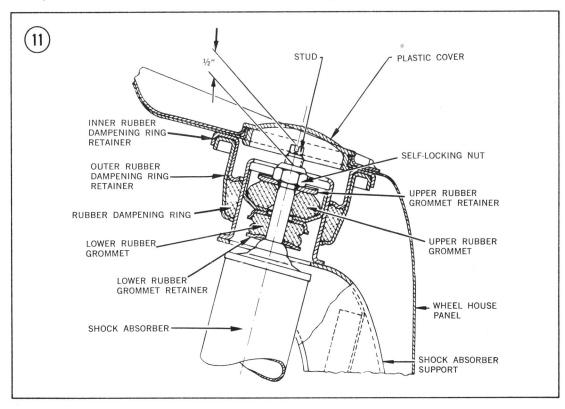

(11)

½″ — STUD — PLASTIC COVER

INNER RUBBER DAMPENING RING RETAINER

OUTER RUBBER DAMPENING RING RETAINER

RUBBER DAMPENING RING

LOWER RUBBER GROMMET

LOWER RUBBER GROMMET RETAINER

SHOCK ABSORBER

SELF-LOCKING NUT

UPPER RUBBER GROMMET RETAINER

UPPER RUBBER GROMMET

WHEEL HOUSE PANEL

SHOCK ABSORBER SUPPORT

10

WHEEL ALIGNMENT

Due to the special equipment required, wheel alignment should be referred to an Opel dealer or specialist in this field. Before having the wheels aligned, the following checks should be performed.

1. Check that tire pressure is correct.

2. Check adjustment of front wheel bearings, as discussed earlier.

3. Check condition of bushings and rubber parts of steering and suspension assemblies. If damage or looseness is apparent, replace the defective parts.

4. Check shock absorber efficiency and replace as required. Specifications for front wheel alignment are shown in **Table 1**.

STEERING

Tie Rod Removal

1. Thoroughly clean tie rods and gear assembly with suitable solvent to prevent dirt from entering the steering gear assembly.

2. Remove cotter pins fixing nuts on tie rod ends. Remove nuts and discard cotter pins.

3. See **Figure 12**. Use a remover to pull outer tie rod ball studs out of steering arms.

4. Remove clamp securing one end of rubber bellows to tie rods. Slip bellows off tie rods to expose nut and/or lock plates, as shown in **Figure 13**.

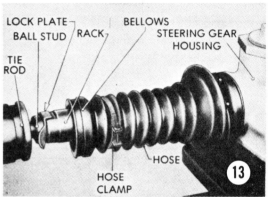

5. *(GT)* Bend up round edges of lock plate from tie rod ball studs. Unscrew ball studs from rack. See **Figure 14**.

Table 1   FRONT WHEEL ALIGNMENT SPECIFICATIONS

Year	Model	Caster (degrees)	Camber (degrees)	Toe-in Min.-Max. (inches)
1966-1968	All	$1\frac{1}{2}, +1, -2$	$\frac{3}{4}, +\frac{1}{2}, -1$	1/32 · 1/8
1969	Kadett	$1\frac{1}{2}, +1, -2$	$\frac{3}{4}, +\frac{1}{2}, -1$	1/32 · 1/8
	GT	$1\frac{1}{2}, +1, -2$	$\frac{1}{2}, +\frac{1}{2}, -1$	1/32 · 1/8
1970	Kadett	2 ± 1	$1 \pm \frac{1}{2}$	1/32 · 1/8
	GT	3 ± 1	$1 \pm \frac{1}{2}$	1/32 · 1/8
1971-1973	1900	$3\frac{1}{2} \pm 1$	$-1 \pm \frac{1}{2}$	1/8 · 3/16
	GT	3 ± 1	$1 \pm \frac{1}{2}$	1/32 · 1/8
	Opel	2 ± 1	$1 \pm \frac{1}{2}$	1/32 · 1/8
1974	All	$+3$ to $+6$	$-1 \pm \frac{1}{2}$	1/8 · 3/16
1975	All	$+3$ to $+6$	$+\frac{1}{4}$ to $-1\frac{1}{4}$	$1/8 \pm 1/32$

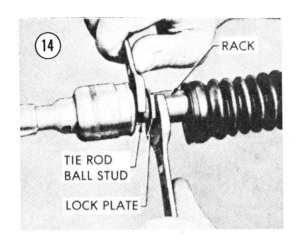

6. Unscrew tie rod from axial joint. Hold rack with wrench to prevent damage to rack teeth.

Tie Rod Installation (GT)

1. Install new lock plates onto tie rod ball studs. Screw ball studs into rack while holding bent tab of lock plates against flat on rack. Torque ball studs to 43 ft.-lb. See **Figure 15**. Hold rack with wrench to prevent damage to rack teeth.

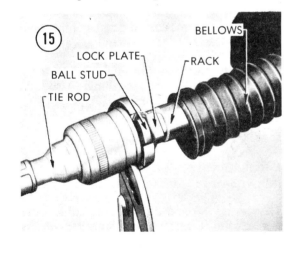

2. Bend round edges of lock plate over flat on ball stud to lock ball stud in position.

3. Install rubber bellows and hose clamps over tie rods and adjust clamp so that wire ends point in same direction as adjusting screw. Check bellows; they must not be twisted and must expand and retract properly.

4. Connect outer tie rod ball stud to steering arm. Install and tighten castellated nut to 29 ft.-lb. Install cotter pin and bend over ends.

Tie Rod Installation (Except GT)

1. Screw tie rod into axial joint.

2. Attach tie rod end to steering arm and tighten nut to 29 ft.-lb. Install new cotter pin and bend over ends.

3. Adjust toe-in to specification. Tighten both tie rod locknuts to 47 ft.-lb.

4. Attach the rubber bellows to the axial joint with hose clamp.

STEERING GEAR

The steering gear is of the rack and pinion type. The steering gear pinion shaft is connected to the lower end of the steering column and moves the rack to the left or right to transmit the turning motion of the steering wheel to the tie rods and steering arms.

The steering gear housing is held to the cross-member by rubber bushings and clamps. The bushings prevent driving noises and vibrations from being transmitted into the passenger compartment. The pinion shaft is seated in the upper part of the steering gear housing and is supported by a needle bearing in the upper housing and a bushing in the lower housing. The pinion is not adjustable. The rack and the pinion shaft are held in mesh by a thrust spring and shell, as shown in **Figure 16**. The pressure of the thrust spring may be changed by the adjusting screw. The spring forces the sintered bronze shell against the rack, which is held against the pinion shaft. **Figure 17** is an exploded view of the steering gear assembly.

Steering Gear Adjustment

1. Set steering gear to high point by positioning front wheels straight ahead with steering wheel centered. The flexible coupling bolt hole must be positioned horizontally (parallel) to the rack.

2. Thread adjusting screw into steering gear housing until resistance is felt.

3. Back off adjusting screw ⅛ to ¼ turn.

4. Tighten locknut to 43 ft.-lb.

5. Fill area under pinion shaft rubber boot with steering gear lubricant and slide boot into position.

10

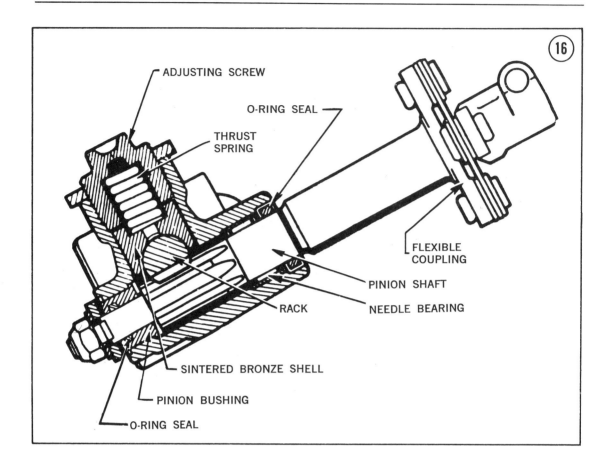

Steering Gear Removal (GT)

1. Remove rubber knee protector pad.

2. Loosen clamp fixing flexible coupling to steering shaft.

3. See **Figure 18**. Remove stop bolt from underside of steering column. Pull steering wheel rearward approximately 3 inches.

4. Remove cotter pins from left and right tie rod ends and unscrew nuts. Discard cotter pins.

5. Use a remover to press tie rod ball studs out of steering arms.

6. Remove 4 attaching bolts fixing steering gear to front suspension crossmember and lift off the steering gear assembly and the tie rods. See **Figure 19**.

7. Inspect all parts for wear or damage. Replace any parts with visible defects.

Steering Gear Installation (GT)

To install, reverse removal procedure and perform the following:

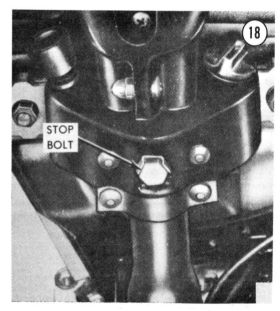

1. Install steering gear on front suspension crossmember. Tighten bolts to 18 ft.-lb.

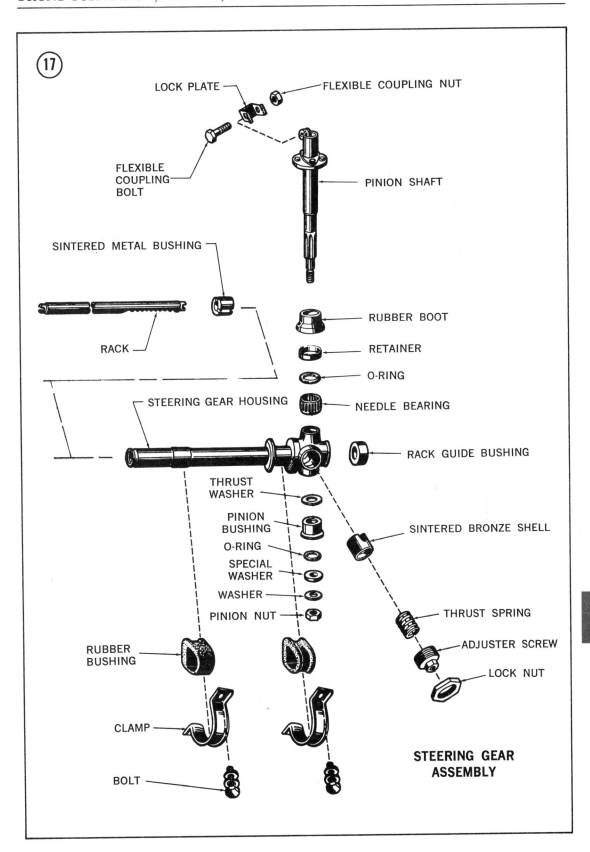

STEERING GEAR ASSEMBLY

10

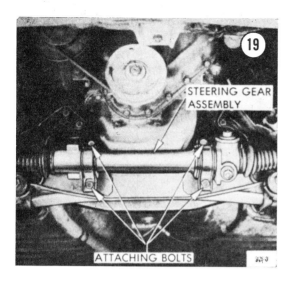

2. Position tie rod ball studs in steering arms. Install nuts and tighten to 29 ft.-lb. Install new cotter pins and bend over ends.

3. Turn steering wheel so that flat or cutout surface on lower part of steering shaft is parallel to flexible coupling bolt hole.

4. Install lower end of steering shaft in the flexible coupling. Adjust dimension between steering wheel hub and direction signal switch housing cove to ⅛ inch. Adjust by tightening flexible coupling bolt and nut to 15 ft.-lb. Lock the bolt and nut in position with lock-plate tabs.

5. Install stop bolt into steering column.

6. Turn steering wheel to full right and left stop. If resistance is felt, the steering column must be removed and the cause corrected.

Steering Gear Removal (Except GT)

1. See **Figure 20**. Remove splash shield from lower deflector panel and both side members.

2. See **Figure 21**. Remove clamp bolt fixing flexible coupling to steering shaft. Remove cotter pins and nuts on left and right tie rod ends. Press tie rod ends out of steering arms.

3. Disconnect steering gear housing from front suspension crossmember. Remove steering gear and tie rods.

Steering Gear Installation (Except GT)

To install, reverse removal procedure and perform the following:

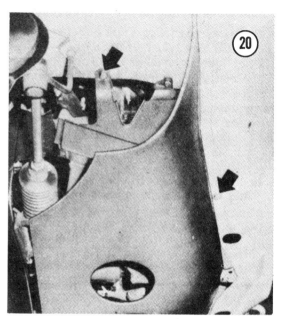

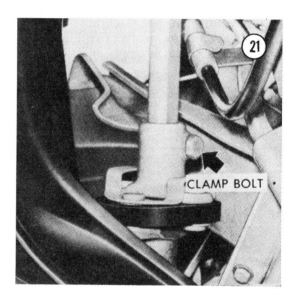

1. Set steering gear to high point. The steering wheel spokes should point downward in an oblique angle and the elongated cutout of the lower steering mast must coincide with the clamp bolt holt of the pinion flange.

2. Install steering gear on front suspension cross member. Tighten nuts to 29 ft.-lb.

3. Install lower end of steering shaft to flexible coupling. Tighten clamp bolt to 22 ft.-lb.

4. Attach guard plate to both side members and lower deflector panel.

CHAPTER ELEVEN

DIFFERENTIAL, REAR AXLE, AND REAR SUSPENSION

This chapter covers 1966-1975 models. See the *Supplement* section, Chapter Eleven, at back of this manual, for 1976 and later models.

Special tools are required for the differential and rear axle procedures. Refer this work to your dealer.

REAR AXLE ASSEMBLY

Removal

Figure 1 shows the rear axle assembly for the 1.1 engine models; **Figure 2** shows the 1.5 and 1.9 engine models.

1. Raise rear of car with jack and place jackstands under rear jack brackets. Remove rear wheels and one brake drum.

2. Disconnect parking brake equalizer and return spring from brake rod.

3. Detach parking brake cable from actuator lever and from brake backing plate at wheel with brake drum removed. Disconnect cable from lower control arm brackets and pull loose end over exhaust system.

4. Disconnect shock absorbers at lower end.

5. Disconnect track rod at left end. On cars equipped with stabilizer rod, disconnect shackles at rear axle housing.

6. Mark position of universal joint and pinion flange relative to each other. Disconnect universal joint from pinion flange. Support or tie-up drive shaft out of the way. If drive shaft is removed, plug rear end of transmission to prevent loss of lubricant.

7. Disconnect brake hose from brake pipe at differential and remove retaining clip.

8. Place a jack equipped with wheels under the differential housing. Support the weight of the rear axle/differential assembly.

9. Lower rear axle assembly far enough to remove coil springs.

10. Remove bolts fixing central joint support bracket to underbody.

11. See **Figure 3**. Disconnect lower control arms at rear axle assembly bracket. Lower the jack and roll the assembly out from under the car.

Installation

1. Roll rear axle assembly under car and loosely attach lower control arms to rear axle housing.

2. Attach central joint support to underbody with bolts. Tighten bolts finger-tight.

3. Lower rear axle assembly and install lower damper rings in spring seats. Install coil springs and upper damper rings. Make certain the damper rings and springs are properly seated.

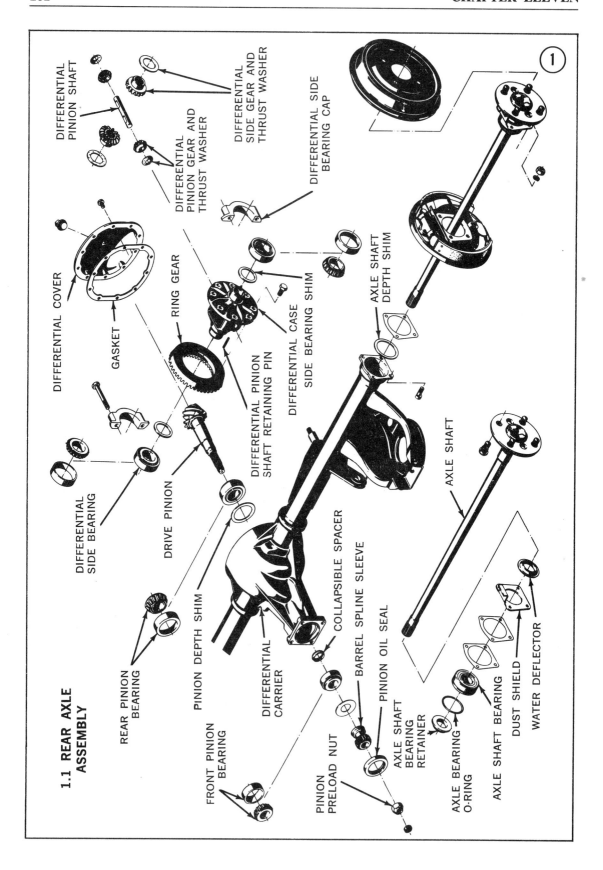

1.1 REAR AXLE ASSEMBLY

DIFFERENTIAL PINION SHAFT

DIFFERENTIAL SIDE GEAR AND THRUST WASHER

DIFFERENTIAL PINION GEAR AND THRUST WASHER

DIFFERENTIAL SIDE GEAR AND THRUST WASHER

DIFFERENTIAL SIDE BEARING CAP

DIFFERENTIAL COVER

GASKET

RING GEAR

DIFFERENTIAL PINION SHAFT RETAINING PIN

DIFFERENTIAL CASE SIDE BEARING SHIM

AXLE SHAFT DEPTH SHIM

DIFFERENTIAL SIDE BEARING

DRIVE PINION

PINION DEPTH SHIM

DIFFERENTIAL CARRIER

COLLAPSIBLE SPACER

BARREL SPLINE SLEEVE

PINION OIL SEAL

AXLE SHAFT

REAR PINION BEARING

FRONT PINION BEARING

PINION PRELOAD NUT

AXLE SHAFT BEARING RETAINER

AXLE BEARING O-RING

AXLE SHAFT BEARING

DUST SHIELD

WATER DEFLECTOR

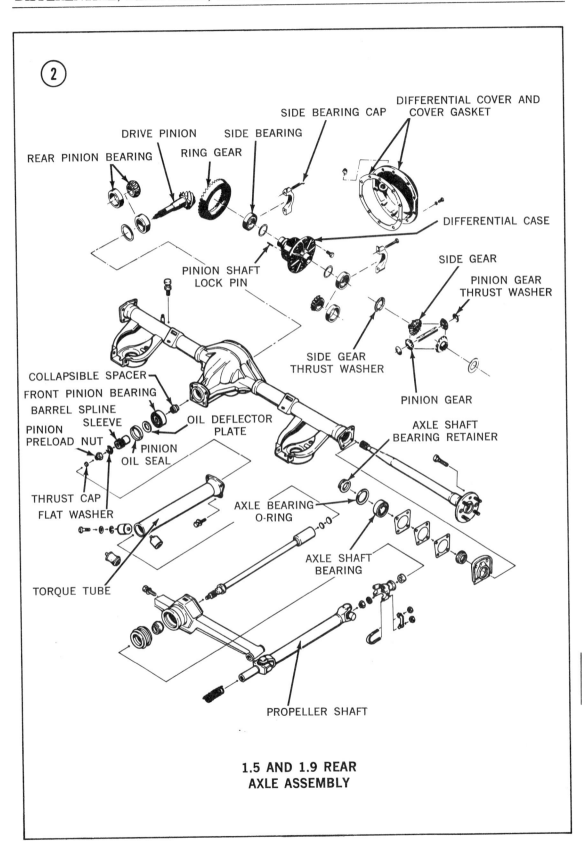

**1.5 AND 1.9 REAR
AXLE ASSEMBLY**

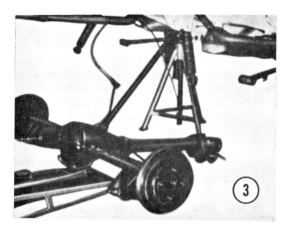

4. Install track rod on axle housing.

5. On Opel and 1900 body styles, put a weight of 350 pounds in the luggage compartment. On GT's, place a 150-pound weight in driver's seat. Raise rear axle far enough for underbody to clear jackstands.

6. Install bolts to connect the following and tighten as specified.

Central joint support to
   underbody   36 ft.-lb.

Lower control arm to axle housing
   Opel and GT   18 ft.-lb.
   1900   22 ft.-lb.

Track rod to rear axle
   Opel and GT   40 ft.-lb.
   1900   76 ft.-lb.

7. Remove weight from luggage compartment or driver's seat.

8. Install shock absorbers and tighten nuts to 15 ft.-lb. on the Opel and GT and to 47 ft.-lb. on the 1900.

9. If the car is equipped with a stabilizer rod, connect the shackles to the axle housing. Tighten the bolts to 25 ft.-lb.

10. Thread parking brake cable over exhaust system. Connect to lower control arm brackets, parking brake actuating lever, and brake backing plate. Install brake drum.

11. Align mating marks made during removal and connect drive shaft to pinion flange. Tighten bolts to 18 ft.-lb. on 1.1 engine cars and to 11 ft.-lb. on 1.5 and 1.9 engine cars. Bend lock plate tabs to secure nuts or bolts.

12. Connect parking brake cable equalizer and

return spring to brake rod. Adjust cable as specified in Chapter Twelve.

13. Bleed brake system, as specified in Chapter Twelve, and replenish the master cylinder as required.

14. Install the wheels and tighten the lug nuts to 65 ft.-lb.

15. Jack up rear of car, remove jackstands, and lower car to floor.

SHOCK ABSORBERS

Location and installation of the shock absorbers are shown in **Figure 4** (1.1 engine) and **Figure 5** (1.5, 1.9 engines). Replace as follows.

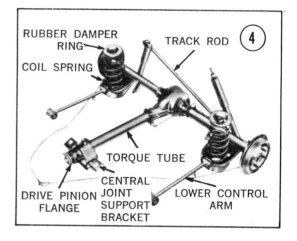

1. Jack up rear end of car and support on jackstands at jack brackets.

2. Remove nuts fixing upper end of shock absorber to car body.

3. Remove bolts and nuts fixing lower end of shock absorber to rear suspension.

4. Remove shock absorber from car. Defective shock absorbers must be replaced.

5. To install, reverse Steps 1-4. Tighten nuts to 15 ft.-lb. on Opel and GT models and to 47 ft.-lb. on 1900 models.

DIFFERENTIAL

Due to the need for special tools and knowledge, it is recommended that all service and repair be referred to an Opel dealer or professional mechanic. Most repairs can be done without removing the differential from the car.

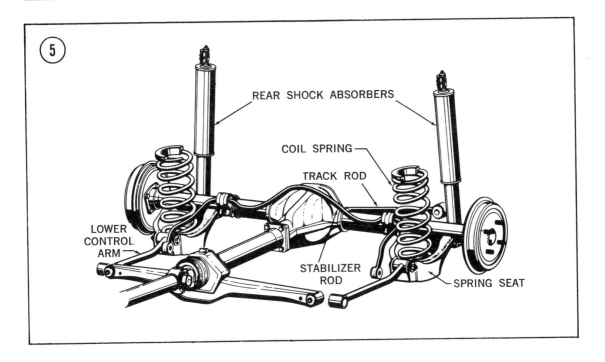

11

CHAPTER TWELVE

BRAKES

This chapter covers the brake system on 1966-1975 models. See the *Supplement* section, Chapter Twelve, at back of this manual, for 1976 and later models.

When working on the brake system, follow these general procedures:

1. Exercise extreme cleanliness when handling brake parts.

2. Never touch rubber seals or internal hydraulic parts with greasy hands or rags.

3. Always use new, high-quality brake fluid to clean hydraulic parts and to fill the reservoir. Never re-use fluid that has been bled from the hydraulic system.

4. Examine all seals carefully. If any damage is evident or suspected, replace the parts with new ones.

5. Take care not to scratch the highly finished surfaces of cylinder bores and pistons.

BRAKE SYSTEM BLEEDING

Whenever any brake system work has been done or leaks repaired, the brake system must be bled to remove any air that may have entered. Each wheel and the master cylinder are equipped with bleeder valves. Bleeding sequence should be master cylinder, left front, right front, left rear, and right rear wheels.

> NOTE: *On drum-brake models, bleeding sequence should be right rear, left rear, right front, left front, and master cylinder.*

Check the fluid level in the reservoir frequently during bleeding so that air will not be taken in through the master cylinder. Do not be satisfied that the bleeding sequence is completed until all signs of bubbles in the fluid have disappeared. If bubbles continue to appear after a reasonable time, there is a leak in the system that must be corrected before the car is driven.

1. Fill master cylinder reservoir with new brake fluid.

2. Remove all dirt and foreign material from around each bleed valve cover. After thorough cleaning, remove the covers.

3. See **Figure 1**. Connect a tube to the bleed valve and immerse the lower end of the tube in a transparent container partly filled with brake fluid.

4. Loosen the bleed valve until fluid escapes into the container. Have an assistant press the brake pedal quickly and allow it to return slowly. Watch for air bubbles at the bleeder hose and

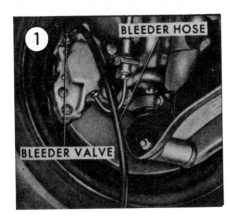

container. Have the assistant pump the brake pedal several times until no further air bubbles appear.

5. When there are no more bubbles, hold down the brake pedal and tighten the bleeder valve. Remove tube and install protective cover.

6. Repeat the bleeding operation for the master cylinder and each wheel. When complete, replenish the master cylinder reservoir with brake fluid and road test the car.

MASTER CYLINDER

Most Opels are equipped with a tandem master cylinder; one half of the unit operates the front disc brakes and the other half operates the rear drum brakes. Early models with drum brakes on all 4 wheels were equipped with a single unit. Details are given for both types of master cylinders. In both systems, hydraulic pressure is transmitted by the driver through the brake pedal and power servo unit (if so equipped) to the piston(s) in the master cylinder. The pressure moves the piston(s) and forces hydraulic fluid through the connecting lines and hoses to actuate the drum brake wheel cylinders and disc brake calipers. The hydraulic pressure applied to the wheel cylinders and brake calipers causes the brake linings and brake pads to come into contact with the brake drums and rotors to stop the car.

Master Cylinder Overhaul (Single)

1. Remove 3 brake lines from master cylinder. Tape or plug end of lines to prevent loss of fluid.

2. Remove 2 bolts fixing master cylinder to firewall. Lift the master cylinder out of the engine compartment.

3. Thoroughly clean outside of master cylinder. Remove reservoir cover and turn master cylinder upside down. Pump the piston with a suitable tool to remove any hydraulic fluid. Discard the fluid.

4. See **Figure 2**. Use snap ring pliers to remove snap ring and stop ring from end of master cylinder.

5. Remove piston with secondary cup, steel washer, primary cup, valve spring seat and spring, check valve, and check valve seat.

6. Unscrew brake fluid reservoir and remove washer and gasket from master cylinder.

> NOTE: *The reservoir is attached to the master cylinder body with left-hand threads.*

7. Clean all parts thoroughly with new hydraulic brake fluid. Inspect for wear and damage. Visible wear or damage is sufficient cause to replace a part.

8. Inspect master cylinder bore for imperfections such as scoring or obvious wear. If defective, replace; honing is not recommended.

9. Check that bypass and compensation ports to the master cylinder bore are not restricted or blocked. Do not use any sharp, pointed object to clean compensating port as this may leave a burr that will cut a groove in the primary cup.

10. To assemble and install, reverse the preceding steps. If an overhaul kit is used, make certain to use all parts in the kit. Coat all parts thoroughly with new brake fluid during installation.

Master Cylinder Overhaul (Tandem)

Figure 3 shows a typical installation on the 1900 and Manta models. **Figure 4** shows a typical installation on the GT's. Operation of the 2 units is essentially the same. The following discussion applies to the 1900 models specifically. **Figure 5** is an exploded view of the 1900 model.

1. Disconnect brake lines from master cylinder. Plug lines to prevent loss of hydraulic fluid.

2. Remove nuts fixing master cylinder to brake

12

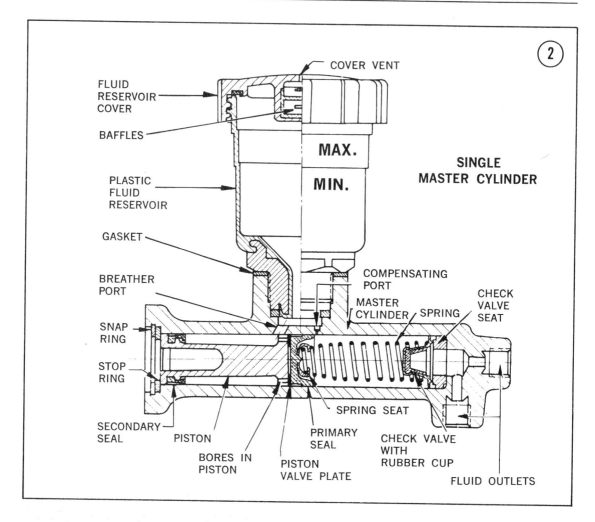

FLUID
RESERVOIR
COVER

COVER VENT

BAFFLES

PLASTIC
FLUID
RESERVOIR

MAX.

MIN.

SINGLE
MASTER CYLINDER

GASKET

BREATHER
PORT

COMPENSATING
PORT

MASTER
CYLINDER

SPRING

CHECK
VALVE
SEAT

SNAP
RING

STOP
RING

SECONDARY
SEAL

PISTON

SPRING SEAT

BORES IN
PISTON

PISTON
VALVE PLATE

PRIMARY
SEAL

CHECK VALVE
WITH
RUBBER CUP

FLUID OUTLETS

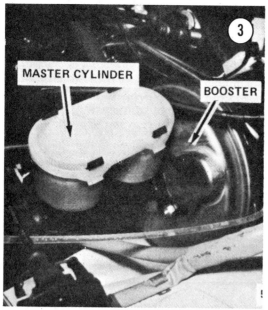

MASTER CYLINDER

BOOSTER

booster. Be careful not to loosen the front housing seal.

3. Remove master cylinder from brake booster. Open and remove reservoir cover. Turn master cylinder upside down and drain fluid. Discard fluid.

4. See **Figure 6**. With snap ring pliers, remove

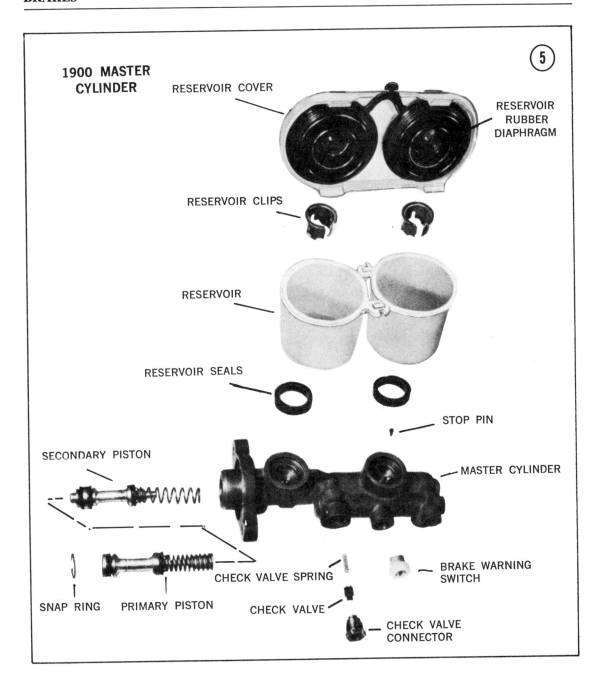

1900 MASTER CYLINDER — RESERVOIR COVER — RESERVOIR RUBBER DIAPHRAGM — RESERVOIR CLIPS — RESERVOIR — RESERVOIR SEALS — STOP PIN — SECONDARY PISTON — MASTER CYLINDER — CHECK VALVE SPRING — BRAKE WARNING SWITCH — SNAP RING — PRIMARY PISTON — CHECK VALVE — CHECK VALVE CONNECTOR — (5)

reservoir clips fixing reservoir to master cylinder body. Remove reservoir from master cylinder body.

5. Remove piston stop screw fitted in master cylinder body.

6. Place master cylinder body in vise equipped with soft jaws. See **Figure 7**. Push piston forward. Insert a rod with a round end into the hole nearest the mounting flange to retain the piston in a forward position and permit removal of snap ring.

7. With snap ring pliers, remove and discard snap ring.

8. Remove primary and secondary pistons from master cylinder body.

9. Remove check valve by unscrewing check valve connection.

10. Clean all parts thoroughly with new hy-

12

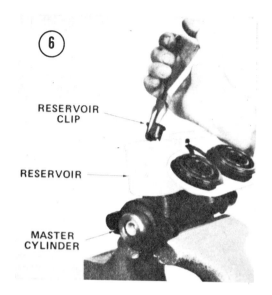

RESERVOIR
CLIP

RESERVOIR

MASTER
CYLINDER

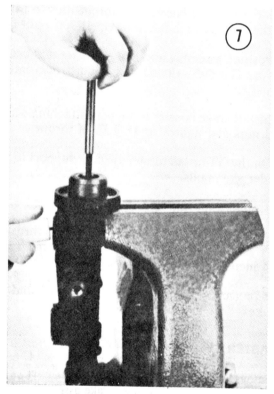

draulic brake fluid. Inspect for wear and damage. Visible wear or damage is sufficient cause to replace a part.

11. Inspect master cylinder bore for imperfections such as scoring or obvious wear. If defective, replace; honing is not recommended.

12. Check that bypass and compensation ports to the master cylinder bore are not restricted

or blocked. Do not use any sharp, pointed object to clean compensating port as this may leave a burr that will cut a groove in the primary cup.

13. To assemble and install, reverse the preceding steps. Use all parts included in the overhaul kit. Perform the following.

14. Coat all parts thoroughly with new brake fluid during installation. Tighten check valve connector to 26 ft.-lb.

15. Inspect condition of seal between master cylinder and brake booster. If defective, replace the seal. As a matter of sound practice, replace the seal whenever the master cylinder is removed.

BRAKE BOOSTER UNIT

Operational Check

Proper operation of the brake booster can be checked as follows:

1. With engine off, depress the brake pedal several times.

2. Depress brake pedal and start engine; leave your foot on the brake pedal.

3. If the brake pedal depresses further when the engine starts, the booster is in proper working order.

4. If the brake pedal does not move downward when the engine starts, the vacuum system is defective. Check the vacuum hose-to-booster and the vacuum control valve-to-engine intake manifold connections.

5. If the above connections and hoses are satisfactory, the defect is in the booster. Check and clean the filter, as discussed following. If operation is still unsatisfactory, the booster must be replaced with a new unit, as it is not repairable.

Filter Servicing

1. See **Figure 8**. Remove protective cap.

2. *(GT)* Pry retainer from housing with a screwdriver.

3. Use a pointed tool to remove noise deadener and filter from control housing bore. Pull it off of the thrust rod.

4. Install new filter and noise deadener. On the GT, the smooth side of the filter must face toward the inside.

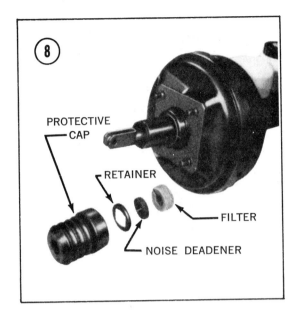

PROTECTIVE CAP

RETAINER

FILTER

NOISE DEADENER

5. Install the filter and deadener so that the radial slots are positioned 180° from each other.

6. *(GT)* Slide retainer over control housing and drive it into place with a plastic hammer.

7. Slide protective cap over control housing and slip it onto brake booster housing.

Vacuum Control Valve Service

The vacuum control valve is installed in the vacuum hose between the intake manifold and the brake booster. It prevents air from flowing backward into the system when the engine is shut off. The control valve is not repairable and must be replaced if defective. During installation, pay attention to the following:

1. Install the short vacuum hose between the intake manifold and vacuum control valve and the long hose between the vacuum control valve and the brake booster.

2. The arrows on the vacuum control valve housing must point toward the intake manifold.

3. Make certain that all hoses are properly installed and that there are no leaks at the connections.

Brake Booster Removal

Defects in the brake booster require that the entire assembly be replaced. To remove a defective unit and install a new one, proceed as follows:

1. Disconnect brake lines from master cylinder. Place a cloth under the master cylinder and brake lines to absorb brake fluid leaks.

2. Disconnect vacuum hose from brake booster.

3. Remove nuts and washers fixing brake booster to brake booster support.

4. *(GT)* Remove master cylinder support-to-fender skirt bolts.

5. *(GT)* Loosen thrust rod locknut. Unscrew the piston pushrod while holding the master cylinder-brake booster assembly.

6. *(Opel, 1900)* Remove nut and bolt attaching clevis on the brake pedal.

7. Remove brake booster unit from car.

8. Disconnect the master cylinder from the brake booster, as previously described.

Brake Booster Installation

To install, reverse the removal procedure and perform the following:

1. Install master cylinder to brake booster. Use a new front seal. Tighten nuts to 14 ft.-lb.

2. Position assembly into brake booster bracket. *(GT)* Thread piston pushrod onto the thrust rod.

3. Install brake booster-to-support washers and nuts. Tighten to 11 ft.-lb.

4. *(GT)* Install master cylinder support to inner fender skirt bolts.

5. Connect vacuum hose to brake booster.

6. *(GT)* Turn the piston pushrod on the thrust rod until the brake pedal free-play is ¼ inch. Tighten the locknut.

7. Connect brake lines to master cylinder and bleed brakes, as previously described.

DISC BRAKES

The front wheel disc brake consists of 2 major parts: the brake disc and the brake caliper. **Figure 9** shows the disc brake assembly.

The brake disc is attached to the inside of the wheel hub flange by 4 bolts. The brake caliper has 2 halves: the mounting half, arranged on the inside of the brake disc, and the rim half. The 2 halves are attached to each other by 4 bolts. Two flanges on the mounting half serve as brake caliper-to-steering knuckle attaching points. The caliper is positioned behind the front

12

HUB AND DISC ASSEMBLY

CALIPER ASSEMBLY

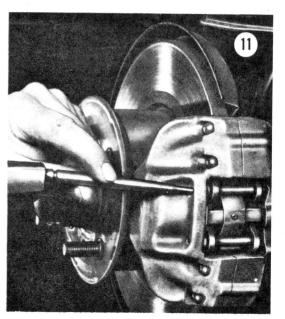

suspension crossmember at steering knuckle spindle level, and is attached to the steering knuckle by 2 bolts.

Both caliper halves act as brake cylinders. Each houses a piston and fluid seal. Inspection of the pads should be done periodically to prevent damage to the brake disc through excessive wear. Adjustment to the front disc brakes is not required. Always replace the pads for both front wheels at the same time, regardless of condition.

Figure 10 is an exploded diagram of the disc brake assembly.

Pad Removal

1. Loosen front wheel lug nuts. Jack up front of car and support it with jackstands. Remove front wheels.

2. See **Figure 11**. Drive dowel pins out of brake calipers toward center of car.

3. Remove pads from calipers, as shown in **Figure 12**. Do not get grease or dirt on the brake pad friction surfaces.

4. See **Figure 13**. Use a micrometer to measure the thickness of the pad and its backing plate. Measure all 4 pads. Minimum permissible thickness of pad and plate is 0.280 in. (7.112mm). If any pad measures less than the minimum, replace all 4 pads.

Pad Installation

To install, reverse the removal procedure and perform the following:

1. With a punch, drive dowel pin from inboard side through caliper and pads to stop. Install new cross-shaped retaining spring under installed dowel pin. Install second dowel pin. If the dowel pins are not snug when installed, replace them.

2. Depress brake pedal several times to seat pads. Check brake fluid level and replenish as required.

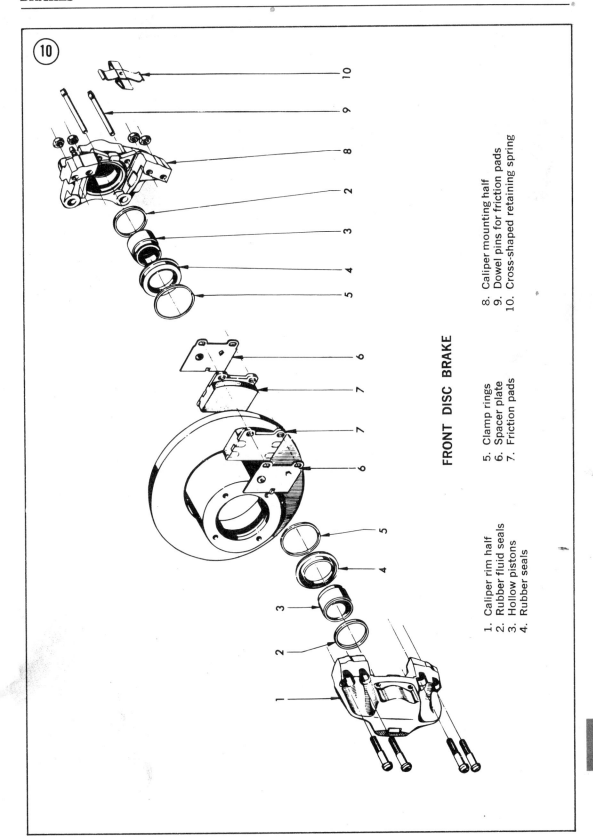

FRONT DISC BRAKE

1. Caliper rim half
2. Rubber fluid seals
3. Hollow pistons
4. Rubber seals
5. Clamp rings
6. Spacer plate
7. Friction pads
8. Caliper mounting half
9. Dowel pins for friction pads
10. Cross-shaped retaining spring

12

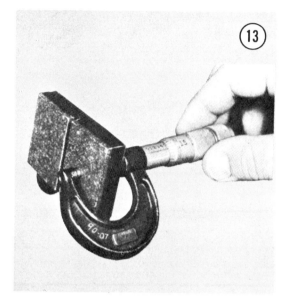

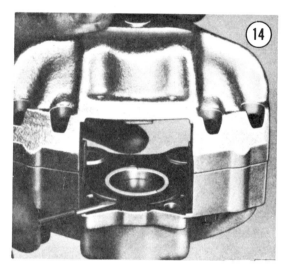

NOTE: *The new brake pads must be broken in. Avoid unnecessary, forceful braking during the first 125 miles after installation of new pads.*

Caliper Removal/Installation

1. Jack up the front end of the car and place it on jackstands. Remove the brake pads as described earlier.

2. Loosen brake line-to-caliper union nut several turns. Detach caliper and brake hose bracket from steering knuckle. Remove caliper from brake disc and swing it sideways. Detach brake line from brake hose, then remove caliper and brake line. Plug end of hose to prevent loss of hydraulic fluid.

3. Disconnect brake line from caliper.

NOTE: *Do not attempt to separate the 2 caliper halves. If a caliper is defective, replace it.*

4. Remove clamp rings with a screwdriver (**Figure 14**). Inspect rubber seal rings around piston. As a matter of sound practice, replace the rubber seal rings whenever the caliper is removed.

5. Use clamp J-22429 (or equivalent) to hold piston in the caliper mounting half. Force the piston out of the rim half with compressed air (**Figure 15**). Then remove the piston from the mounting half (**Figure 16**).

WARNING
The pistons may come out with considerable force. Regulate air pressure carefully and keep fingers out of the way.

6. See **Figure 17**. Pry rubber fluid seals out of the annular grooves in the caliper bores.

7. Check all parts of the caliper for wear. If the bores are scored or rusted, replace the caliper with a new one. Small, light rust spots in the caliper bores may be removeable with fine emery

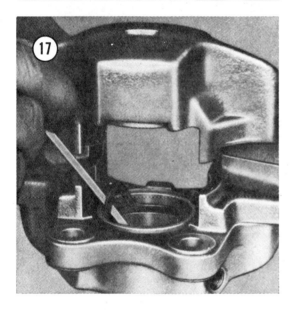

2. Remove the caliper assembly as described earlier.

3. Check both sides of the disc for scoring, corrosion, obvious wear, and burns (blue-tinted areas).

4. Remove front wheel bearing grease cap and spindle nut cotter pin. Tighten spindle nut until all free-play is eliminated from wheel bearings.

5. See **Figure 18**. Use a dial gauge to check disc runout at a point ½ in. from outer edge. Rotate the disc and read the gauge. Maximum permissible runout is 0.004 in. (0.101mm).

If the brake disc is defective, have it skimmed (trued) by a dealer or machine shop. Minimum thickness is 0.394 in. (10.001mm). If the disc is thinner than this after skimming, it must be replaced.

Brake Disc Removal/Installation

1. Jack up the front of the car, place it on jack-stands, and remove the front wheels.

2. Without detaching the brake hose, remove the caliper together with pads as described earlier. Tie the caliper up out of the way.

3. Remove the front wheel hub and disc assembly, together with the wheel bearings.

4. Place the hub and disc assembly in a vise with soft jaws.

cloth. If the pistons are damaged in any way, replace them. Always replace the 4 rubber seals in each caliper, as well as the clamp rings.

8. To assemble and install, reverse the preceding steps. Coat pistons and rubber seals with brake fluid during assembly. Tighten the caliper-to-steering knuckle bolts to 72 ft.-lb. (1966-67 models: 50 ft.-lb.). After installation, bleed the brakes and road test the car.

Brake Disc Inspection

Brake discs should be inspected whenever the pads are replaced.

1. Jack up the front of the car, place it on jack-stands, and remove the front wheels.

12

5. Make alignment marks on the brake disc and wheel hub so they can be reassembled in the same relative positions. Use a star wrench to remove star head bolts and lockwashers fixing brake disc to hub (**Figure 19**).

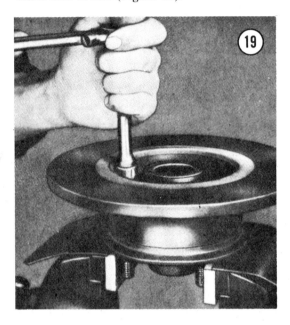

6. Inspect the brake disc as described earlier. Have it skimmed if necessary. Be sure the disc meets minimum thickness specifications.

7. Installation is the reverse of these steps. Line up the match marks made during removal, then tighten the disc-to-hub bolts to 36 ft.-lbs. Make sure there is enough grease n the hub and bearings. Repack the bearings if the grease is old or dirty.

8. After installation, adjust the wheel bearings as described in Chapter Ten. Bleed the brakes and road test the car.

DRUM BRAKES

All models are equipped with drum brakes on the rear wheels. Some early models also used drum brakes on the front wheels. Adjustment of the drum brakes is periodically required as the brake shoes become worn. Adjustment procedures are given later.

Each drum brake assembly uses 2 brake shoes that are actuated by a single wheel cylinder. The centers of the brake shoes are held against the backing plate by a hold-down pin,

spring, and retainer. The bottoms of the shoes pivot in a support plate, and the tops rest directly on the wheel cylinder push rods. The brake shoes are connected by upper and lower return springs, which pull the shoes back to resting position after application of the brakes. The mechanical parking brake works on the rear wheels only.

Figure 20 shows a typical drum brake assembly.

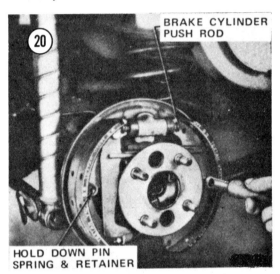

BRAKE CYLINDER PUSH ROD

HOLD DOWN PIN SPRING & RETAINER

Drum Brake Adjustment

Two adjusting eccentrics at each wheel provide individual adjustment for each brake shoe to obtain clearance with the brake drum. An arrow on the brake backing plate circumference shows the direction that eccentrics must be turned to make adjustment. See **Figure 21**.

1. Jack up rear of car and support it with jackstands. Make certain parking brake is off.

2. Turn each wheel to make certain it rotates freely.

3. Rotate wheel in forward direction and turn front brake shoe eccentric with a wrench in direction of arrow until brake shoe contacts brake drum. Turn eccentric in opposite direction until brake drum is just free to turn.

4. Adjust rear brake shoe in the same way but revolve brake drum in backward direction.

5. Remove jackstands and road test car. Readjust brakes if they grab or pull to one side.

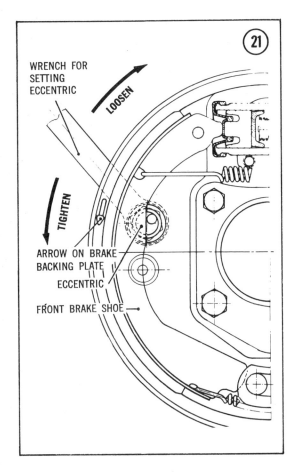

Parking Brake Adjustment

Adjustment of the parking brake cable is necessary whenever the rear brake cables have been disconnected, or when cables have been stretched through extended use. Adjustment is required whenever the parking brake handle can be engaged with 8 or more ratchet clicks and the foot brake system is in good condition and adjusted properly. **Figures 22 and 23** show typical parking brake levers for the 1900 and GT, respectively.

1. Adjust brake shoes, as previously described.

2. Fully release the parking brake lever. Check the parking brake cable for free movement.

3. Loosen equalizer nut or adjusting nut, depending upon whether tension is to be increased or decreased on the cable.

4. Pull parking brake lever on to 3 ratchet clicks. Adjust equalizer with adjusting nut and locknut so that rear brakes just begin to bind

when rotated. Make certain brake action is identical on both wheels. In case of unequal brake action, apply lubricant to equalizer and brake cable.

5. After adjustment, tighten locknut. Make certain equalizer is in horizontal position.

6. Road test car and apply parking brake at slow speed. If brakes grab or pull, readjust parking brake. Check the condition of the brake shoes and the drums if satisfactory adjustment cannot be made.

Brake Shoe Replacement

1. Jack up the rear of car and support it on jackstands.

2. Remove wheel and drum assembly.

3. Remove upper and lower brake shoe return springs.

4. Remove retaining pins and springs, as shown in Figure 20.

5. Clean all dirt and foreign material out of brake drum. Inspect for wear, scoring, and burns (blue-tinted areas). If defective, have brake drum turned or replace with new drum. After turning, check drum diameter. Inner diameter must not exceed 7.900 in. or 9.090 in. (200.68 or 230.886mm), depending on model.

6. Blow all dirt from brake assemblies and inspect for any abnormal condition. Look for oil, grease, and rust.

12

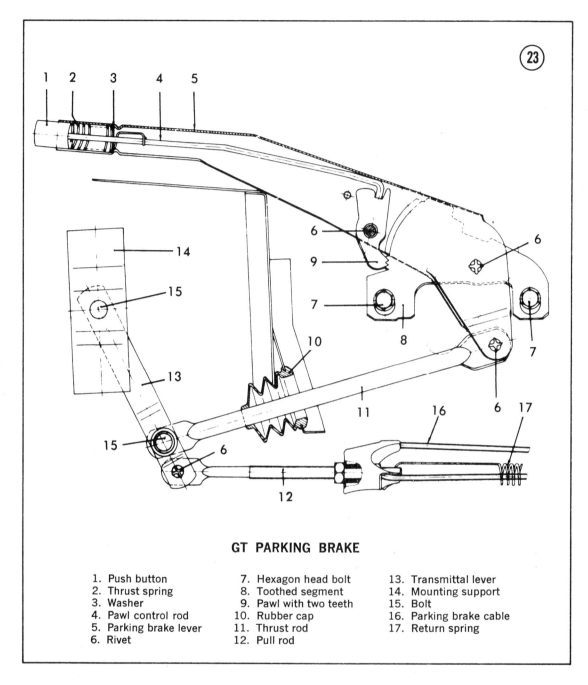

GT PARKING BRAKE

1. Push button	7. Hexagon head bolt	13. Transmittal lever
2. Thrust spring	8. Toothed segment	14. Mounting support
3. Washer	9. Pawl with two teeth	15. Bolt
4. Pawl control rod	10. Rubber cap	16. Parking brake cable
5. Parking brake lever	11. Thrust rod	17. Return spring
6. Rivet	12. Pull rod	

7. See **Figure 24**. Carefully pull lower edges of wheel cylinder boots away from cylinders and note whether interior is wet with brake fluid. Fluid indicates leakage past a piston cup, which requires overhauling or replacement of the wheel cylinder. Overhaul kits are available that include all parts that should be replaced. To overhaul, disassemble the wheel cylinder as shown in Figure 24 and inspect cylinder bore. Lightly hone

(if required) and reassemble with new parts. If the cylinder bore is scratched or defective, replace entire wheel cylinder assembly. After installation and road test, inspect for leaks.

8. Inspect all brake line and hose connections for evidence of fluid leakage. Tighten connections, apply heavy pressure to brake pedal, and recheck connections. If leaks are still apparent, replace defective parts.

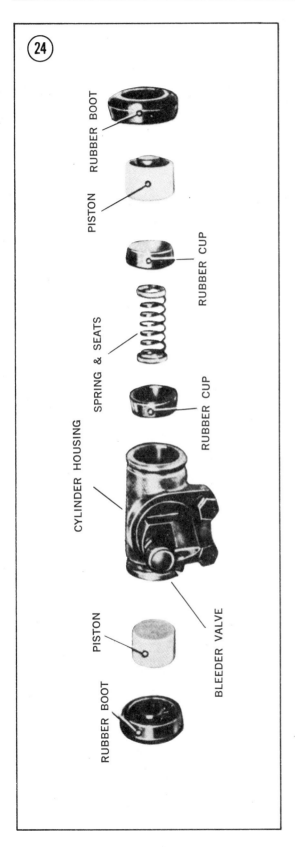

24

RUBBER BOOT

PISTON

RUBBER CUP

SPRING & SEATS

RUBBER CUP

CYLINDER HOUSING

PISTON

BLEEDER VALVE

RUBBER BOOT

9. Inspect backing plate for oil leak past rear wheel bearing oil seals. If leaks are apparent, replace oil seals.

10. Check all backing plate attaching bolts to make sure they are tight. Use fine emery cloth to clean all rust and dirt from shoe contact surfaces on backing plate.

11. Inspect condition of shoes and linings. If the linings are obviously worn or are worn unevenly, replace them with new parts. Always replace full set of shoes and linings at the same time.

12. To assemble and install, reverse steps used during removal and disassembly. After installation, bleed brakes and road test car. If new linings were installed, avoid sudden, hard stops until the linings have had the opportunity to seat correctly.

SUPPLEMENT

1976-1977 SERVICE INFORMATION

The following supplement provides procedures unique to the 1976 and later Opel. All other service procedures are identical to earlier models.

The chapter headings in this supplement correspond to those in the main portion of this book. If a change is not included in the supplement, there are no changes affecting the 1976 and later models.

CHAPTER TWO

LUBRICATION, MAINTENANCE, AND TUNE-UP SUPPLEMENT

This chapter includes only information for 1976 and later models that is different from that found in Chapter Two for earlier models.

PREVENTIVE MAINTENANCE

The preventive maintenance procedures for Opels from 1976 on are identical to previous models, except for the time and/or mileage intervals between servicing. Refer to **Tables 1 and 2**.

ENGINE TUNE-UP

Refer to the *Quick Reference* section in the front of this manual for tune-up specifications for all models.

Valve Clearance Adjustment

1. Prior to adjusting the valve clearance, tighten rocker arm shaft bracket nuts to 16 ft.-lb. See **Figure 1**.

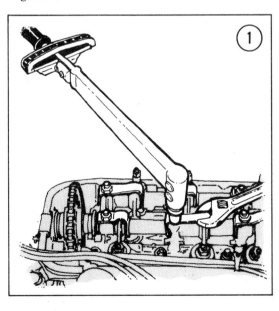

2. Bring piston in either No. 1 or No. 4 cylinder to TDC (top dead center) on compression stroke by turning crankshaft until notched line on crankshaft pulley is in line with zero mark on front cover.

3. Hold crankshaft steady and adjust valve clearance. Refer to *Quick Reference* section in front of this manual.

4. Turn crankshaft one full turn and adjust remaining valves. Refer to **Figure 2** for correct order for setting valve clearance.

	CYL Cylinder No.	1	2	3	4
Valve					
Intake		⊗	⊗	△	△
Exhaust		⊗	△	⊗	△

⊗ When piston in No. 1 cylinder is at TDC on compression stroke

△ When piston in No. 4 cylinder is at TDC on compression stroke

Breaker Point Replacement

1. Release distributor cap clamps and lift off distributor cap.

2. Remove rotor and dust shield.

3. Remove breaker point assembly by loosening retaining screws and lifting out breaker point set. See **Figure 3**.

4. Disconnect the wire lead from the terminal assembly.

5. Position new breaker point set and install retaining screws (do not tighten completely).

Table 1 LUBRICATION AND MAINTENANCE SCHEDULE

Every 6 months or 7,500 miles:

- Lubricate chassis and body; check fluid and lubricant levels; change engine oil; tighten drive shaft flange bolts to 18-20 ft.-lb.

- Rotate tires.

- Check brake lines and hoses; tires and wheels; suspension and steering; exhaust system; and disc brakes.

Every 12 months or 15,000 miles:

- Perform complete engine tune-up.

- Change oil filter.

- Lubricate brake and clutch pedal springs, clutch bushing, and clevis pin; check clutch pedal free play; clean radiator (exterior) and pressure test cooling system; tighten hose clamps and inspect cooling and heating hoses; inspect drum brakes and parking brake; drive belts; throttle linkage; lighting system; underbody; and bumpers.

Every 30,000 miles:

- Replace spark plug and ignition coil wires; change air cleaner element.

- Check external components of brake power assist unit, master cylinder, reservoir, disc brakes, and drum brakes.

- Replace drive belts; ignition rotor; and ignition distributor cap.

- Replace cooling system hoses; drain, flush, and refill cooling system with new coolant.

- Change manual transmission and differential lubricant (every 15,000 miles under severe operating conditions) and clean and repack front wheel bearings.

Every 60,000 miles:

- Change automatic transmission fluid and service pump filter.

- Replace rubber components of brake system; replace brake combination valve and brake hoses.

6. Plug lead wire onto terminal assembly.

7. Turn crankshaft pulley until rubbing block heel is on high point of cam hole. Adjust point gap with a feeler gauge and a screwdriver, to 0.018 in. Tighten set screws.

8. Install dust shield, rotor, and distributor cap.

Breaker Point Adjustment

1. Bring XX notched line on crankshaft pulley into alignment with zero mark on front cover by turning crankshaft pulley (Figure 1).

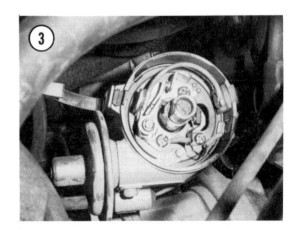

Table 2   RECOMMENDED LUBRICANTS

Component	Fluid/Lubricant
Engine	"SE" oil only
Manual transmission	"SE" oil, SAE 10W-30 (below 50°F), or SAE 40 (above 50°F)
Differential	GL-5, as indicated: SAE 10W-30, below 50°F SAE 40, above 50°F SAE 30, between 0° and 90°F
Automatic transmission	DEXRON II ATF
Brake system and master cylinder	Delco Supreme II or DOT-3 fluids
Clutch linkage Pivot points and clevis pin	Engine oil EP chassis grease meeting GM 6031-M requirements
Automatic transmission shift linkage	Engine oil
Hood latch Pivots and spring anchor, and release pawl	Engine oil EP chassis grease meeting GM 6031-M requirements
Distributor advance mechanism; hood hinges; and heater water valve	Engine oil
Chassis lubrication	EP chassis grease meeting GM 6031-M requirements
Parking brake cables	EP chassis grease meeting GM 6031-M requirements
Front wheel bearings	Grease GM 1051344 (or equivalent meeting requirements of GM 6031-M)
Body door hinge pins and latch	Engine oil
Windshield washer solvent	GM Optikleen washer solvent Part No. 1050001 (or equivalent)
Battery	Distilled water
Engine coolant	Mixture of water and Ethylene Glycol base type anti-freeze conforming to GM 1899-M

2. Loosen 2 retaining screws and open or close breaker point gap by changing position of the breaker point plate in relation to the breaker point arm. Refer to Figure 3.

3. Tighten retaining screws.

Dwell Angle Adjustment

1. Connect dwell meter according to meter manufacturer's instructions.

2. Start engine and allow it to idle. Read the cam dwell angle on the meter. If it is less than 52°, reduce breaker point gap; if it is more than 52°, increase breaker point gap.

3. Stop engine and disconnect dwell meter.

4. Set ignition timing (refer to *Ignition Timing*, following).

Ignition Timing

1. Start engine and allow to warm up to normal operating temperature.

2. Connect tachometer and timing light to No. 1 cylinder, per instrument manufacturer's instructions.

3. Aim timing light at notch on crankshaft pulley. If ignition timing is incorrect, loosen distributor mounting bolts and turn distributor body. See **Figure 4**.

13

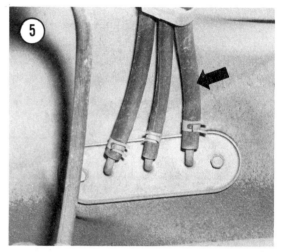

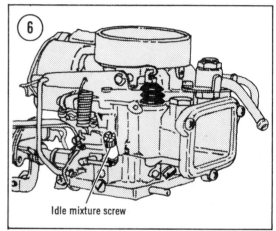

Idle mixture screw

NOTE: *The ignition timing advances as distributor body is turned clockwise; it retards when distributor body is turned counterclockwise. Correct timing is 6° BTDC @ 900 rpm.*

4. Tighten distributor mounting bolts securely (Figure 4).

5. Stop engine and disconnect tachometer and timing light.

Idle Adjustment

1. Set parking brake securely, block rear wheels, and place transmission in NEUTRAL.

2. Start engine and allow to warm up to normal operating temperature.

3. If car is equipped with an air conditioner, turn it off. Block choke open and disconnect and plug distributor vacuum line and idle compensator vacuum line. See **Figure 5**.

4. Turn idle mixture adjustment screw in until it lightly "bottoms," then back it out 3 full turns. See **Figure 6**.

5. Adjust idle speed screw until engine idles at 900 rpm (refer to Figure 6).

6. Adjust idle mixture screw until engine idles at maximum speed.

7. Readjust idle speed screw until engine idles at 900 rpm.

8. Turn idle mixture screw clockwise to lean the mixture until engine idles at 850 rpm.

9. Turn idle mixture screw ½ turn counterclockwise to richen the mixture.

10. Readjust idle speed screw until engine idles at 900 rpm.

11. Unplug and reconnect both vacuum lines. See Figure 5.

12. On cars equipped with air conditioner, perform the following:

   a. Turn air conditioner on maximum cold and blower on high.

   b. Open throttle approximately ⅓ of the way, then allow it to close (this will allow the solenoid to reach its full travel).

   c. Adjust speed-up controller screw until engine idles at 900 rpm.

CHAPTER FOUR

ENGINE SUPPLEMENT

The 1.8 liter, 4-cylinder engine used in Opel models from 1976 on is a straightforward design similar to previous Opel models. Refer to Chapter Four in the front of this manual for basic disassembly/assembly procedures; use the specifications in this supplement (**Tables 3, 4, and 5**), however.

In addition, refer to the following illustrations to further clarify the differences as they apply to 1976 and later engines:

a. **Figure 7** (aligning marks on camshaft and No. 1 bracket during valve timing adjustment)

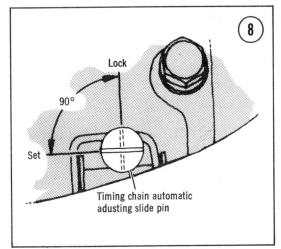

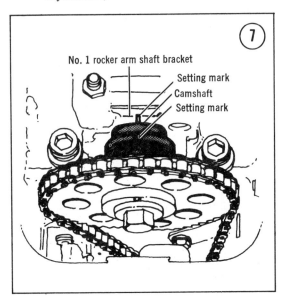

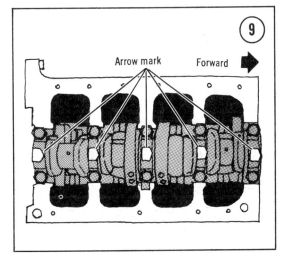

b. **Figure 8** (locking the chain adjuster during removal of the rocker arm shaft and camshaft)

c. **Figure 9** (installing main bearing caps with arrow pointing toward front of engine)

d. **Figure 10** (position of piston rings on piston during piston ring installation)

e. **Figure 11** (position of piston when correctly installed in cylinder)

f. **Figure 12** (installing timing chain guide)

13

Table 3 ENGINE COMPONENTS SPECIFICATIONS

	Standard Value (in.)	Value indicating Need for Servicing (in.)	Limit for Use (in.)
Cylinder bore	3.307	0.0079 (or more)	3.354
Crankshaft			
Runout	0.0012	0.0039	——
Journal diameter	2.205	0.020	2.1555
Crankpin diameter	1.929	0.020	1.8799
Finishing accuracy (journal-to-crankpin)	0.00004	——	——
Journal-to-bearing clearance	0.0008-0.0025	0.0047 (or more)	——
Crankpin-to-bearing clearance	0.0007-0.0030	0.0047 (or more)	——
End play	0.0024-0.0094	0.0118 (or more)	——
Pistons			
Piston-to-cylinder clearance (measured at 1.575 in. below piston head)	0.0018-0.0026	——	——
Piston-to-cylinder clearance (at piston skirt)	0.0001-0.0026	——	——
Piston rings			
1st compression ring (when in cylinder bore)	0.008-0.0016	——	0.059
2nd compression ring (when in cylinder bore)	0.008-0.0016	——	0.059
Oil control ring	0.008-0.035	——	0.059
Ring-to-ring groove clearance (1st and 2nd compression rings)	0.0010-0.0024	——	0.0059
Ring-to-ring groove clearance (oil control ring)	0.0008	——	0.0059
Connecting rods			
Connecting rod-to-crankpin clearance	0.0079-0.0130	0.0138 (or more)	——
Cylinder head			
Distortion	0.0020 (or less)	0.0079 (or more)	0.0157

(continued)

Table 3   ENGINE COMPONENT SPECIFICATIONS (continued)

	Standard Value (in.)	Value indicating Need for Servicing (in.)	Limit for Use (in.)
Valves			
Seat width	0.0472-0.0630	0.0079 (or more)	——
Valve guide-to-valve stem clearance	0.0009-0.0022 (intake);	0.0029, or more (intake);	——
	0.0015-0.0031 (exhaust)	0.0098, or more (exhaust)	——
Valve stem diameter	0.315 (intake and exhaust)	——	0.3102 (intake); 0.3091 (exhaust)
Valve head thickness	0.0433 (intake); 0.0512 (exhaust)	——	0.0315 (intake); 0.0394 (exhaust)
Valve spring free height	1.8465 (outer spring); 1.7835 (inner spring)	——	1.7874 (outer spring); 1.7244 (inner spring)
Valve spring inclination (when free)	——	——	0.0787
Outer valve spring tension (at height of 1.614 in.)	32.2-37.0 lb.	——	30.9 lb.
Inner valve spring tension (at height of 1.516 in.)	18.7-21.5 lb.	——	16.5 lb.
Camshaft			
Height (both intake and exhaust sides)	1.4508	——	1.4311
Journal diameter	1.3362-1.3368	——	1.3307
Camshaft runout	0.0020	0.0039 (or more)	——
Camshaft end play	0.0020-0.0059	0.0079 (or more)	——
Journal-to-bearing clearance	0.0016-0.0035	0.0059 (or more)	——
Rocker arm shaft runout	0.0079 (or less)	0.0157 (or more)	——
Rocker arm shaft diameter	0.8071	——	0.8012
Rocker arm-to-shaft clearance	0.0002-0.0018	0.0079 (or more)	——

g. **Figure 13** (install the oil jet during installation of the timing chain)

h. **Figure 14** (installing automatic adjuster lock plate during installation of chain guide, tensioner, and adjuster)

i. **Figure 15** (installing the timing sprocket and timing chain)

j. **Figure 16** (installing the camshaft timing sprocket)

k. **Figure 17** (aligning the oil pump for installation of the front cover)

l. **Figure 18** (checking position of the punch mark during installation of the front cover assembly)

13

Table 4   GENERAL ENGINE SPECIFICATIONS

Engine type	Water cooled, 4-cycle, 4-cylinder
Valve mechanism	Single overhead camshaft
Combustion chamber type	Hemispherical
Bore and stroke	3.31 x 3.23 in.
Piston displacement	110.8 cu. in.
Compression ratio	8.5:1
Ignition timing	6° BTDC @ 675-725 rpm
Firing order	1-3-4-2
Idle speed	675-725 rpm
Valve clearance (cold)	
Intake	0.006 in.
Exhaust	0.010 in.
Carburetor type	2-barrel downdraft
Fuel pump type	Electrical
Fuel filter type	Paper
Water pump type	Centrifugal
Thermostat type	Wax pellet
Cooling system capacity	1.7 gal.
Air cleaner type	Wet paper filter
Battery type	N 50 - 12V
Alternator type	12V - 40A
Starter type	12V - 1.0KW
Lubricating system	Pressurized with full-flow oil filter
Oil capacity	5 qt.

Table 5   ENGINE TIGHTENING TORQUES

Component	
Rocker arm shaft bracket nuts	16 Foot-pound
Timing sprocket bolt	58 Foot-pound
Cylinder head bolts	72 Foot-pound
Crankshaft pulley bolt	87 Foot-pound
Flywheel bolts	69 Foot-pound
Crankshaft bearing cap bolts	72 Foot-pound
Connecting rod bearing cap bolts	33 Foot-pound
Oil pan bolts	3.6 Foot pound
Cylinder head cover cap nuts	3.6 Foot-pound

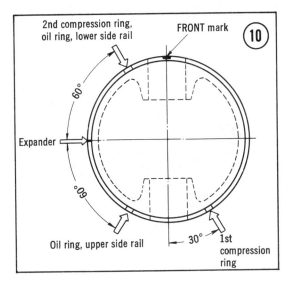

⑩

2nd compression ring, oil ring, lower side rail

FRONT mark

60°

Expander

60°

Oil ring, upper side rail

30°

1st compression ring

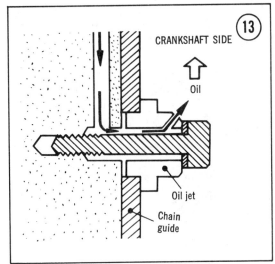

⑬

CRANKSHAFT SIDE

Oil

Oil jet

Chain guide

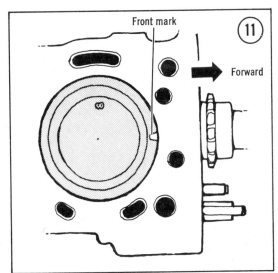

⑪

Front mark

Forward

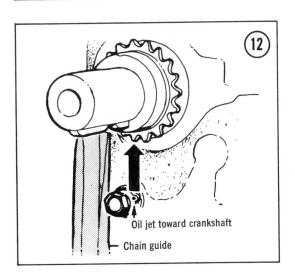

⑫

Oil jet toward crankshaft

Chain guide

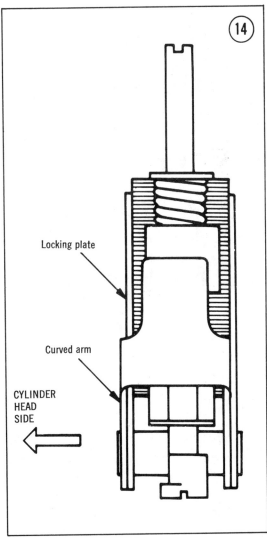

⑭

Locking plate

Curved arm

CYLINDER HEAD SIDE

13

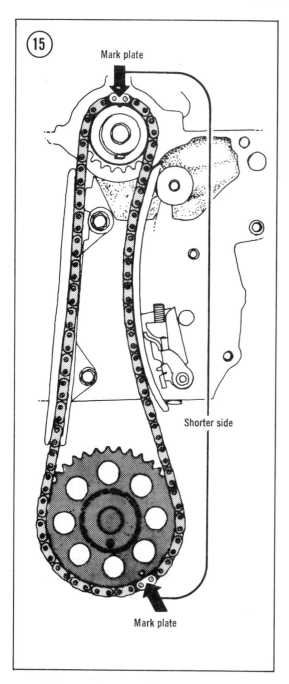

Mark plate

Shorter side

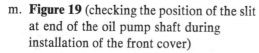

Mark plate

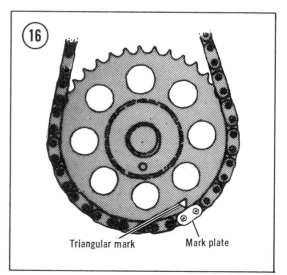

Triangular mark   Mark plate

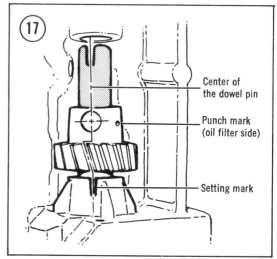

Center of
the dowel pin

Punch mark
(oil filter side)

Setting mark

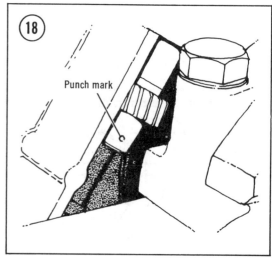

Punch mark

m. **Figure 19** (checking the position of the slit
at end of the oil pump shaft during
installation of the front cover)

n. **Figure 20** (installing cylinder head gasket)

o. **Figure 21** (cylinder head bolt tightening
sequence)

p. **Figure 22** (installing the camshaft, rocker
arm shafts, and rocker arm shaft brackets)

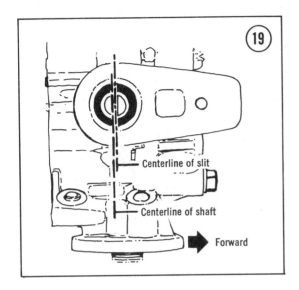

Centerline of slit

Centerline of shaft

Forward

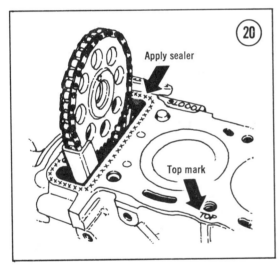

Apply sealer

Top mark

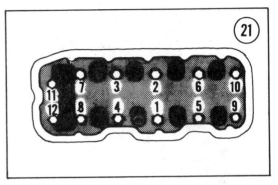

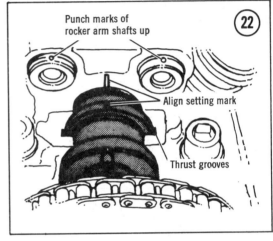

Punch marks of rocker arm shafts up

Align setting mark

Thrust grooves

q. **Figure 23** (locking the automatic adjuster during installation of the camshaft timing sprocket)

r. **Figure 24** (installing rocker arm assembly)

s. **Figure 25** (installing oil pump)

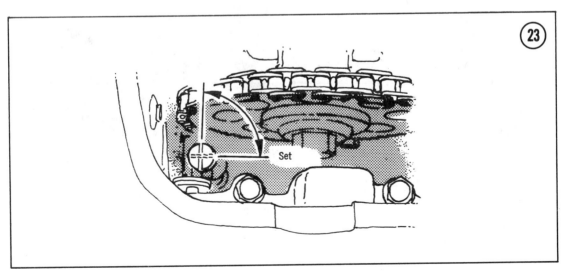

Set

13

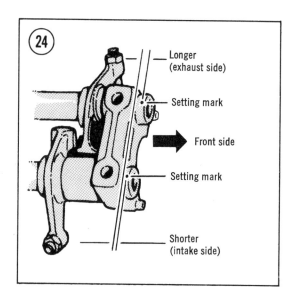

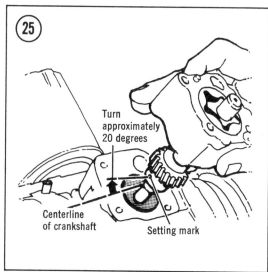

CHAPTER FIVE

FUEL AND EXHAUST SYSTEMS SUPPLEMENT

The fuel system used on 1.8 liter Opel engines from 1976 on consists of a fuel tank; electric fuel pump (built into the fuel tank); fuel filter (cartridge type); 2-barrel carburetor; fuel return pipe line; and a closed crankcase type evaporative emission control system. Refer to **Figure 26**.

The exhaust system consists of a single exhaust front pipe; a main muffler with center pipe; a rear muffler with rear pipe; and clamps connecting the various components together. The mufflers "float" on rubber rings to prevent vibrations. Insulation under the floor over the mufflers and catalytic converter keep heat transfer to the interior of the car at a minimum. Refer to **Figure 27**.

FUEL TANK

Removal

1. Disconnect fuel return hose from pipe and drain fuel. Refer to **Figure 28**.

2. Remove fuel tank cover and fuel filler cap.

3. Disconnect fuel return hose, evaporator hose, and fuel hose from floor panel. Then disconnect fuel pump and fuel tank sending unit wiring at the connector. See **Figure 29**.

4. Disconnect radio speaker wires and remove speaker assembly.

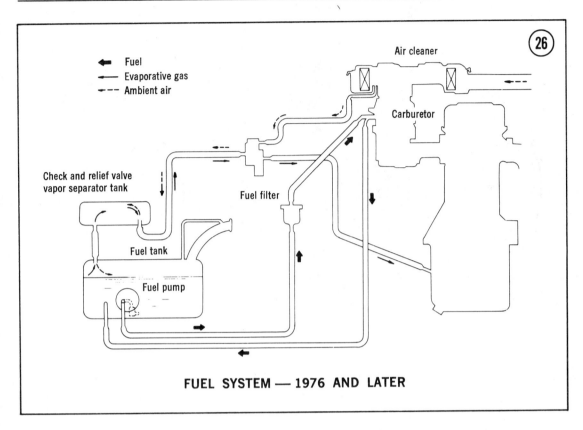

FUEL SYSTEM — 1976 AND LATER

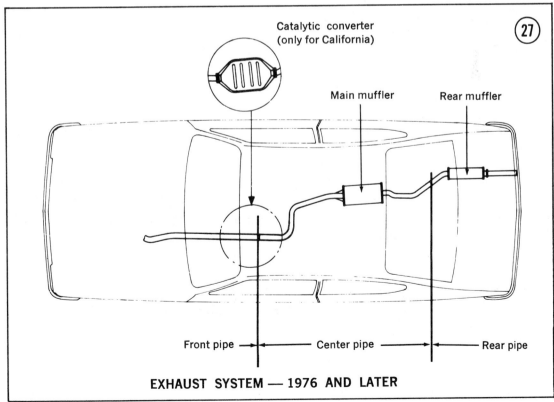

EXHAUST SYSTEM — 1976 AND LATER

13

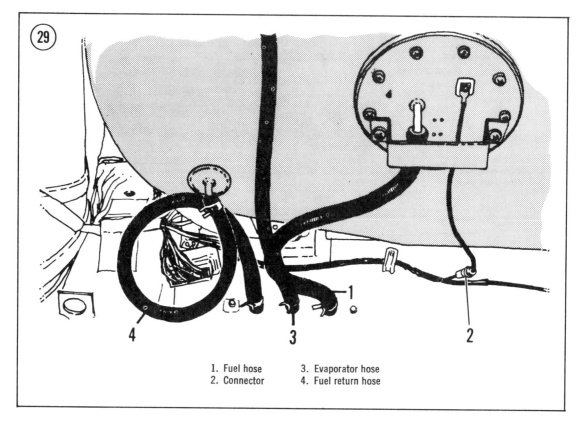

1. Fuel hose 3. Evaporator hose
2. Connector 4. Fuel return hose

5. Remove bolts holding fuel tank in place, then remove fuel tank, along with filler neck seal ring. When tank is out of car, remove seal ring.

6. Remove fuel pump and fuel tank sending unit from fuel tank, if necessary.

Installation

1. Install fuel pump and fuel tank sending unit on fuel tank.

2. Place end of fuel filler neck into fitting hole. Install and loosely tighten 4 bolts holding fuel tank.

3. Remove fuel tank in toward filler cap side.

4. Lubricate seal ring with soapy water. Work lipped portion of the seal ring into the flange at fuel filler recess.

CAUTION
Do not damage the lip during installation process. Check to be sure seal ring is properly fitted to the flanged portion of fuel filler recess, as viewed from inside of luggage compartment.

5. Tighten 4 bolts holding fuel tank in place.

6. Connect hoses and wiring, and fuel return hose. Check for leaks.

FUEL PUMP

Removal/Installation

1. Disconnect fuel return hose from pipe, and drain fuel.

2. Remove fuel tank cover and 2 screws holding fuel pipe cover. Remove the fuel pipe cover.

3. Disconnect fuel hose from fuel pipe.

4. Disconnect fuel pump wiring. Refer to **Figure 30** for fuel pump wiring diagram.

5. Remove 9 screws holding fuel pump in place and take out fuel pump assembly from fuel tank. See **Figure 31**.

6. Install fuel pump by reversing preceding steps.

WARNING
Start engine and check for fuel leaks around gasket. Leaking fuel could cause a fire.

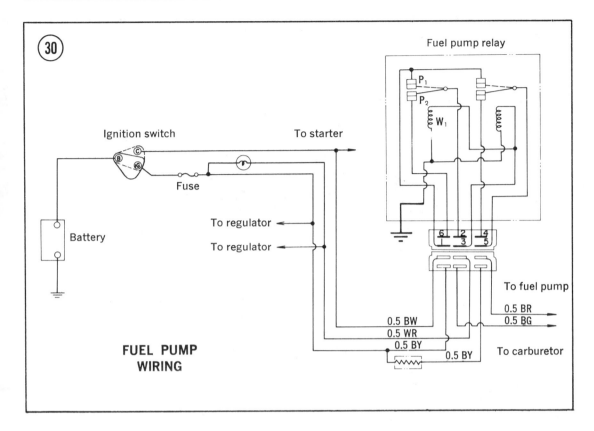

FUEL PUMP WIRING

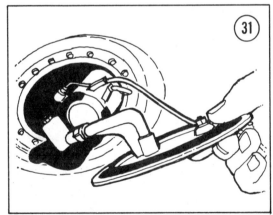

FUEL FILTER

Removal/Installation

1. Disconnect 2 fuel hoses from fuel filter.
2. Remove fuel filter from clip.
3. Install by reversing preceding steps.

WARNING
Start engine and check for fuel leaks at hose joints. Leaking fuel could cause a fire.

CARBURETOR

The 2-barrel, down-draft carburetor is designed and constructed so that a primary side of the carburetor is operated when engine is running at low speed and light load; a secondary side is brought into use when engine speed and load increases. Due to the double venturi action, airflow is maintained at a velocity for efficient operation.

The carburetor is equipped with an electric automatic choke. The engine exhaust gas control system features a coasting richer system that operates only when the engine is coasting, and an anti-dieseling solenoid valve. Refer to **Figure 32** for an exploded view of carburetor.

Removal

1. Disconnect PCV hose from cylinder head cover.
2. Disconnect ECS hose from air cleaner body.
3. Disconnect air hose from AIR pump.
4. Disconnect CCS hose (from hot idle compensator to intake manifold) from the manifold.

13

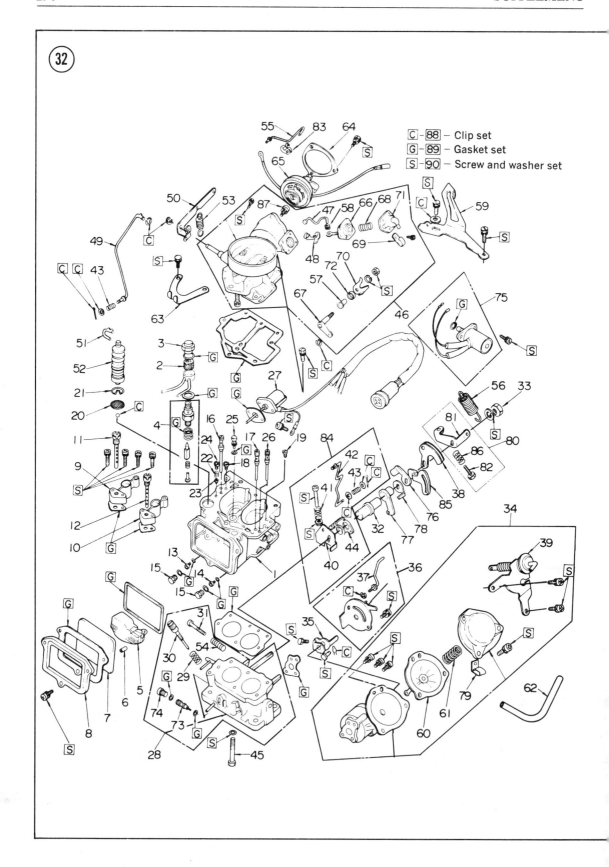

CARBURETOR — 1976-1977

1. Float bowl
2. Strainer
3. Union cap nut
4. Float valve
5. Float assembly
6. Float pin collar
7. Glass
8. Float chamber cover
9. Primary small venturi
10. Secondary small venturi
11. Primary main air bleed
12. Secondary main air bleed
13. Primary main jet
14. Secondary main jet
15. Main passage plug
16. Slow jet
17. Step jet
18. Slow air speed
19. Step air bleed
20. Accelerator pump strainer
21. Strainer clip
22. Discharge check valve spring
23. Discharge check valve
24. Outlet valve plug
25. Power valve jet
26. Coasting jet (except federal, automatic transmission)
27. Anti-dieseling solenoid
28. Throttle body
29. Idle adjust screw spring
30. Idle adjust screw
31. Throttle adjust screw
32. Throttle shaft sleeve
33. Throttle shaft nut
34. Diaphragm chamber assembly
35. Secondary throttle shaft arm
36. Secondary throttle return arm
37. Throttle link
38. Throttle wire lever
39. Choke piston assembly
40. Choke piston arm
41. Fast idle adjust spring
42. Select lever rod
43. Select lever rod spring
44. Select lever
45. Bolt
46. Air horn assembly
47. Choke diaphragm rod

48. Link holder
49. Pump connecting rod
50. Pump arm
51. Pump link
52. Accelerator pump plunger
53. Pump arm return spring
54. Throttle adjust screw spring
55. Choke piston link
56. Throttle return spring
57. Tape bearing bushing
58. Teflon bushing
59. Throttle return spring hanger
60. Diaphragm
61. Diaphragm spring
62. Automatic choke vacuum hose
63. Clamp
64. Thermostat case cover
65. Thermostat case
66. Automatic choke diaphragm
67. Select arm lever
68. Automatic choke diaphragm spring
69. Lead wire clip
70. Select arm
71. Automatic choke diaphragm cover
72. Washer
73. Idle nozzle
74. Idle nozzle plug
75. Coasting richer solenoid (except federal, automatic transmission)
76. Dashpot arm (only for manual transmission)
77. Throttle valve cable (only for automatic transmission)
78. Throttle valve cable stopper (only for automatic transmission)
79. Lead wire clip
80. Fast idle lever assembly
81. Fast idle lever
82. Speed up controller adjusting screw
83. Link holder
84. Throttle adjust arm assembly
85. Primary throttle arm
86. Speed up controll adjusting spring
87. Screw and washer
88. Clip set
89. Gasket set
90. Screw and washer set

13

5. Remove bolts holding air cleaner in place, and loosen clamp bolt. Lift air cleaner and disconnect CCS hose (from thermosensor to intake manifold). Remove air cleaner assembly.

6. Disconnect fuel hoses at main and return side joints. Disconnect distributor vacuum hose and EGR vacuum hose from carburetor. Refer to Figure 32.

7. Disconnect accelerator control cable from carburetor throttle lever.

8. Disconnect automatic choke and solenoid valves wiring at connector and remove clip from water outlet pipe (**Figure 33**).

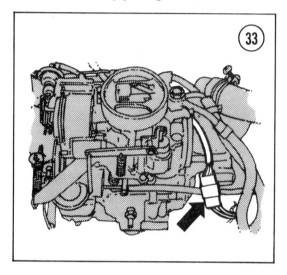

9. Remove 4 nuts holding carburetor in place, then remove carburetor assembly.

Installation

1. To install, reverse steps under *Removal* section, preceding. In addition, perform the following steps:

  a. Start engine and check to be sure fuel hose joints do not leak.

WARNING
Leaking fuel could cause a fire.

  b. Check to be sure that accelerator control cable play is within specifications. Refer to *Control Cable Adjustment,* this chapter.

  c. Adjust engine idle. Refer to Chapter Two, *Lubrication, Maintenance, and Tune-up Supplement, Idle Adjustment* section.

Control Cable Adjustment

1. Turn the accelerator control cable adjusting nut until carburetor throttle valve begins to open (**Figure 34**).

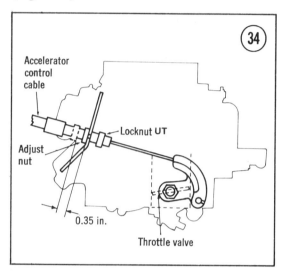

2. Move control cable in toward carburetor about 7-7.5 full turns of the adjusting nut (approximately 0.35 in.). Lock the control cable in position with the locknut (Figure 34).

3. Press accelerator pedal slowly downward. Check that carburetor throttle valve does not open while accelerator switch plunger is in contact with accelerator pedal (**Figure 35**).

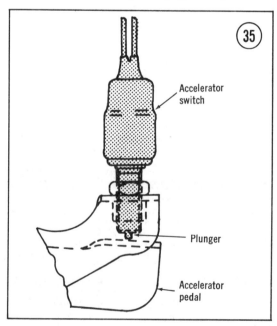

FRONT EXHAUST PIPE

Removal/Installation

1. Raise vehicle and support on jackstands.

2. Remove 2 nuts holding front exhaust pipe to exhaust manifold.

3. Remove 2 bolts holding front exhaust pipe bracket to transmission rear cover.

4. Loosen clamp bolt and disconnect front exhaust pipe from center exhaust pipe.

> NOTE: *On California models, remove bolts holding front exhaust pipe to catalytic converter.*

5. Remove front exhaust pipe assembly.

6. Install by reversing preceding steps.

CENTER AND REAR EXHAUST PIPE

Removal/Installation

1. Raise vehicle and install jackstands.

2. Loosen center and front exhaust pipe clamp bolts.

> NOTE: *On California models, remove bolts holding center exhaust pipe to catalytic converter.*

3. Remove 2 rubber rings from front of main muffler.

4. Flatten tab on rubber ring mounting bracket. Remove rubber ring from its bracket, together with rear exhaust pipe.

5. Loosen center and rear exhaust pipe clamp bolt, then remove center and rear pipe assemblies.

6. To install, reverse preceding steps.

> NOTE: *Use muffler sealer on pipe joints. Overlap front pipe on center pipe by 2.8 in.; overlap center pipe on rear pipe by 2.4 in.*

CATALYTIC CONVERTER

Removal/Installation

1. Raise vehicle and install jackstands.

2. Disconnect thermosensor wiring.

3. Remove front and rear flange bolts, then remove catalytic converter (**Figure 36**).

4. Install by reversing preceding steps.

1. Rear flange bolts   2. Front flange bolts

13

CHAPTER SIX

COOLING AND HEATING
SYSTEMS SUPPLEMENT

The 1.8 liter engine used in Opels from 1976 on is equipped with a pressure circulation type cooling system consisting of a water pump, radiator, wax pellet-type thermostat, cooling fan, fan belt, and cooling hoses.

See **Table 6** for cooling system specifications.

Table 6   COOLING SYSTEM SPECIFICATIONS

Method of cooling	Pressurized circulation
Cooling system capacity	6½ qt.
Water pump	Centrifugal impeller type
Radiator	
Type	Flat tube type with corrugated fins
Pressure valve opening pressure	15 psi
Vacuum valve opening pressure	0.6-0.7 psi
Thermostat	
Type	Wax pellet type with jiggle valve
Valve opening temperature	177-182°F
Temperature at which thermostat valve is wide open	203°F
Valve lift (at 203°)	0.32 in. or more
Amount of leak-off (when tested with valve held in cold water and a pressure of 2.8 psi)	0.11 qt./min. or less
Cooling fan	
Type	Resin
Drive method	Direct drive (models without air conditioning); fluid coupling, thermo-modulate type fan clutch (models with air conditioning)
Number of cooling fan blades	4 (models without air conditioning); 5 (models with air conditioning)
Fan belt	
Type	Plain low-edge type
Fan belt deflection	Approximately 0.4 in.

CHAPTER SEVEN

EMISSION CONTROL SYSTEMS SUPPLEMENT

Due to the increasing complexity of the emission control devices needed to meet U.S. government standards, it is recommended that any emission control systems work be done by your dealer.

CHAPTER EIGHT

ELECTRICAL SYSTEM SUPPLEMENT

This chapter covers the removal and installation of the starter, distributor, and alternator.

Starter Removal/Installation
(Models Without Air Conditioning)

1. Disconnect negative (—) battery cable and wiring from solenoid.

2. Remove starter-to-flywheel housing top and bottom retaining nuts and washers. Refer to **Figure 37.**

3. Lift starter forward to clear stud, and remove it from engine compartment.

4. Install by reversing preceding steps.

Starter Removal/Installation
(Models With Air Conditioning)

1. Disconnect negative (—) battery cable and wiring from solenoid.

2. Jack up front of car and support with jackstands.

3. With a U-joint and extension, reach over front crossmember and behind solenoid to remove starter-to-flywheel housing upper retaining nut and washer.

4. Remove starter-to-flywheel housing lower retaining bolt, and lift starter forward to clear stud. Remove starter.

5. Install by reversing preceding steps.

13

Distributor Removal/Installation

1. Release distributor cap retaining clips and remove cap. Note position of rotor for correct installation.

2. Disconnect vacuum advance hose. Refer to **Figure 38**.

3. Remove distributor clamp bolt and clamp and lift distributor out of engine. See **Figure 39**.

4. To install, rotate rotor to same position as when removed. Then slide distributor shaft into engine with shaft aligned with slot in oil pump drive shaft.

5. Install distributor retaining bracket with bolt just finger-tight.

6. Check and correct dwell and timing. Refer to *Supplement,* Chapter Two, *Engine Tune-up* section, for procedures.

7. After dwell and timing adjustments are made, tighten distributor clamp bolt and connect vacuum hose.

Alternator Removal/Installation

1. Disconnect negative (—) battery cable.

2. Remove stone shield; 2 lower alternator attaching bolts; and horn.

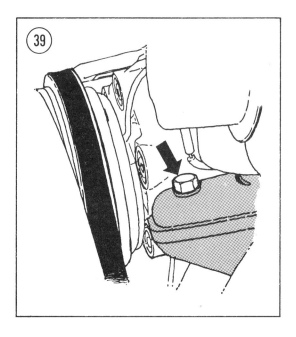

3. Disconnect alternator wiring. Refer to **Figure 40**.

4. Remove top alternator bolt and disengage the belt.

5. Remove alternator belt adjusting bracket and bolt, then remove alternator.

6. Install by reversing preceding steps.

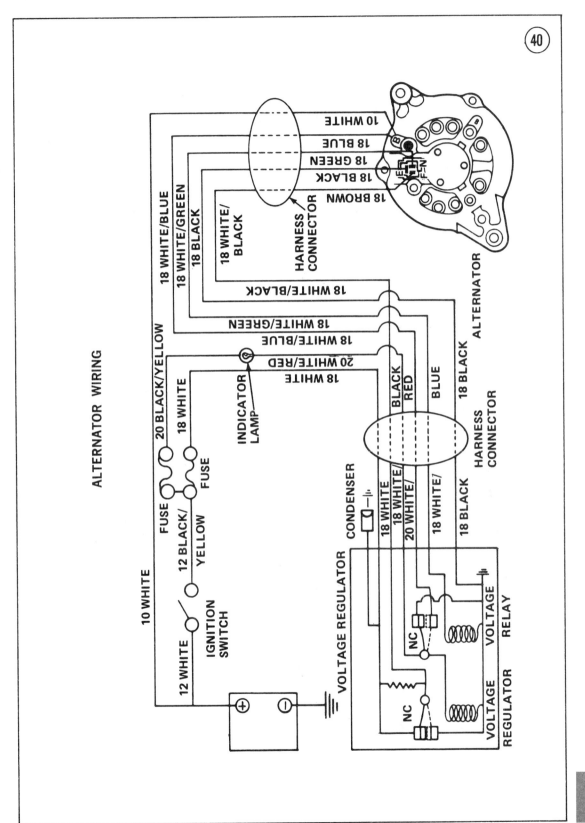

CHAPTER NINE

CLUTCH, TRANSMISSION, AND
DRIVE SHAFT SUPPLEMENT

This chapter covers removal, installation, and adjustment of the clutch; replacement of the clutch cable; removal and installation of the manual transmission; and removal and installation of the drive shaft. (The automatic transmission requires highly specialized tools and knowledge to accomplish repairs. This work should be done by a qualified automatic transmission repairman.)

Clutch Removal/Installation

1. Remove transmission. Refer to *Manual Transmission Removal/Installation* section, this chapter.

2. Scribe a mark on clutch assembly and flywheel so they can be assembled in same position.

3. Install Opel aligning tool J-26509 (or equivalent) and remove 6 retaining bolts (**Figure 41**).

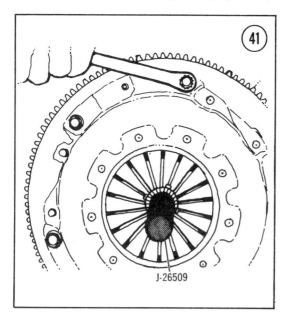

4. Remove release bearing-to-yoke retaining springs, then remove release bearing with support (**Figure 42**).

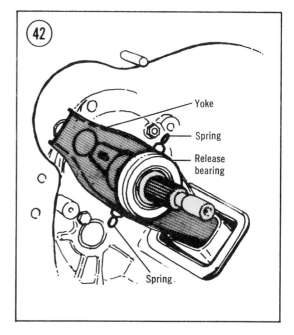

5. Remove release yoke from transmission ball stud.

6. To install clutch, lube the ball stud and install release yoke.

7. Lube the support and install release bearing and support-to-release yoke with retaining springs. Refer to Figure 42.

8. Insert Opel aligning tool J-26509 (or equivalent) and install clutch assembly in original position (match up the scribe lines). Tighten the bolts evenly to 13 ft.-lb.

9. Install transmission. Refer to *Manual Transmission Removal/Installation*, this chapter.

Clutch Adjustment

1. Loosen lock and adjusting nuts on clutch cable (**Figure 43**).

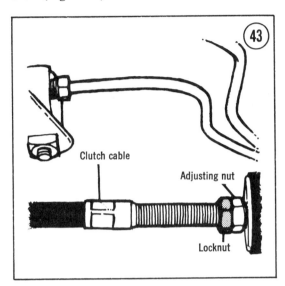

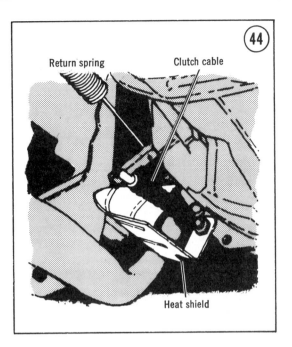

2. Take up slack in cable by pulling it forward (toward front of car).

3. Turn adjusting nut inward until clutch pedal free play is approximately ⅝ in. Tighten locknut.

Clutch Cable Replacement

1. Loosen clutch lock and adjusting nuts (Figure 43).

2. Raise car and install jackstands. Remove heat shield and return spring from release yoke (**Figure 44**).

3. Remove clutch cable from release yoke. Slide it forward through the retaining bracket.

4. Disconnect cable from clutch pedal and remove it.

5. To install clutch cable, slide it through bulkhead and attach it to clutch pedal. Then perform the following steps:

   a. Install cable in original position (through retaining bracket) and attach it to the release yoke.

   b. Install clutch return spring and heat shield.

   c. Adjust cable and tighten locknut. Refer to *Clutch Adjustment,* this chapter.

Drive Shaft Removal/Installation

1. Raise rear of car and support with jackstands.

2. Disconnect parking brake return spring from rod.

3. Scribe a line across mating parts of the U-joint and drive pinion extension shaft flange. Refer to **Figure 45**.

4. Loosen bolt locks and remove bolts (or nuts).

5. Pull drive shaft slightly forward, lower rear end of shaft, and slide assembly rearward. Remove thrust spring from front of drive shaft.

6. Install plug in transmission extension housing to prevent loss of lubricant.

13

7. To install, remove plug from rear of transmission. Refer to Step 6, preceding. Slide the thrust spring onto transmission output shaft and slide drive shaft through oil seal and onto transmission output shaft.

8. Align pinion flange and U-joint scribe marks (refer to Step 3, preceding) and install bolts and new lock plates (see CAUTION under Step 6, preceding). Torque bolts to 18 ft.-lb.

9. Connect parking brake return spring to brake rod.

Manual Transmission Removal/Installation

1. Disconnect negative (—) battery cable.

2. Remove shift lever assembly (from inside of car).

3. Loosen clutch cable adjusting nuts (left side of engine compartment).

4. Remove upper starter mounting bolt, then disconnect starter wiring.

5. Raise car and install jackstands.

6. Remove drive shaft. Refer to *Drive Shaft Removal/Installation,* this chapter.

7. Disconnect speedometer cable.

8. Remove clutch cable heat shield and cable, and lower starter retaining bolt and starter.

9. Disconnect exhaust pipe from manifold.

10. Remove flywheel inspection cover and rear transmissision support mounting bolt.

11. Support transmission with a jack and remove rear transmission support from frame. Lower the transmission to a position approximately 4 in. below where it is normally mounted.

12. Disconnect back-up light and CRS (coasting richer system) switch wires.

13. Remove transmission housing-to-engine block bolts, and move the transmission straight back and down, away from the car.

14. To install, reverse preceding steps, and perform the following, in addition:

    a. Lubricate drive gear shaft with a light coat of grease before installing.

    b. Adjust clutch. Refer to *Clutch Adjustment,* earlier in this section.

    c. Fill transmission to level of filler hole with SAE 30 engine oil.

CHAPTER TEN

FRONT SUSPENSION, WHEELS, AND STEERING SUPPLEMENT

This chapter covers adjustment of the front wheel bearings; tie rod end replacement; shock absorber replacement; and torque specifications (**Table 7**) for the front suspension, wheels, and steering.

Front Wheel Bearing Adjustment

1. Remove grease cap, cotter key, and spindle nut. Discard the cotter key.

2. Tighten spindle nut to 21 ft.-lb. while turning the wheel by hand (this will allow bearings to seat).

3. Back spindle nut off ¼ turn. If slot and cotter key hole are staggered, back nut off more (until next slot in nut aligns with hole in spindle).

Table 7   TORQUE SPECIFICATIONS

Component	
Wheel lugs nuts	50 Foot-pound
Lower control arm ball-joint-to-steering knuckle	72 Foot-pound
Lower control arm bolt-to-crossmember	43 Foot-pound
Lower control arm bolt-to-body	43 Foot-pound
Upper control arm ball-joint-to-steering knuckle	40 Foot-pound
Upper control arm ball-joint-to-upper control arm	29 Foot-pound
Shock absorber-to-upper control arm	29 Foot-pound
Brake backing plate-to-steering knuckle	58 Foot-pound
Brake caliper-to-steering knuckle	36 Foot-pound
Brake disc-to-front wheel hub	36 Foot-pound
Tie rod castle nut	29 Foot-pound
Toe-in adjustment locknut	47 Foot-pound

4. Install a new cotter key.

5. Check the bearing. (A properly adjusted wheel bearing has a slight amount of end play and a loose nut when adjusted in the manner described.)

Tie Rod End Replacement

1. Raise car and support on jackstands.

2. Remove tie rod end cotter key and castle nut (discard the cotter key). Loosen tie rod end with Opel tool J-21687-1 (or equivalent). Refer to **Figure 46**.

3. Loosen locknut and unscrew tie rod end from tie rod assembly. Refer to **Figure 47**.

4. Screw the tie rod into a new tie rod end and attach the tie rod end to the steering knuckle. Tighten the castle nut to 29 ft.-lb. and install a new cotter key.

5. Remove jackstands and lower car. Have the toe-in adjusted by a professional front end alignment shop and tighten locknut to 47 ft.-lb.

Front Shock Absorber Replacement

1. Raise car and support with jackstands. Remove front wheels.

13

2. Disconnect shock absorber from upper control arm (**Figure 48**).

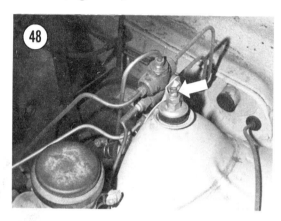

3. Remove shock absorber nuts from engine compartment (**Figure 49**).

4. Remove shock absorber.

5. Install new grommets and washers on the replacement shock (**Figure 50**) and tighten the thicker nut to the end of the threads on the rod. Install the locknut.

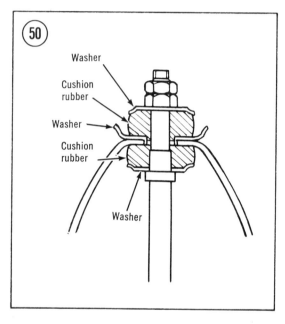

6. Connect shock absorber to upper control arm and tighten nut to 29 ft.-lb. Refer to **Figure 48**.

7. Install wheels and tighten wheel lug nuts to 50 ft.-lb. Remove jackstands and lower car.

CHAPTER ELEVEN

DIFFERENTIAL, REAR AXLE, AND REAR SUSPENSION SUPPLEMENT

This chapter covers the removal and installation of the lateral rod, control arm, rear coil springs, and rear shock absorbers. Torque specifications are found in **Table 8**.

Lateral Rod Removal/Installation

1. Raise car and support with jackstands. Remove the rear wheels.

2. Remove lower shock absorber bolt. Refer to *Rear Shock Absorber Replacement,* this chapter.

3. Remove bolt holding lateral rod to body, and nut holding lateral rod to axle case. Refer to **Figure 51**.

4. Remove lateral rod assembly.

5. To install, attach lateral rod to axle case and body and torque lateral rod bolt (to body) to 43

Table 8   TORQUE SPECIFICATIONS

Component	
Shock absorber-to-axle	29 Foot-pound
Lateral rod-to-body bracket	43 Foot-pound
Lateral rod-to-axle	49 Foot-pound
Control arm bolts	29 Foot-pound
Wheel lug nuts	50 Foot-pound

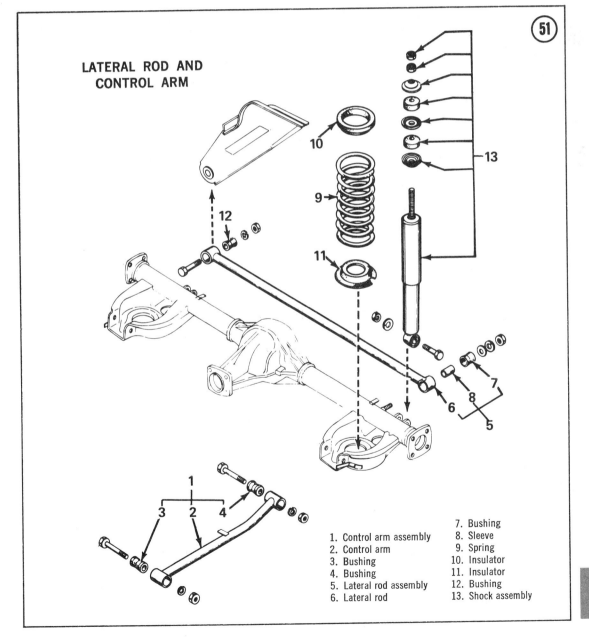

**LATERAL ROD AND
CONTROL ARM**

1. Control arm assembly
2. Control arm
3. Bushing
4. Bushing
5. Lateral rod assembly
6. Lateral rod
7. Bushing
8. Sleeve
9. Spring
10. Insulator
11. Insulator
12. Bushing
13. Shock assembly

13

ft.-lb. Torque lateral rod nut (to axle case) to 49 ft.-lb.

6. Install lower shock absorber bolt. Refer to *Rear Shock Absorber Replacement,* this chapter, and torque to 29 ft.-lb.

7. Install wheels and tighten wheel lug nuts to 50 ft.-lb. Remove jackstands and lower car.

Control Arm Removal/Installation

1. Raise car and install jackstands. Remove rear wheels.

2. Remove bolt holding control arm to axle case, and bolt holding control arm to body. Refer to Figure 51.

3. Remove control arm assembly.

4. To install, connect control arm assembly to body and to axle case. Torque bolts to 29 ft.-lb. Refer to **Figure 52**.

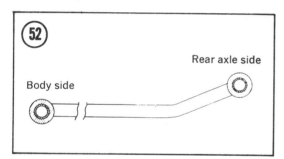

5. Install wheels and torque wheel lug nuts to 50 ft.-lb. Remove jackstands and lower car.

Rear Coil Springs Removal/Installation

1. Raise car and install jackstands. Remove rear wheels.

2. Raise rear axle with a jack.

3. Disconnect lower end of rear shock absorber from rear axle. Refer to *Rear Shock Absorber Replacement,* this chapter.

4. Lower rear axle with the supporting jack until coil spring can be removed.

5. To install, position the spring and raise the rear axle slowly with the jack. Then perform the following steps:

  a. Connect lower end of rear shock absorber to rear axle. Refer to *Rear Shock Absorber Replacement,* this chapter.

b. Remove jack under rear axle.

c. Install wheels and tighten wheel lug nuts to 50 ft.-lb.

d. Remove jackstands and lower car.

Rear Shock Absorber Replacement

1. Raise car and support with jackstands. Remove rear wheels.

2. Disconnect lower end of shock absorber from axle (**Figure 53**).

3. Remove fuel tank cover from inside the trunk and disconnect upper end of shock absorber (**Figure 54**).

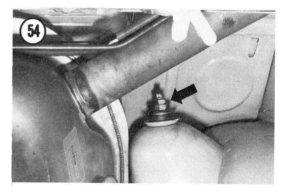

4. Remove shock absorber.

5. To install, attach shock absorber to rear wheel arch. Then perform the following steps:

  a. Install fuel tank cover.

b. Connect lower end of shock absorber to axle and torque nut to 29 ft.-lb.

c. Install wheels and tighten wheel lug nuts to 50 ft.-lb.

d. Remove jackstands and lower car.

CHAPTER TWELVE

BRAKES SUPPLEMENT

This chapter covers the replacement of the front disc brake pads; removal/installation procedures for the front disc brake calipers and discs; replacement of the rear drum brake shoes; and adjustment of the rear parking brake. Torque specifications are found in **Table 9**.

DISC BRAKE

Brake Pad Replacement

1. Raise front end of car and support with jackstands. Remove front wheels.

2. Remove clips, pins, "M" type spring, pad shims, and brake pads (**Figure 55**).

3. Clean dirt or foreign material from brake pad recess in caliper and inspect piston seals for leakage.

4. Apply grease included in brake pad repair kit to the area shown in **Figure 56**.

5. Push pistons into bores with Opel tool J-22430 (or equivalent). Open bleeder valve slightly to prevent brake fluid from overflowing reservoir (continue to push pistons into their bores during this operation). Tighten bleeder valve when pistons have bottomed.

6. Install anti-rattle shims on brake pads with arrow marks pointing in direction of normal disc rotation. Install in caliper.

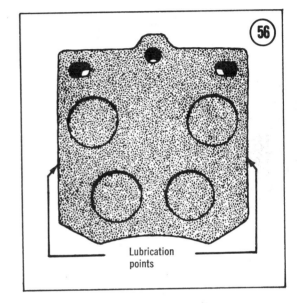

Lubrication points

7. Install "M" type spring, pins, and clips.

8. Install wheels, remove jackstands, and lower car.

Caliper Removal/Installation

1. Raise front end of car and support with jackstands. Remove front wheels.

2. Disconnect caliper brake line from brake hose. Cover ends of hoses and lines to protect against dirt. Refer to **Figure 57**.

Table 9   TORQUE SPECIFICATIONS

Component	
Backing plate retaining nuts	28 Foot-pound
Wheel cylinder retaining bolt	7 Foot-pound
Front disc brake caliper attaching bolt	36.2 Foot-pound
Front disc brake pipe flare nut	11.6 Foot-pound

13

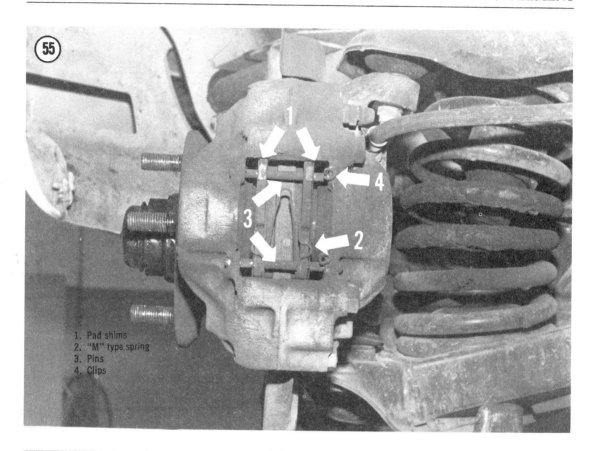

1. Pad shims
2. "M" type spring
3. Pins
4. Clips

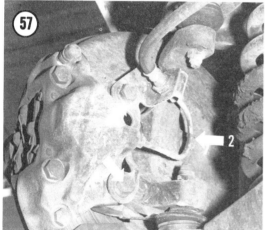

1. Caliper attaching bolts   2. Caliper brake pipe

3. Remove caliper attaching bolts. Refer to Figure 57. This will allow brake hose and bracket to hang normally.

4. Remove caliper.

5. To install, reverse preceding steps. Torque caliper attaching bolts to 36.2 ft.-lb., and brake pipe flare nut to 11.6 ft.-lb.

6. Bleed brakes. Refer to Chapter Twelve, *Brake System Bleeding* section, in front of this manual.

Caliper Disassembly/Assembly

The caliper is of an integral design and cannot be disassembled. Replace entire caliper assembly if brake fluid leaks from caliper joint.

> **WARNING**
> *Never disturb bridge bolts, or breakage of bolts or brake fluid leaks could result. This could cause a loss of braking action, which could result in a serious accident.*

Brake Disc Removal/Installation

1. Raise front end of car and support with jackstands. Remove front wheels.

2. Remove caliper retaining bolts. Refer to Figure 57. Support caliper with a piece of wire so that no strain is placed on brake hose and line. See **Figure 58**.

3. Remove hub and disc assembly and clamp in a vise.

CAUTION
Use protective pads in vise jaws to prevent disc from being marred.

4. Remove disc-to-hub retaining bolts. Refer to **Figure 59**.

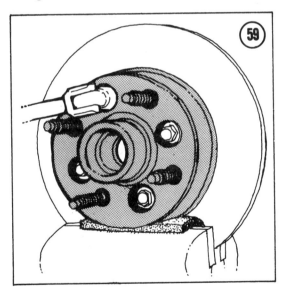

5. To install, reverse preceding steps. Tighten disc-to-hub bolts and caliper attaching bolts to 36.2 ft.-lb.

6. Adjust wheel bearings. Refer to Chapter Ten, *Front Suspension, Wheels, and Steering Supplement,* under *Front Wheel Bearing Adjustment* section.

DRUM BRAKES

Removal

1. Raise rear of car and install jackstands. Remove rear wheel/drum assemblies.

2. Remove return springs, shoe holding pins, cups, and springs (**Figure 60**).

3. Move automatic adjuster all the way in the direction of expansion and disconnect strut. Remove primary shoe (**Figure 61**).

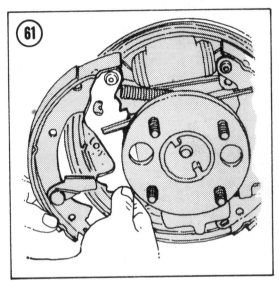

4. Disconnect parking brake cable from parking brake lever and remove secondary shoe (**Figure 62**).

13

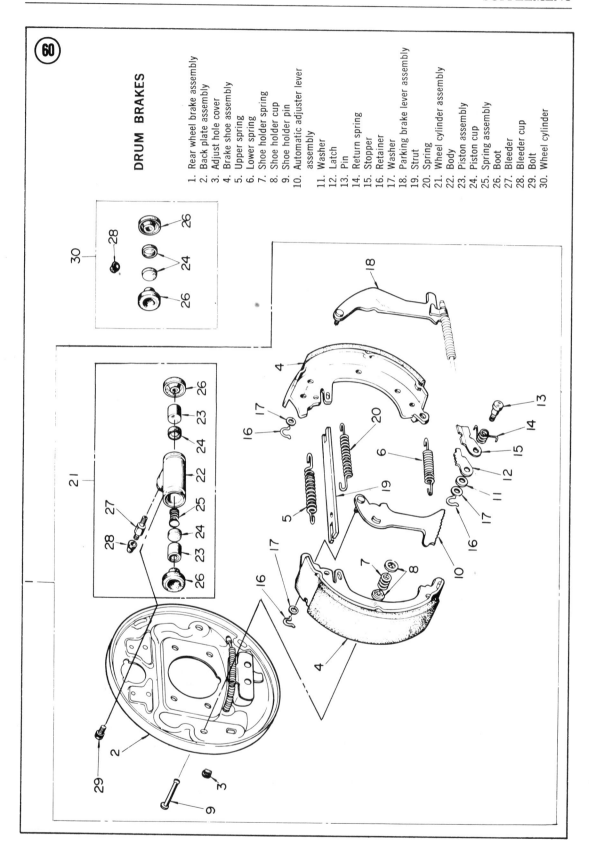

60

DRUM BRAKES

1. Rear wheel brake assembly
2. Back plate assembly
3. Adjust hole cover
4. Brake shoe assembly
5. Upper spring
6. Lower spring
7. Shoe holder spring
8. Shoe holder cup
9. Shoe holder pin
10. Automatic adjuster lever assembly
11. Washer
12. Latch
13. Pin
14. Return spring
15. Stopper
16. Retainer
17. Washer
18. Parking brake lever assembly
19. Strut
20. Spring
21. Wheel cylinder assembly
22. Body
23. Piston assembly
24. Piston cup
25. Spring assembly
26. Boot
27. Bleeder
28. Bleeder cup
29. Bolt
30. Wheel cylinder

5. Pry on the spring cup with a 12mm wrench and pull cable out from rear face of back plate (**Figure 63**).

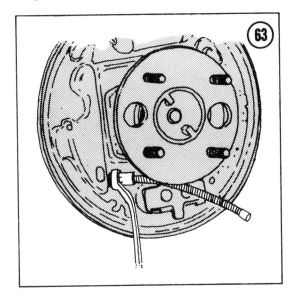

6. Remove wheel cylinder attaching bolts from back plate. Disconnect brake pipe and remove wheel cylinder assembly.

CAUTION
Cap ends of brake hoses and pipes to prevent dirt from entering. Dirt could result in a loss of braking action and could result in a serious accident.

Disassembly

1. Remove retainer, washer, and adjuster lever from primary shoe. Remove retainer and washer and pull pin out. Remove the ratchet, stopper, and springs (**Figure 64**).

2. Remove strut, retainer, and washer from secondary shoe (**Figure 65**). Remove parking brake cable lever.

3. Remove boots, pistons, piston cups, spring, and bleeder screw from wheel cylinder. See **Figure 66**.

Inspection

1. Wash disassembled wheel cylinder parts in clean brake fluid and inspect carefully for wear.

2. Measure wheel cylinder bore with a cylinder bore indicator; it should measure 0.812 in. Measure piston outside diameter; the difference between that and the wheel cylinder bore should give a clearance of 0.003 in. (the limit for use is 0.006 in.). Replace entire wheel cylinder if this clearance is exceeded. Check the wheel cylinder wall for uneven wear, rust, or scuff marks. Replace cylinder if necessary. Inspect return spring for weakening. Replace if necessary.

CAUTION
Replace used piston cups and boots with new ones whenever wheel cylin-

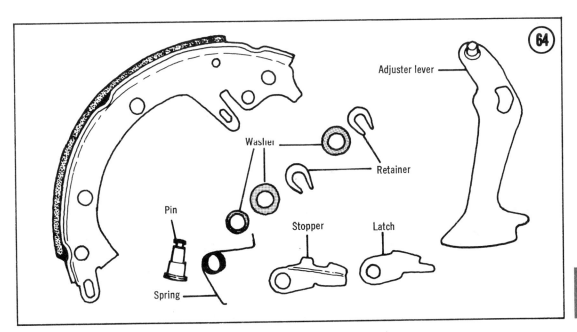

13

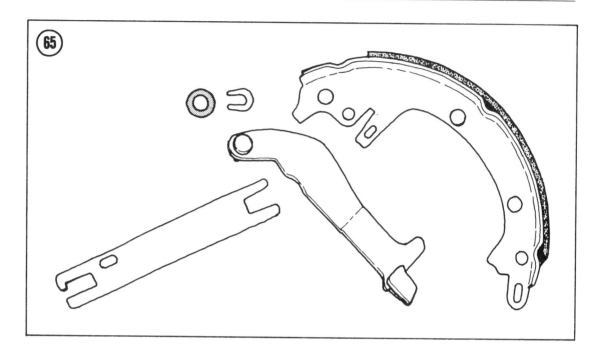

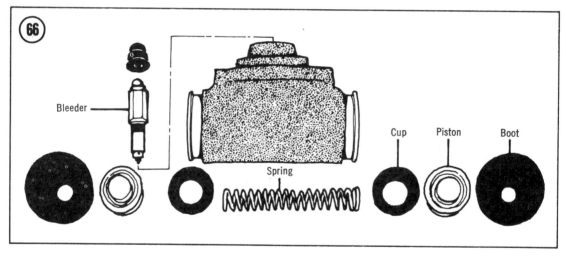

der assembly is disassembled, to avoid possibility of brake failure.

3. Measure thickness of brake shoes; they should measure 0.190 in. Replace if they measure 0.040 in. or less.

4. Measure the brake drum. Normal diameter is 8.980 in. The maximum machining limit is 9.040 in., and the discard limit is 9.060 in. The drum out-of-round should be 0.003 in. (or less).

5. Check automatic adjuster, parking brake lever, automatic adjuster lever, latch, strut, and parking brake cable lever for distortion or wear.

Check brake back plate for cracking or distortion. Check brake shoes for distortion or cracking, and return spring fitting holes for wear.

Assembly

1. Soak sliding parts of wheel cylinder assembly in clean brake fluid. Assemble into cylinder so that piston cups are as shown in **Figure 67**.

2. Attach automatic adjuster lever and latch to the primary shoe, then connect parking brake cable lever to secondary shoe. Refer to **Figure 68**.

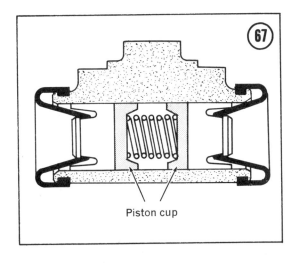

Piston cup

NOTE: *During installation, tighten back plate nut to 28 ft.-lb., and wheel cylinder bolts to 7 ft.-lb.*

2. Bleed hydraulic brake system. Refer to *Brake System Bleeding* at the beginning of Chapter Twelve in the main part of the book.

3. Remove jackstands and lower car to ground.

PARKING BRAKE

Adjustment

1. Release parking brake lever and check parking brake cable for free movement. Remove excessive cable play by turning brake lever rod adjustment nut (**Figure 69**).

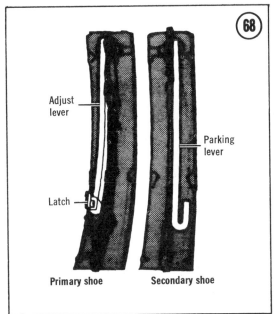

Adjust lever

Latch

Parking lever

Primary shoe   Secondary shoe

Installation

1. To install, reverse steps under *Removal,* this section.

2. After adjustment, be sure parking brake lever travel is 5-8 notches before parking brake is firmly set. If travel exceeds 5-8 notches, readjust with lever rod adjusting nut.

13

INDEX